MY BOYFRIEND'S BACK

My Boyfriend's Back

True Stories of
Rediscovering Love with a
Long-Lost Sweetheart

DONNA HANOVER

HUDSON
STREET
PRESS

HUDSON STREET PRESS
Published by Penguin Group
Penguin Group (USA) Inc., 375 Hudson Street, New York, New York 10014, U.S.A.
Penguin Group (Canada), 10 Alcorn Avenue, Toronto, Ontario, Canada M4V 3B2
(a division of Pearson Penguin Canada Inc.)
Penguin Books Ltd, 80 Strand, London WC2R 0RL, England
Penguin Ireland, 25 St Stephen's Green, Dublin 2, Ireland (a division of Penguin Books Ltd)
Penguin Group (Australia), 250 Camberwell Road, Camberwell, Victoria 3124, Australia
(a division of Pearson Australia Group Pty Ltd)
Penguin Books India Pvt Ltd, 11 Community Centre, Panchsheel Park, New Delhi – 110 017, India
Penguin Books (NZ), cnr Airborne and Rosedale Roads, Albany, Auckland 1310, New Zealand
(a division of Pearson New Zealand Ltd)
Penguin Books (South Africa) (Pty) Ltd, 24 Sturdee Avenue, Rosebank,
Johannesburg 2196, South Africa

Penguin Books Ltd, Registered Offices: 80 Strand, London WC2R 0RL, England

First published by Hudson Street Press, a member of Penguin Group (USA) Inc.

First Printing, February 2005
10 9 8 7 6 5 4 3 2 1

REGISTERED TRADEMARK — MARCA REGISTRADA
HUDSON
STREET
PRESS

LIBRARY OF CONGRESS CATALOGING-IN-PUBLICATION DATA
Hanover, Donna.
My boyfriend's back : true stories of rediscovering love with a long-lost sweetheart / Donna Hanover.
    p.   cm.
    ISBN 1-59463-010-0 (hardcover : alk. paper)
    1. First loves.   2. Love.   3. Reunions.   4. Soul mates.   5. Interpersonal relations.   I. Title.
    HQ801.H3227 2005   2004020940

Printed in the United States of America
Set in Goudy
Designed by Eve L. Kirch

This book is printed on acid-free paper. ∞

To Andrew and Caroline,
Whose love has been my strength and
Who carry my heart
Wherever they go.

To Mom and Dad,
Who are always in my corner
With steadfast love.

And to the man
Whose tenderness fills me with joy,
My dear sweetheart, Ed,
Who came back.

CONTENTS

PART TWO

Why So Many People Are Rekindling Love Now

PART THREE

How to Find Rekindled Love

HOW IT ALL STARTED

The Phone Call

THE SEEDS OF THIS BOOK WERE PLANTED WHEN MY HIGH SCHOOL sweetheart called more than 30 years after we broke up.

It was August 2002, a stifling hot afternoon in New York. After 18 years of marriage, my divorce had become final a month earlier, and I was adjusting to single life as a working mom. Besides serving as host of the nationally syndicated TV show *Famous Homes & Hideaways*, I was raising my 16-year-old son, Andrew, and 12-year-old daughter, Caroline, and renovating our apartment on the Upper East Side of Manhattan. Thirty-five floors up, it faces north and east, offering sights such as the graceful Triborough Bridge and countless planes taking off from La Guardia Airport. My kids like the view because we can tell when the Yankees are home by checking the stadium lights.

Nothing stood out about that day until the phone rang.

"Donna, it's Ed. Ed Oster."

I sat down. Ed Oster was my high school love. He was also my college love—until he broke my heart. I tried to hear Ed's voice over the pulse pounding in my ears.

"I was wondering," Ed asked tentatively, "if you're planning to go to the Stanford reunion?"

This was interesting to say the least. What was going on here? This was the guy who had dumped me freshman year and had spoken to me for maybe two minutes at our reunion five years ago.

"Yes," I said and then waited. Silently I prayed, "Please don't let this be about fund-raising."

"Well, the reunion isn't until October," Ed said, "but my work is bringing me to New York next week. I was wondering if I could take you out for coffee."

I thought to myself, "I gotta call somebody—no one's going to believe this." Oh-so-casually I responded, "Let me check my calendar." After flipping through several weeks of blank "date" pages, I said, "I think I can free up a little time."

Ed had read the news stories, so he knew that I was on my own these days after eight years as New York City's First Lady. He was divorced, too; he had three grown daughters, and was living in Newport Beach, California, where he practiced law.

The sound of his voice brought back memories of our young romance. Ed wasn't a cad in college. In fact, he was tender and dear. But he was 17 then and just didn't want to go steady. I didn't take that news so well at the time, but here we were 30 years later. (Maybe he had reconsidered!) Coffee was sounding better and better.

The Past Love Phenomenon

Over the next few weeks Ed and I saw each other frequently, were quickly smitten, and soon realized that we wanted to spend the rest of our lives together. "Whoa, slow down," you say? So did my girlfriends!

They thoroughly interrogated Ed, probing and prying until he felt he'd been worked over by experts. But he passed the test with flying colors. He was warm, smart, and charming. What was not to like?

People loved hearing our story, which was fortunate because we couldn't stop telling it. When we explained that we were getting married more than 30 years after our breakup, they would grin, sigh, or get teary-eyed. One guy from Ed's athletic club got right to the point: "That's the damned coolest thing I ever heard." People often responded with their own stories of a cousin or friend who had reconnected with a long-ago sweetheart and fallen in love. In each case the past had waltzed straight into the present and taken both parties by surprise. Ed and I discovered that we were part of a growing phenomenon.

In the weeks before our wedding, a close friend suggested that I write a book. "There are lots of good, intelligent women and men who are lonely and would love to know that reuniting is a possibility."

The idea intrigued me, but I was bodice deep in planning a wedding. I wanted to be fully present to enjoy the white gown, the flowers, the vows, the joy and meaning of this beautiful moment in our lives. So any idea about writing a book was put on hold.

But after the honeymoon the thought really appealed to me—because of our personal experience, of course, but also as a journalist. I told Ed it would be no small task pulling together people's stories from across the country. But he got right on board. "Go for it," he encouraged. "I'll help you all I can. We can eat takeout for a few months." I don't think he fully realized that, book or no book, takeout was going to be a way of life from now on. Nevertheless, I was touched by his all-out support.

An Innocent Time

When a relationship ends, people tend to look up previous loves. "Way before we were thrown against the rocks of life and were whooped around by the tides," says Los Angeles therapist Suzanne Lopez, "many of us knew a sweet encounter with a boyfriend or girlfriend."

The love and excitement we felt then may be possible again—and with the same person. No wonder it is so tempting to explore the prospect. But the very idea of bringing the past into the present raises a number of issues that will be examined in *My Boyfriend's Back*:

- In Part One, we discover how reuniting is different, and sometimes more powerful, than falling in love with someone new.

- Part Two looks at why so many former sweethearts are reconnecting *now*.

- Part Three offers suggestions on how to go about finding rekindled love, important precautions to keep in mind, and some happily-ever-after wedding stories.

My Boyfriend's Back shares the experiences of dozens of couples who have reunited after years apart. We will hear from Dr. Hilly Dubin who says, "When I realized my former sweetheart Cheryl Kagan was on the phone after 17 years, I felt like Roger Rabbit, with my heart pounding right out of my chest." We'll meet Kate Coyne and Ron Martucci who came back together after his eagle-eyed mom noticed Kate wasn't wearing a wedding ring during a TV interview. There are Sam and Joy (Jemison) Nichols who reunited more than 50 years after being separated by World War II. And there is Janet Jacobson who felt so bad about turning down Mark Davis's invitation to the prom 20 years earlier that she hung a mirrored disco ball in their living room to recreate it!

Some celebrities have also reconnected with former sweethearts. We'll hear from Carol Channing about her recent marriage to her junior high school love, Harry Kullijian. Suzanne Pleshette and Tom Poston, both veterans of Bob Newhart's TV shows, tell us how they reconnected. And we'll talk with a star of TV's *Passions*, Liza Huber, who remet and married Alex Hesterberg, the boy who sat behind her in second grade.

It was a great pleasure—truly a gift—to talk with the many wonderful reunited couples in this book. They were charming, romantic, funny, and generous in sharing their experiences. And they are so much in love! Their stories illustrate the strong biological and psychological forces that drive the rekindled love experience. We will hear about these influences from scientists and therapists who have studied human behavior and relationships, and have considered what causes and nurtures rekindled love.

Reunitees, to coin a term, report finding it easy to feel close again quickly. These feelings derive, at least in part, from what took place in their brains when they were young sweethearts. "There is an actual neurological attachment that happens," says Linda Waud, Psy.D., who wrote her dissertation for The Professional School of

Psychology in Sacramento, California, on the subject of rekindled love, "and that's why it's enduring. The attachment is there forever and ever." You *look* young to one another, and you *feel* young around each other. In a sense you win a fresh start with an old love, something that is at once familiar and exciting.

It Can Happen to You

Adolescence, when most of us look back on it, may seem like a vast romantic wasteland. But if you really think about it, there could be someone from that time you'd like to find and get to know again. You had classmates, teammates, lab partners; there were people you dated, had crushes on, were friends with, loved and lost. Perhaps there was someone you ignored or, in a hormonal moment, decided you absolutely hated. How about the one who got away? The reasons we did not end up with certain people may be different from what we thought; years later we might learn that there was another side to the story. Digging deep into long-forgotten feelings can turn up buried treasure.

Sometimes the reasons an early love didn't work out *are* worth noting. Later in the book we'll hear some cautionary tales about unrealistic expectations. But even a rekindled romance gone flat may have a silver lining: Finding out that "the perfect guy" is not so perfect may free you to find the one who is right for you.

The Beauty of Rekindled Love

Ed's phone call that sultry August afternoon triggered extraordinary life changes for both of us. We are sometimes sad that we missed being there for each other as we learned so many of life's lessons. But for each opportunity lost, several have taken its place. We adore each other's children, and we look forward to spoiling the grandchildren (no pressure, kids!), traveling together, and cheering each other on in the prime of our careers.

A word about the title of this book: Sometimes there is a song that perfectly commemorates a special moment. In December 1998 my friend, comedienne Joan Rivers, threw a beautiful, lavish wedding for her daughter, Melissa, at the Plaza Hotel in New York. Joan went all out and spent a fortune replicating a Russian winter, complete with fake snow and icicles. When she strolled down the aisle, the choir broke into "Hey Big Spender" and the guests went wild.

When Ed and I married on August 3, 2003, our first slow dance was to "How Do I Live?" the romantic ballad recorded by Trisha Yearwood. Predictably, our guests got a little misty-eyed and applauded warmly. But when the bandleader segued into the 60s hit by The Angels, the roof came off!

> *He's been gone for such a long time*
> *Hey la, hey la!*
> *My boyfriend's back.*
>
> *Now he's back and things'll be fine.*
> *Hey la, hey la!*
> *My boyfriend's back.*

People laughed and cheered and filled the dance floor, rockin' and rollin' to what everyone agreed was, for this sweet occasion, the perfect song.

When you read through the following pages, if you're already crazy in love, just enjoy the stories of the couples who finally got there, too—and maybe share their experiences with your single friends. If you're looking for love, keep in mind that even if it doesn't work out, you might heal a wound that's standing in the way of your happiness now. The best that can happen is what happened to me: marrying and building a joyous life with the wonderful man who was my high school sweetheart.

PART ONE

How Reuniting Is
Different, and Sometimes
More Powerful, Than
Falling in Love with
Someone New

Chapter 1

He Doesn't See My Cellulite

Ed Oster may have been my high school sweetheart, but he was also my adversary. At weekend debate tournaments our schools were traditional rivals. My team, Fremont High in Sunnyvale, California, was a perennial powerhouse. Ed led the team for Bellarmine College Preparatory, a Catholic boys' school in San Jose that treated debate like a varsity sport, expecting cogent arguments and intense competitive spirit. I remember thinking that Ed was a smart and persuasive debater with a deep voice and a strong intellect. I also thought he was pretty darn cute.

Fast forward to August 2002. Having finalized my divorce a month before, I was adapting to a new life. And I was about to have coffee with Ed, who broke up with me during our freshman year at Stanford. It was more than 30 years since our young romance had ended.

I was nervous. I was happy. I considered canceling.

This wasn't exactly a *date*, I told myself. It was more like getting together with an old friend to catch up. I studied my face in the mirror. A few more wrinkles, I guess. Okay, a couple more pounds. The page-boy haircut from my past was gone (thank goodness), but at least I was still blond. I'll admit it: I spent lots of extra time fussing with my hair and makeup that day. I wanted Ed to think that I had been naturally gorgeous 34 years ago and that I was still naturally gorgeous today, no matter how much work it took!

I confronted my closet, looking for something that would suddenly make me tall and slim and glamorous, but the "lose-10-pounds-overnight" fairy had not stopped by. I settled on a gray silk suit and black high heels—after all, if you can't *be* tall, you can at least *think* tall.

I was so glad that Ed hadn't suggested going to the beach—no bathing suit, no cellulite on display! However this meeting turned out, I wanted to look my best. (And it is possible that I wanted him to eat his heart out since he broke mine so many years before!)

I was happy he hadn't seen me during some of my past phases—trying to lose weight gained during pregnancies or growing out a disastrous hairstyle. Launching into an internal pep talk, I reminded myself that I wasn't the only one who had gotten older. And if I was this eager to see the man I had once loved and who had loved me, he might be feeling the same way. Maybe his formal tone on the phone came from the same nervous excitement I was feeling.

We had agreed to meet in Ed's hotel lobby. Of course, I was ready way too early. I passed the time straightening photographs in the living room: my children, now teenagers, playing with Legos when they were little; Andrew in his football uniform; and Caroline at six, missing her front teeth, hugging my dad and a stuffed Minnie Mouse doll. My mother looked so proud holding her new grandson on the day we brought him home from the hospital. In a later picture Andrew appeared angelic as he hugged his little sister, when he actually had her in a headlock.

In another shot, I played evangelist Ruth Carter Stapleton in

Milos Forman's film *The People vs. Larry Flynt*, actor Woody Harrelson posed with us. We looked pretty angelic as a group that day in our white robes for a scene where I baptized him in a lake. Next to that was a photo from my early reporter days interviewing Steelers quarterback Terry Bradshaw in Pittsburgh. Then several screaming roller-coaster shots and a collection of Christmas card pictures of the kids over the years, stretching from the backyard of Gracie Mansion to the Eiffel Tower to the Golden Gate Bridge.

In the car heading toward midtown I wondered what to tell Ed. How do you catch someone up on 30 years of your life? (Should I pick the 10 best to start with? Would we feel comfortable? What if he didn't notice I was thinking tall?)

I arrived, called him on the house phone, and practiced my Lamaze breathing. Finally he answered and said in a professional tone, "I'll be down in a few minutes. I'm just finishing a business call." But when he stepped out of the elevator, he looked so freshly showered that I couldn't help but kid him.

"There *wasn't* really a business call, was there?"

Busted! He gave me exactly the same mischievous grin I remembered from school and admitted he might have taken a little extra time to look good for me. We both felt instantly at ease.

"When I was getting ready to see Donna," Ed later told some of his friends, "I couldn't help but wonder if time and circumstances had taken their toll, but she looked absolutely great! It was her glow and, as corny as it may sound, the light in her eyes that transported me back. It was as if nothing had changed. She exuded so much energy and magnetism, I immediately felt comfortable. And attracted. It was as if time had stood still." (A girl can't hear too much of this stuff. I sometimes ask him to repeat it.)

Ed was wearing a classic blue blazer and gray slacks. His hair was the same luminous brown I remembered. It took about two seconds for me to notice that he was in terrific shape—slim, muscular, and agile. He had been quite the athlete in his youth, a pitcher with a no-hitter under his belt and a quarterback who could throw a spiral right on the numbers. It was obvious that he still worked out. And then there was that handsome face! Friends have kidded me that I'm lucky; he is a definite "10." But I would have been equally attracted even if he weren't so smashingly gorgeous. There was an immediate chemistry between us just as there had been when we were kids.

This was going to be fun.

The Walk

More than three decades after we last dated, Ed and I began our first walk through Central Park. I pointed out some of my favorite sights: Bethesda Fountain, the Great Lawn, Belvedere Castle. We passed the world-famous Central Park restaurant Tavern on the Green, and I shared with Ed some of my experiences there. It had been the scene of several live broadcasts when I was a correspondent for *Good Day New York*. I had cheered on the winners of the New York marathon when they crossed the finish line at that very spot. As New York City's First Lady, I had been honored to blow the air horn near the landmark restaurant to start 30,000 women gallantly battling breast cancer in their 5K "Race for the Cure."

Ed told me he was a trial attorney in Newport Beach, California, with the firm Barger & Wolen. He loved his work and had more than 50 jury trials and appellate cases behind him, including malpractice defense and business and insurance litigation. As we strolled, Ed, ever the gentleman, always made sure he walked closest to traffic, on the curb side of the path. It was endearing to be treated with such care.

At West Eighty-first Street we headed toward the American Museum of Natural History, where the children and I had celebrated the millennium. When I pointed out the remarkable new Hayden Planetarium and Rose Center for Earth and Space, Ed seemed to share my sense of wonder. I learned that he had become quite a stargazer. He loved to pack up his daughters and go to their vacation home at Big Bear Lake in California's San Bernardino Mountains, where he liked watching the nighttime skies.

"The light show is magnificent up there," he said. "No city lights to interfere with the real ones."

Would we be watching them together one day, I wondered? It was much too soon to know, but I was happy to hear of his close relationship with his daughters. My children are my number one priority, and it was clear that Ed was equally devoted to his three girls. He told me that Lauren was a Stanford graduate and a published poet. Emily, an aspiring teacher, was a student at Stanford, majoring in French. And Joanna was a talented artist studying at the University of Southern California. I would later learn for myself how fabulous, witty, and smart each of them is.

We headed along Columbus Avenue on the Upper West Side and slipped into a small Chinese restaurant. Over an order of fried rice we talked more about our kids, comparing notes about reading to them at night. Ed had read his girls the classics. I naively took that to mean *Little Women* and *Jane Eyre*, but apparently Ed's daughters were raised on such feminine fare as *Treasure Island*, *Lord of the Rings*, and, his personal favorite, Sherlock Holmes.

I told Ed stories about living in Gracie Mansion and some of the fascinating people I'd met along the way. When the New York Rangers won the NHL championship, we had a reception for the team in our backyard. Superstar goalie Mike Richter didn't seem to feel it was a compliment that our Labrador "Goalie" was named after him and commented, "I sure hope he's a smart dog!" That day I urged all my single girlfriends to have pictures taken with the famous trophy, teasing that "a photo with the Stanley Cup is surefire 'man bait.'"

Ed told me that every few years he and his brothers Dave, Ron, and Steve went on what they called "OBWs," Oster Brother Weekends, to places like Monument Valley, the American River in Sacramento, and Mountain Ranch in Calaveras County. They would barbecue, talk politics, and feel like boys again, playing baseball games like "three flies up." Much more often he and Ron would venture up to Big Bear for "Operation New Frontier." Ed explained: "We go hiking part of the day and spend the rest working on the house; we've built the deck, added a toolshed, and put in new lighting."

What more could a girl want? In addition to having a terrific career as an attorney, he could also do carpentry, repair the car, and install plumbing. He could fix things that inevitably broke down in the nitty-gritty of life. I found this aspect of him enchanting; actually, everything that day was enchanting.

As he recounted his past, I was surprised to learn that his mother had remembered me as "Ed's best girl" and on occasion had asked if he'd heard how I was doing. Ed knew that I had studied journalism in graduate school at Columbia University, and he had seen me now and then on television.

We finished our walk by strolling to Lincoln Center, the home of great cultural institutions such as the New York City Ballet. We admired the fountain in front of Alice Tully Hall and the glorious Chagall paintings showcased through the huge windows of the Metropolitan Opera House. Illustrating one of the more humbling aspects of broadcasting, I told Ed about the time at Lincoln Center that I was decked by a Muppet. While I earnestly interviewed Kermit the Frog, Big Bird turned, and his heavy tail feathers knocked me flat. Graceful it wasn't.

We had a million things to talk about. But one moment will forever stand out in my memory: Ed took my hand and apologized for the way he had ended our early romance.

"It was all my doing," he assured me. "I had no reservations about you. I didn't wish you were different or want you to change. And there was no one else. I just didn't want to be tied down. But it was the dumbest thing I ever did," he said. "Besides, at Stanford so few women would date a freshman guy that letting go of you was nuts. I was just too young to know what I had, and I'm sorry I hurt you."

I was shocked that he had carried the memory of those feelings for more than 30 years. I'd been very sad when we split up, and it touched my heart to hear what he was saying now. He was young and inexperienced back then—we both were—and while it had been painful, I could understand it, too. Now, as he apologized for his actions of so many years ago as if they were still fresh in his mind, his strength of character and kindness were compelling.

When Ed and I finally parted that day, neither of us knew what the future held. I only knew that I had spent an incredible afternoon with my high school love. He was a little older but no less handsome or thrilling than I remembered him. In fact, he still looked young to me—an improved version of his former wonderful self, complete with new wisdom and compassion. Clearly, I was seeing him through young eyes, and I liked how that made me feel.

So although we lived a continent apart, as quickly as you could sing "Hey la, hey la, my boyfriend's back," we decided to take full advantage of a second chance together—a veritable miracle in both of our lives.

Wanting a Life Partner

In choosing to go forward, Ed and I were about to discover that reuniting with a former sweetheart can be deeply fulfilling. "There is something about capturing that youthful time that is very powerful," says Los Angeles psychologist Vicki Hillman Firstenberg who has been in private practice for 10 years. "If we could do it all over again with what we know now, we'd do better. We would get to feel young again and hopefully end up with a better outcome this time around." The experts I interviewed say rekindling love is also especially appealing because most of us yearn for a life partner, and few people like the idea of looking for new people to date.

In big cities like Los Angeles and New York it is easy to feel lost or anonymous. Just getting around requires massive effort, and people rarely know their neighbors, much less the boy next door. City dwellers often feel that they are not part of a community and can therefore feel invisible to other like-minded people. In less populous areas there is a sense that the pool of potential mates is just too small or simply not diverse enough.

The fear of rejection is another major impediment to dating, even when we deeply want a partner. In her study, entitled "Does

Rejection Hurt?" (originally published in the journal *Science*), UCLA psychologist Naomi Eisenberger investigated why many of us are so frightened of rejection. Each subject underwent a brain scan while playing a virtual ball game with two other players that was actually rigged to make the first participant feel left out. Reporting on the experiment in New York's *Daily News* (October 10, 2003), journalist Paul H. B. Shin cited the results of the MRI scans in the Eisenberger study: "A social snub activates the same part of the brain that is switched on when a person feels physical pain."

"You really do experience pain when you're rejected," Eisenberger said. No wonder we try to avoid being emotionally vulnerable!

One's physical safety is also a concern when dating someone new. For many women the idea of searching for Mr. Right on the Internet feels too risky. While online dating has been successful for some people, it is natural and even wise to question the honesty of the biographical profile you are reading. It is difficult to know if the online photo you are viewing is current or even a digital scan of a picture from a magazine. How many people lie about their age, interests, or marital status, and how would you know?

These roadblocks to meeting the "genuine article" can feed our insecurities. Who hasn't wanted to curl up in a ball at home? No question: The obstacles increase our ambivalence about how best to search for a true life partner.

In the past, as a married woman, I had looked around at my single girlfriends, and in some ways, their situations had seemed discouraging. These beautiful, accomplished women, many of whom wanted to be in committed relationships, could not find the right man. Once I was on my own again, I wondered if I would be in the same position. Would finding companionship require huge compromises? How would I find a man with the intelligence, wit, and compassion that I wanted in a partner?

Of course I realized I was more fortunate than many: My children, my close friends, and my work were all wonderful. But I had to face the fact that I was newly single, and as so many women my age already knew, there were far fewer eligible men out there than when I was in my twenties—"less popcorn in the popper," so to speak. I had many blessings, but I still felt I was missing one of the great joys of life: a loving partner.

So why shouldn't it be someone we already know, albeit from long ago? Nancy Kalish, Ph.D., is a professor of psychology at California State University, Sacramento. Author of *Lost and Found Lovers* and founder of the popular Web site Lostlovers.com, Kalish conducted a four-year research project on rekindled relationships with more than a thousand participants. Her results showed that lost-love reunions were common in all age groups, and the overall "staying together" success rate for reunited couples was a whopping 72 percent. This compares to U.S. Census Bureau conclusions from 2002 that only 50 percent of first marriages and 40 percent of second marriages last. Dr. Herb Barrett, a Westport, Connecticut, clinical psychologist who has counseled hundreds of couples, is not surprised that rekindled-love marriages seem to have a better chance at success. "I would think it would have a greater guarantee of permanency than a completely new relationship because it's the known person meeting the known person. Whatever time has done to separate them, there is that early feeling of safety."

When Ed and I started seeing each other regularly, I was grateful to be spared the typical dating miseries: a series of uncomfortable dinners, awkward fix-ups, and torturous coffee dates. Instead it felt good to have a "gentleman caller" whose character I knew from years ago. Ed was someone I could proudly introduce to my children. Spending time with a former sweetheart was a promising and delightful proposition.

This path to happiness is actually pleasantly crowded. Rekindled love has changed the lives of many people, and it is a phenomenon that is gathering steam. In researching this book I collected the funny, inspiring, poignant stories of hundreds of reunited couples. Since publishing her book in 1997, Dr. Kalish has added at least a thousand additional reunited pairs to her database. Internet Web sites such as Classmates.com and Reunion.com, which reunite people, also report thousands of rekindled romances.

The hope, appreciation, and beauty of rekindled love are wonderfully demonstrated by an engaging couple I first met several years ago when I was hosting a show for the Food Network.

Carol and Gary

"THE INTENSITY . . . WARPED THE RICHTER SCALE"

Gary Puetz, 58, and Carol Pedersen, 56, live near Portland, Oregon, where Gary cooks, consults, and acts as national spokesman for the state's seafood commissions. Carol, still a beauty who won the Miss Oregon title in 1964, has enjoyed a flourishing career as a clothing sales representative.

This reunited couple swears they are happier than they ever imagined possible, and they appreciate every minute because their reunion almost didn't happen. Fourteen years prior, Gary was struck with a vicious strain of testicular cancer that spread to his neck and shoulders. After 18 months of chemotherapy, combined with what he calls a good dose of laugh therapy, he conquered the cancer. Today he is in good health and remains eternally grateful to his doctors.

I had interviewed Gary in his capacity as a gourmet seafood chef many times, but it wasn't until I told him about Ed and me that he said, "You know, Donna, that's my story, too."

He and Carol originally met during high school in Newport, Oregon, in a tiny café called The Townhouse. Gary recalls Carol as a little freshman beauty and even remembers what she ordered: a Crab Louis (he never forgets a seafood dish). Carol recalls Gary in his junior year as "a sweet, kind fellow" reputed to be quite a good dancer. A humble man, Gary says Carol must have been easy to impress because when he asked her to the Christmas formal that was to take place in four days, she immediately said yes. What Gary didn't know was that Carol considered his invitation a dream come true.

Gary didn't own a suit or tie, but he bought them especially for the formal. "People think teenagers don't know what real love is," Gary says, "but I disagree. I was 16 and she was 15 when we met, and the intensity of our relationship warped the Richter scale. I never had a deeper and more passionate love than Carol at any time in my life."

Carol's mom, a seamstress by trade, was up for two nights making her daughter a formal dress. "It was pearly white with half an inch of baby blue trim," Carol recalls, "with—what do you call those things, pasta straps?"

"She means spaghetti straps," chef Gary teases. Carol remembers every detail of that dress. Gary remembers how delicious Carol smelled and how it felt to put his arms around her, albeit a bit tentatively, the first time they danced together. From that night on they were inseparable, going to school carnivals and weekend movies. Carol says he was quite the gentleman, opening doors for her, and she felt proud being treated that way. They were the best of friends—until a college man came along and tempted Carol away.

"He was a good-looking guy with a cool car. What chance did I have?" Gary says. He moved on, having no other choice, but he never forgot his first love.

Carol went on to win the beauty pageant title, after which she married and joined the corporate world. Gary married, too, had a son, and, like Carol, after many years he divorced. They were both single when they met once again three decades later at a "high school reunion shindig" back in Newport, Oregon.

"I hadn't thought much about him beforehand," says Carol. "I was just sitting at a table with friends, and when Gary walked up, this warm feeling crept right up my spine. I was stunned since I hadn't seen him for what felt like a century. But when I heard that unmistakable laugh—his soul pours out when he laughs—I knew I was hooked again."

For Gary's part, "The minute I saw her, my mouth went dry, my palms got wet, and I absolutely came unglued."

They dated for about a year and a half, which gave Carol a chance to make sure that Gary was the same "heartful" man she remembered from so long ago. Seeing that he was still generous, strong, and loving, she jokes that she used the feminine version of pursuit: "I tripped him, and he caught me." They married during a trip to Spain in 1995.

"I consider myself the luckiest man in the universe," says Gary.

They both feel fortunate despite the fact that Carol battles emphysema. Weakened by her degenerative physical condition, she has difficulty performing certain tasks. According to Carol, Gary is the greatest caregiver in the world. "He's my Atlas," she says. "He takes care of me so beautifully, he gives 400 percent of his soul."

When I asked Gary about taking care of Carol, he smiled and said, "There are two ways to look at everything. Carol has trouble taking a shower, so when I help her, I get to see the most beautiful woman in the world naked every morning. Why would I complain about that?"

Gary found that reactions to their rekindled love were far stronger than he had ever expected. "I was on a plane soon after the wedding, and when I showed the flight attendant our picture and told her our story, she broke down into gushing tears and went all goofy-eyed. She sent me off the plane with a bunch of little Cognac bottles and a big bottle of champagne."

According to Gary, guys also react positively, but they're a little more profane. "No s—!" they say, all smiles and backslapping. "They like it just as much as the women do," he says. "I think everybody has a memory of a first love that they carry through life with them."

Young Eyes

Stories like mine and Ed's and Carol and Gary's inspire some intriguing questions:

- What is the phenomenon that allows us to overlook what some might view as imperfections and see our rekindled love partners as beautiful and youthful no matter what their age?

- Why do reunited sweethearts look at each other through young, optimistic eyes?

- Why don't these guys see our cellulite?

Carl Jung probably wasn't thinking of "dimpled-thigh anxiety" when he wrote his celebrated book *Memories, Dreams, Reflections,* but he did express some insight that helps us understand the concept of seeing the world—or one's sweetheart—through young eyes: "[a] childhood memory can suddenly take possession of consciousness with so lively an emotion that we feel wholly transported back to the original situation."

This can be a great benefit of reuniting with an old boyfriend or girlfriend. He looks as handsome to you as he did the night of the senior prom. You look as fresh and lovely to him as you did on your Sweet Sixteen birthday. And this makes both of you feel remarkably young again.

Reunited couples that we'll meet in these pages express it best:

Arnold Spitz was 88 and Millie was 72 when they reunited. They married in 2003. He says, "When I picked her up in front of her store after more than 50 years apart, I saw her as she was at 17. She's beautiful and I feel young again."

Tom Anton says of his wife, Sandi: "Even more than 20 years later, I see that 15-year-old girl. The bounce is still there, and so is her love of life."

Linda Hart, 50, says of her partner, Ken Kohn, 51: "When I look at him, I flash back to when we were young, and that's what I see in him now."

Such feelings are understandable, says Dr. Herb Barrett. "When you meet new friends, the face they encounter is that of the 45- or

55- or 65-year-old person, with all the experiences and wrinkles. In a reencounter with an old friend we very quickly get back to how we thought as kids."

The quest to recapture youth is practically eternal, and the ways in which people pursue it aren't always terribly productive. Some go through the old "midlife crisis," including a fast car and much younger trophy spouse. Others opt for new noses, chins, or breasts. But rekindling a past love can be a far more exhilarating way to drink from the fountain of youth.

There are powerful psychological forces underpinning reunited lovers' feelings of youth and attraction that will be examined in the next few chapters. But there is also a biological component.

The Biology of Rekindled Love

"Falling in love is one of the most profound and powerful experiences on earth," says Helen Fisher, Ph.D., a professor at Rutgers University. "When something is that novel and exciting, the brain encodes it through networks of neurons in long-term memory. There is an imprinting in the brain."

A highly regarded anthropologist, Dr. Fisher has studied what actually occurs in the biology of the brain when people fall in love. Her research included taking functional MRI brain scans while subjects looked at photographs of their sweethearts, and she found that when you fall in love, the primitive portion of the brain shows increased activity. She concludes from this study and her other work that the need for romantic passion is hardwired into our brains by evolution.

With rekindled love, Dr. Fisher says, the gestures, tone of voice, and facial expressions of your former sweetheart, the way you walked and talked and danced together, were probably encoded in your memory. "You fell in love with this person for a specific constellation of reasons," says Dr. Fisher. "Why wouldn't the brain be quite impressed by certain things that a lover does and then cause you to feel comfort and joy when those things are reproduced?"

Sometimes reunited lovers are startled by the intensity of their feelings for each other. They may not realize that subconscious as well as conscious memories drive their mutual attraction. In her dissertation on rekindled love, Linda Waud, Psy.D., explains, "During the initial attachment process of the young couple, the implicit memory system permanently and unconsciously encodes feelings of love and intimacy . . . the basis for the enduring attachment of reunited couples."

Reunitees often fervently declare that their physical passion for each other is greater than what they would expect with a new love. Probably not so, says Dr. Fisher. She suspects that the levels of testosterone—which she calls "the hormone of desire"—is similar for both groups. What's actually happening, Dr. Fisher suggests, is that reunited sweethearts face fewer barriers in creating thrilling sexual intimacy.

"It can be very awkward starting a sexual relationship with someone new as opposed to somebody you already know. With a person who is familiar, some of the intense awkwardness is not there." She thinks that in many cases of rekindled love the partners have confidence they are being seen in a flattering light by each other. So they might have fewer inhibitions and feel sexually adventurous more quickly. This may happen even when the reunited sweethearts' earlier experience involved mostly holding and kissing rather than a full physical relationship.

Reunitees who feel passion beyond what they imagined possible at this point in their lives often express it eloquently. Sam Nichols gave Joy (Jemison) her first kiss when they were teenagers in Tennessee before he headed off to the join the navy in World War II and then built a life on the West Coast. After long, happy marriages and the deaths of their respective spouses, they met again in the year 2000 and then wed in July 2001, more than 50 years after their early romance. At age 79, Sam writes in one of his love notes to Joy about the "marvels" of their relationship: "fun and laughter, kissing impromptu . . . and hugging one another with no excuse. Thank God for our reunion."

Love letters like Sam's and the astounding "staying together" rate of 72 percent gleaned from Dr. Kalish's study indicate something powerful is under way as people find love and companionship with sweethearts or friends from their past. When they reunite, they feel transformed, confident, strong, and enthusiastic. The loving gaze of a rekindled sweetheart makes them feel attracted and attractive.

By the way, Ed and I have been married for more than a year now. He's seen it all, and he really doesn't see my cellulite. They say that love is blind, but our experience and the experiences of other reunited couples lead me to believe that rekindled love actually has a unique kind of vision that transcends time.

Chapter 2

He Loves the Real Me

THERE IS A POWERFUL TRUST THAT COMES WITH THE BELIEF THAT "he cared for me when I was young, so I know he loves the *real me*." No pretense, no worrying about keeping up a front or polishing an image. If he has already seen you in your gawky stage, what worse can he see? If he remembers your youthful hurts, he knows some of your permanent scars.

The flip side is that you probably also know the real him. You remember his personality from your early days together, so you have a pretty good read on his character. Of course you don't approach the relationship as though he hasn't changed, but some of the getting-to-know-you dance is over. You are able to decide more quickly than with a new person whether it is safe to cut to the chase and reveal your vulnerabilities.

That sense of being loved for "the real me" makes Hollywood dream team Suzanne Pleshette and Tom Poston big believers in reunited love.

Suzanne and Tom

"WE HAD NO RIGHT NOT TO GRAB THIS"

Suzanne Pleshette* holds nothing in—not her salty comments, not her feelings. And certainly not her stomach. This is just one of the many benefits of her marriage three years ago to old flame **Tom Poston**. "I remember saying to him, 'Look, you saw me at my best. I'm never holding this tummy in again, and you don't have to hold yours in.' There is no pressure. I see my girlfriends running for Botox and liposuction, but he puts his hand on my fat little belly and we're happy.

"Tell her how much you love me, honey," Suzanne prompted Tom during a recent interview.

"I have to tell you how much I love her," says straight man Tom.

"And tell her how flat my belly is, darling."

"I have to tell you how flat her belly is."

The couple, probably best known for their roles in separate Bob Newhart sitcoms (Suzanne was sardonic, smoky-voiced Emily Hartley on *The Bob Newhart Show*; Tom was hapless, hopeless handyman George on *Newhart*), have their timing down pat. Then again, they've had plenty of time to perfect it. They first met in a New York acting class in the late 1950s; they renewed their acquaintance the next year when Tom was starring in a play bound for Broadway and Suzanne was brought in to replace the leading lady.

She began playing his leading lady offstage as well. "Tom suggested that I come to his room to run lines, and I said that I

*Couples whose names are in boldface appear in the photo insert.

was in my robe," recalls Suzanne, who for the record looks trim and lovely. "And he said, 'Well, that would be fine.' Well, it was fine for *him*."

The romance ran about as long as the play—10 weeks. Suzanne lived in California. Tom, then recently separated from his wife, and the father of a young daughter, was living in New York and appearing as a panelist on the game show *To Tell the Truth*. And to tell the truth, he wasn't urging Suzanne to move east or to move in. "I think he thought I was too young for him"—Tom is 16 years Suzanne's senior—"and his personal life wasn't resolved. But we always adored each other personally, professionally, and sexually. We were always extremely compatible."

And always very happy to see each other. After the breakup of her brief marriage to Troy Donahue in the early 60s, Suzanne returned to New York. "I sent him a telegram reading, 'Help. Help. Trapped at the Plaza Hotel in need of your services.'" Tom showed up immediately—ready to serve.

Suzanne stayed in town as long as she could, but then a movie called. So did a romance with businessman Tommy Gallagher. Their marriage lasted 33 years, until Gallagher's death in 2000. Tom took his own walk down the aisle with Kay Hudson, a dancer and critical-care nurse, the same year that Suzanne married. "But we were always friends," she says. Her cousin was his jeweler. He was a guest star (as the zany Peeper) on *The Bob Newhart Show*, and she famously guested on the last episode of *Newhart*. Since the two had friends in common, she was often at assorted Poston family events, and he turned up at Pleshette family gatherings. "Tom knew Tommy, and I knew Kay. I was crazy about her. She was just a fabulous dame."

Both Tom and Suzanne had that rare Hollywood commodity: long, happy marriages. Both watched their spouses struggle with viciously debilitating illnesses: Kay was afflicted with ALS (Lou Gehrig's disease), Tommy with cancer. "He was so brave," Suzanne says quietly. "It was just one thing after another after another. The paramedics came to our house so many times that I used to call 911 and just say, 'It's Susie. Tell them it's Tommy.'" He died after a six-year struggle—within 12 months of Kay's passing.

Suzanne swore to her friends that she would never go out on another date and that she would certainly never marry again. But when Tom called to extend belated sympathies—he had been out of town for nearly a year and had just heard the news—"He was my old pal. We were commiserating. I said, 'This is the Widow Gallagher. Is this Widower Poston? This widow stuff sucks, doesn't it?'"

They made a date for dinner—nothing fancy, just the local deli with a bunch of Tom's comedian cronies. But somewhere over the tuna melt when she took Tom's arm, Suzanne felt herself starting to melt. "I went: 'What the hell is this feeling?' It was awkward because I didn't in any way want to disrespect Tommy."

It all seemed a little too fast, a little too soon, a little too everything. And yet this was her old friend Tom, a man she had always loved and trusted with all her heart. "It became a matter of 'Do you spit in the face of this gift and walk away, or do you embrace it?'"

They decided to embrace it even though they were having a little bit of trouble with the embracing part of this rekindled romance. When Tom came over once to watch the fights on TV and put his arm around Suzanne, she was uncomfortable. "I called him later and said, 'I feel like I'm in high school. I don't even know how to do this anymore.' So we made a date to neck."

What with Suzanne's very possessive Yorkshire terriers—one tried to bite Tom and the other stuck its tongue in Tom's mouth, "before I could," cracks Suzanne—the couple didn't make a lot of headway with necking, that night anyway.

What this romance needed, she told her beau, was a little bling bling. "Just because you slept with me before does not mean you get to sleep with me again" is how she put it—unless Tom came across with a ring. A ring, let's be clear, "with a very big rock," she specified.

Some weeks later, when the two were sitting in the bar at Los Angeles's Bel Air Country Club, Tom suddenly got down on one knee. "I thought he fell," remembers Suzanne. "I tried to pick him up, and he said, 'No, no, I *want* to be down here.'"

With a flourish he said, "This is for you," and handed Suzanne a ring box. Her mind was a tangle of confused emotions: "This is too soon. I can't do this. What will I say? I care about him so much and don't want to hurt his feelings, but . . ."

Stalling for time, she opened the box. Nestled on a bed of cotton was a platinum ring, the classic Tiffany setting supporting a 57-carat stunner. To be precise, a rock. Not a diamond but an actual piece of gravel.

"And, I mean, after that you gotta marry the guy, right? We were madly in love and acknowledging that we just had no right *not* to grab this and be grateful."

(Fifty-seven carats, by the way, comes to a little less than half an ounce.) Suzanne has kept this one-of-a-kind ring as a laughable, lovable souvenir.

Initially, they contemplated a big wedding, but when the guest list hit 800 names—"And those were just the people we had in common," says Suzanne—eloping seemed like the way to go. The ceremony was in New York where their romance had its roots.

"I gave Tom my father's cuff links. And I said, 'You were my first love and you are my last,'" says Suzanne, who wore a white satin dress (and a red thong). The groom wore a delighted expression. He's still wearing it.

"This is what I imagined love would be like when I was a little boy," he confides. "It's like a miracle to me. I thought I had imagined something that couldn't happen."

"When a man says that to you, when he sings you love songs, when he brings you flowers, when you swoon in his arms as you dance across the floor, that's worth everything," says Suzanne. Equally valuable is the couple's sense of their marriage as a safe haven where anything and everything can be put on the table. "Tom is obliged to talk more about things than he ever has," says Suzanne. "I just think that you should get things out there so they don't burn a hole in your gut."

"But I have nothing to hide," deadpans Tom, "except Bubbles."

"I know about Bubbles," assures his wife.

Suzanne has nothing to hide, either. She readily explains what it is about Tom that has her atwitter and aglow: "Tom and I were made for each other. We had other marriages and they were wonderful in their own ways, but this is the gift at the end. We shared so much in the early years. He knew my grandfather; he visited the apartment I grew up in. So it's almost like a very old marriage with all of that history."

Between acting jobs—Suzanne did recent stints on *8 Simple Rules* and *Will & Grace* while Tom had roles in the feature films *Christmas with the Kranks* and the sequel to *The Princess Diaries*—the couple has "just a really pleasant life," says

I bent over and kissed her right on the lips. It was innocent, but suddenly we heard the door close behind us. Carol's dad had seen it. But all I cared about was looking into her eyes."

After a couple of years they grew apart. Carol was busy with singing and dancing lessons, and, Harry admits, "I was too immature. Although I was proud of her accomplishments, I wanted all of her time on weekends." Then they went to different high schools and subsequently lost touch—for 70 years. They agree that although they were not together, they always remained connected spiritually. Carol says, "We formed each other and our principles—integrity and honesty. And they lasted all my life."

Carol needed that strength at the start of her career. The rough patches were discouraging before she found fame. "There were bleak years," she says. Breaking into the New York theater world was daunting, and whenever she was rejected, she thought of Harry. "Isn't that funny?" she says. "I would think of Harry because being with him was the happiest time in my life. When a producer would say hurtful things like 'No, you won't do. You're over six feet tall in heels, and you just don't fit,' I knew that Harry could straighten me out in two sentences."

Carol went on to smashing success in the 1950s Broadway musical *Gentlemen Prefer Blondes*. Lorelei's anthem, "Diamonds Are a Girl's Best Friend," is still considered Carol's signature song. Then in 1964 she tore up the Great White Way as matchmaker Dolly Gallagher Levi in *Hello, Dolly!* In the years since, Carol has been in great demand for revues and nightclub shows, and she gave a spectacular performance in the film *Thoroughly Modern Millie*. It's no surprise that Carol has won Tony Awards and a Golden Globe.

Harry flourished in business as a land developer and was

happily married for 60 years, until his wife died. On occasion over the years he tried to contact Carol just to send his regards but was never able to get through. "Why would a big celebrity answer me?" he thought, but actually she never received his messages.

On the personal front, Carol had tried marriage, including a lengthy one that she ended with a divorce after years of being mistreated. By her early eighties, she felt lonely and sad, doubting her spiritual beliefs. Did God really love her, and was he watching out for her? One night she took a walk outside her condo and began to pray. "Look," she told God, "I know that You exist. I know we were all created by You. Help me, please! I don't know how to handle life." She wanted a sign.

At about the same time, shortly after his wonderful wife died, Harry got down on his knees and also spoke to God. "Lord," he prayed, "I'm lonely, and if you want it so, I'll be alone. But if you want me to be married again, then please present that person to me."

Their prayers were answered. Carol had written her autobiography, *Just Lucky I Guess*, and in a few pages of it she reminisced about Harry. She described him as "exotic and beautiful," and recalled that she had loved hugging him. Mervyn Morris of the Mervyn department stores was a neighbor of Carol's near Palm Springs. Miraculously enough, Merv also knew Harry, because he happened to be one of Merv's office landlords. Merv read Carol's book and found a matchmaking opportunity as irresistible as it would have been to Dolly herself. He called Carol in late January 2003 and said, "Harry Kullijian is absolutely the most honest man I've ever dealt with. I just read how dearly you felt about him in the past, so I gave him your number."

Carol recalls that even after 70 years she was not nervous while awaiting Harry's call, "I knew him too well," she says, "and I'd loved him. We never really broke up. He went off to military school because it was the natural course of things." Harry agrees and feels that the joy of having shared his youth with her never left him even though he had been a happily married man.

Their reunion at her condo was explosive. The moment they hugged, Harry thought, "That's my girl, and she's going to be my wife. No doubt in my mind." Carol explained to Harry that she didn't cook, so they fixed a lunch of cottage cheese and apples. Their romance took off from there.

They were engaged within two weeks. "He proposed to me at a breakfast for 35 people who were his neighbors. I said yes, and it was the most natural thing in the world. It just evolved. I relaxed completely; I was so safe with him. I couldn't stop hugging and kissing him. It was plain old ordinary magnetism." Harry began to help Carol with work problems, such as planning her performance schedule and making sure her management was honest.

Harry and Carol were blissfully married in the presence of her cousin, Richard Long, and Harry's daughter and son, on May 10, 2003, at Merv's home near San Francisco. The invitation showed a picture of Carol and Harry from their junior high days. Merv walked Carol down the aisle, and though she had been married previously, she felt this was her first real wedding. "Harry just made me feel so girlie and feminine even though I was wearing a silk pants suit and low heels. I felt good next to him in his dark suit." They laugh at the memory of their quick modern-day courtship and admit that part of the reason for the rush is that they waited to be intimate until they were man and wife. After the wedding they escaped to charming Carmel, California, for a glorious four-day honeymoon.

People are so intrigued by their romance that when they appeared on the *Larry King Live* on CNN, all lights on the incoming phones lit up. Carol recalls, sporting that broad Channing smile, "People all over the world wanted to know: 'Where's *my* Harry Kullijian?'"

To this day Harry does the cooking and Carol washes and dries the dishes so they can be alone together. No staff. "I never knew there could be such romance," says Carol. "He's funny, he's tender, and he makes love to me like beautiful music. It's just *rrrrrrrrrrrr*! It's his warmth, the way he puts his arms around me and holds me. There's an ease with a man who wants to take care of his wife and considers her precious and sacred."

They are a testament to the phenomenon of reunited lovers never growing old in each other's eyes. When Carol emerges from the shower with wet hair and no makeup, Harry sees her as his young girlfriend. "She's the most beautiful woman in the world," he says. "She's extremely shapely, such a beautiful figure. It's hard to believe that at 83 she could be that lovely. But our compatibility was there in junior high school, and it hasn't gone away."

Carol has been performing her one-woman show to rave reviews across the country and overseas. "I tell stories about my friends Ethel Merman, Pearl Bailey, and Mary Martin," she says. "And Rosie O'Donnell and the Lunts. And I get to sing 'Razzle Dazzle.'" But she doesn't travel constantly anymore. She and Harry treasure time together at their house in Modesto, California, where their pool is surrounded with Armenian statuary in a nod to Harry's ancestry. "Before we reunited," says Carol, "I was on tour all the time, going from theater to hotel to dressing room. But I've slowed down a little for the first time in my life. Now I call our home an Armenian farmhouse, and I love to be with Harry in the sunshine."

In the mornings they pick fresh apricots, peaches, and figs to have with milk for breakfast. Carol says they feel like Adam and Eve in the Garden of Eden. She looks lovingly at her wedding ring, with a central diamond and several more around a gold flowerlike setting. It is the very ring Harry's mother wore, and Carol remembers admiring it when she was 12 years old. She says, "I never had this feeling with anyone else. Just his hand on my shoulder means the world."

Holding her hand, Harry nods in agreement. "Our story is all about hope," he says. "Society is at a place in history where love and respect seem to be fading away, but we are helping to change that by respecting the institution of marriage. A man and a woman are without doubt the most beautiful of God's creations. The love we have is invigorating, and it makes us feel young. It's a real miracle for Carol and me to be together again."

Hollywood is as smitten as the rest of us with rekindled love stories and has produced a ream of films about them. Some of the best loved (and most wept over) are *Casablanca*, *Forrest Gump*, *Splendor in the Grass*, *Dr. Zhivago*, *An Affair to Remember*, and, more recently, *Before Sunset* and *The Notebook*. Of course it makes a better drama if the lovers are parted heartbreakingly once again after they have reunited!

The entertainment industry has a reputation for real-life relationships that fail and bloom again (and sometimes fail once or twice more). Elizabeth Taylor and Richard Burton, Natalie Wood and

Robert Wagner, and Melanie Griffith and Don Johnson are couples whose personal lives made headlines with their marriage-divorce-remarriage scenario. The plot line is so dramatic (and sometimes comedic) that it has been the basis for such popular movies as *The Philadelphia Story*, *When a Man Loves a Woman*, and *The Parent Trap*.

Reunitees have been thoroughly mined for laughs in such films as *Bridget Jones's Diary*, *Splash*, *Soapdish*, and *Sweet Home Alabama*. Rekindled love has even crossed over into animation in *The Lion King*. Simba and Nala were cubs together in the veldt equivalent of kindergarten before their tragic separation and eventual reunion.

Kindergarten was also the real-life setting for the meeting of soap opera star Liza Huber and her future husband. Alex Hesterberg had a big crush on Liza when they were in elementary school. But he never told her. She went on to star in the daytime TV drama *Passions*, and to have a great passion of her own with her dorky-turned-dashing former classmate.

Liza and Alex

"I HAD A CRUSH ON HER IN THIRD GRADE"

Alex Hesterberg was sweating bullets. He should have hidden the ring somewhere else. His girlfriend, **Liza Huber,** was painstakingly applying her makeup over the dresser where the sparkler was concealed under his socks. He had told friends that this was the big night, and they had been waiting for over an hour with champagne ready to pop.

"Shouldn't you go to the bathroom?" he tried.

"No, don't need to." She leaned into the mirror.

"It's a long walk to the restaurant," he coaxed.

"Can you believe, I really don't have to go." She rummaged through her suitcase. "I like my outfit, but the accessories are off."

A lucky break. Reaching past her for the box as he went down on one knee, 27-year-old Alex delivered the best line of his life: "I have just the accessory for you. Will you marry me?"

It was a long road from St. Joseph's kindergarten where they first met in Garden City, New York. Their first grade class picture shows him standing behind her. "She's so cute in the front row, with her straight blond hair and freckles," says Alex, "and I'm the dorky-looking kid in the back with my tie messed up. By third grade, I had a real crush on her." He was not dissuaded by the navy jumper and green knee socks. "She was the prettiest girl in school."

"He was an old soul even when he was young," recalls Liza. "He was never snotty or bratty. He was a leader."

And secretly he was also her knight in shining armor. "Once at recess another girl pushed her and Liza fell down. I walked up to that girl and asked what her problem was."

What did Alex think of Liza's mom, renowned actress Susan Lucci? He loves her now that she's his mother-in-law, but at the time "I wasn't watching *All My Children*. Why would a third grader care who starred in it?"

He recalls one day when Liza rode her bike to the ice cream store with another boy. "I was so jealous," Alex reveals. His ardor became a case of love postponed when Liza transferred in fourth grade to another school.

Over the years Liza and Alex ran into each other at "spring fling" dances. He was also one of 50 kids at her Sweet Sixteen party but they were dating others. After attending different colleges he worked as business development manager for a software company in northern California, and she on television.

Then one night in the spring of 2002 they both went to Manhattan for a band performance honoring a Garden City classmate. Alex and Liza were surprised to see each other. "It was a very dark bar, but she lit it up," he smiles.

"My, didn't he turn out well!" she thought. "We were scrawny 16-year-olds when we last saw each other," she explains. "Now he was six-foot-three and very handsome."

They talked all night. When she was about to leave with her girlfriends, she invited him to go uptown. But Alex, having ignored his buddies, said he would call her sometime when it wasn't so late. Five minutes later she tapped him on the shoulder. "I told my friends to go because I want to be with you. Will you come uptown with me now?"

"She had a lot of chutzpah, and I admire that. She told me what was in her heart," praises Alex. "I said, 'Sorry, fellas. I gave you a shot, but I'm going with her.'" They headed out into a rainstorm, with Alex holding his leather jacket over their heads.

"It was special the moment I saw him again," Liza says. "His aura was different from the other guys I'd dated. He's open to people and nonjudgmental. He's every bit a man's man, but there's such a sweetness and kindness about him."

They started dating long distance; she re-upped with her show and moved back to California. A year later Alex asked Liza's dad, Helmut Huber, for his daughter's hand in marriage. In 2004 they married in the parish where they had first met.

As for the public nature of her work, Liza says, "Alex has never gotten upset about my being in the limelight or walking the red carpet. He innately knows how to handle himself. It's wonderful to have a man who's proud of me and helps keep the highs and lows of the business in perspective."

"Because we knew each other growing up and our families knew each other," says Alex, "we had a lot of trust right from the get-go. It allowed us to fall in love faster."

"Ain't No Mountain High Enough" was their wedding song because they believe nothing could have kept them apart. Says Alex, "I definitely feel that our being together was meant to be."

"He's extremely independent," says Liza. "He doesn't care what other people are saying. He does what's right for him and me and our family. That I love."

Ed and I attended Liza and Alex's wedding in March 2004. It was a jubilant celebration, with each family clearly thrilled to welcome the new son or daughter they had watched grow up.

High-profile people in other professions have also found themselves looking back for love. Muriel Humphrey Brown briefly succeeded her husband, former vice president Hubert Humphrey, in the Senate after he died in January 1978. She did not seek election that fall, choosing instead to go home to Minnesota. The next year she married Max Brown, whom she had met when the two were sixth graders in Huron, South Dakota. In a 1986 *Minneapolis Star Tribune* interview she was quoted as saying, "This is a whole new life for me. I don't live a life of politics anymore. Max and I have so much fun and a wonderful companionship."

Famed designer Nicole Miller is another believer in rekindled love. Recognized worldwide as the reinventor of the little black dress, her clothing collections are hugely successful, and her name is now on leather goods, shoes, and sheets. But one of the best places she ever put her name was on her wedding license to Kim Taipale.

Nicole and Kim

"IT'S EASIER TO RECONNECT THAN TO START FRESH"

Nicole Miller met Kim Taipale at a bridal shower for a mutual friend in Manhattan. Because they had other friends in common, they often ended up at the same clubs and cultural events.

It was the end of 1989 when she and Kim decided to be more than friends. "We dated a few months," Nicole says, "but I was more into him than he was into me. It was complicated turning a friendship into a romance. We ended up hating each other, and we both stopped calling."

About three years later, in 1992, still part of the same social group, they ran into each other at a wedding. "Kim was being friendly," says Nicole, "and I was a little mistrustful of him, but I figured I'd let bygones be bygones. Maybe we could go back to being friends."

Kim called Nicole a few months later and asked her out to dinner. She said her life was too busy right then and she would call him back, but she never did. Most of the summer went by before she ran into him at another party. "I apologized immediately and said I was sorry. Finally, in September, I made the call. I didn't plan it, but I think not being so available made me more attractive to him."

This time they clicked. "But as usual in my life we did things backwards. When he told me he really wanted kids, we decided on a family first, before we ever planned a wedding."

They married in February 1996, and Nicole now suits up for rollerblading with son Palmer and plays video games and basketball with him. This designer of many a frilly dress says, "I love doing 'boy' things with our son, and I love being with Kim. I think we got along so well the second time around because we already knew each other. When you're a little older, it's easier to reconnect than to start fresh with someone you don't know."

Kim is founder and executive director of the Center for Advanced Studies in Science and Technology Policy, a research and advisory group, as far from the garment business as you can get. "We balance each other out," says Nicole. "In the end I believe that knowing each other before and sharing mutual friends helped us make everything gel."

Clinical psychologist Ginny Fleming, who has a private practice in Los Angeles, agrees. "There can be a built-in trust with someone you knew before. There is a sense that this person is not intimidated by your success or your difficulties and has fallen in love with the real you." That's what sports reporter Scott Clark of WABC-TV felt when he looked back for love. A down-to-earth guy who values his Lima, Ohio, upbringing, Scott hit one out of the park romantically when he headed home for a friend's wedding. His teenage crush, Heather (Lynn), was the celebrity when they first met. She was a ninth grade cheerleader while Scott was a lowly eighth grader.

Heather and Scott

"THERE'S ONLY SO MUCH TO CELEBRITY, AND THEN YOU GO HOME"

Though Scott Clark would become a well-known sportscaster in New York, he never thought he had a chance with

Heather (Lynn) back in junior high. "She had status. The skirt, the sweater—that was status. And she was beautiful."

"The red skirt with the white inside pleat," Heather says with a laugh. "I thought I was hot stuff." She had long, straight blond hair, and Scott had a major crush.

"He was a little guy with a Prince Valiant haircut who used to say hi to me in the hall," remembers Heather. "We frequented the same make-out spots," he adds with a grin, "a place behind the funeral home and another behind the church, but definitely not together. We met once in a while at the local hangout spot, a hamburger joint called the Kewpee."

Heather moved to Michigan when she was a junior. It would be 25 years before they saw each other again.

Scott studied broadcast journalism and progressed from Ohio through Washington, D.C., to the Big Apple in 1986. After graduating in the class of 1970, Heather married, had three children, divorced, and worked as a kitchen designer in Ann Arbor, Michigan. When their mutual friend, Julia, got married in 1992, Heather and Scott both made the trek to Lima for the festivities.

At the reception, "I couldn't take my eyes off Heather. The middle-aged thunderbolt hit me," Scott says.

"People had been talking about our famous classmate," says Heather. "He was a lot taller now and had a better haircut. And he was handsome." They flirted all weekend, but because she has three kids she saw how complicated any future would be. When he invited her to visit a month later, she called Julia. "He's a big shot in New York, and I don't even know him that well."

"Go have a wonderful time," advised Julia, "but don't fall in love with him." She was aware of Scott's reputation with the ladies and his penchant for drinking.

It was a whirlwind weekend of fancy restaurants, a football game at West Point, and a boat ride around Manhattan. After dozens of people recognized him and ignored her, the two of them decided to have some fun. He began introducing her as Lady Victoria, and people bought it. "I curtsied, and they were impressed. Scott and I couldn't stop laughing." They loved realizing that they had both grown up on the same Betty Crocker recipes, like salmon patties with Spanish rice. "Even our speech patterns and relationships with our siblings were similar. Our values were all the same," Scott says. "I really trusted Heather because we both came from Lima. We had a sense of comfort with each other. I liked everything about her."

A week after Heather and Scott reunited he stopped drinking and has stayed sober ever since. "I don't think she would have stuck around if she had seen me as a party animal."

What mattered most to Heather was that although Scott had fame and made a great living, at heart he was still a hometown boy. "I'm crazy in love with him," she says. After commuting for two years they married in their hometown on New Year's Day 1995, in front of old classmates, family, and friends. Heather would have preferred that Scott move to Michigan but realized that for professional reasons they were better off in New York.

He leaves his TV-star status at work. "There is only so much to the celebrity situation," says Scott. "Then you go home. Heather has common sense, warmth, and kindness. I like that she has no airs. When you're with someone from your hometown, all the celebrity stuff goes away. That's one of the best things about it for me."

"He's supercharged at work," explains Heather, "but he's comfortable coming home and sitting at the kitchen table in his surgery scrubs. Honestly, we try to avoid the celebrity life for the most part on weekends. We stay home, rent a video, and order a pizza."

Scott says he feels excitement and passion for Heather at the same time that he feels comfort and confidence. "She loves me for who I am." How lucky does he feel? He smiles. "She was a cheerleader, for crying out loud. I'm on top of the world!"

Celebrity or not, we all wonder how much we can trust someone we find attractive. We all hope a potential partner has only one agenda: building a caring relationship with us.

Fortunately, I very quickly knew this was true of Ed. Because we had known each other as adolescents, when we came together as adults it didn't take long to feel that he knew and cared for the real me. We were drawn by each other's core qualities. Once Ed and I realized how serious we were, I wanted him to meet Caroline and Andrew. Paramount in my thoughts was making the occasion comfortable for the kids. I needn't have worried.

A little nervous, I approached Caroline first and started to say, "If I was ever invited out by a gentleman caller—"

She interrupted. "Mom, that sounds so Victorian."

I started again. "Okay, then, what would we be looking for in a gentleman who wanted to spend time with me and take me out to dinner?"

"Well," Caroline said, mulling the question thoughtfully, "we'd want him to be trustworthy. He should bring you flowers. And he should take you to a very nice place for dinner unless *you* specifically ask for fast food." She also said it would be good in the long run if he liked traveling since I like it so much. "But," she added, "we shouldn't be too strict about that one. We don't want so many requirements that nobody could meet them."

I immediately called Ed *sotto voce*. "You need to arrive with flowers." He assured me that a dozen roses were already part of his plan.

That night at about nine, Andrew and Caroline were both home to meet this man whom they knew was my high school sweetheart. When the doorbell rang, I made sure I was still "getting ready" so that Andrew would greet Ed on his own. Hospitable as usual, Andrew invited him to have a seat and brought him water in a World Series plastic cup. They immediately started talking baseball, which set them both at ease. When I walked into the living room, I received compliments on my dress and a kiss on the cheek from Ed. Andrew grinned. It was a good beginning.

Caroline took a break from instant-messaging her friends on the computer to sit down and join us. My kids wanted Ed to tell them what I was like as a girl. They were particularly delighted when he divulged how we had "decorated" people's houses late at night with rolls of toilet paper. I added that a girlfriend and I once tried a more fashionable version; we tied several hundred red ribbons to the tree branches in Ed's front yard.

At 9:30, Ed helped me with my shawl, and we were off on our first official dinner date. When I returned home, Caroline was waiting up. Smiling broadly, she asked, "Did you feel that Andrew and I were kind of like your parents checking him out?"

She had put the flowers Ed brought in a vase and suggested I keep the plastic wrapper because it was decorated with little pink hearts. She was happy; she foresaw a real romance for her mom.

Andrew simply said, "Mom, he's a great guy!"

I was thrilled. The kids were relaxed and comfortable, and so was Ed. He had even set a good example, getting me home before midnight. Who knew rekindled love would bring a rekindled curfew?

Chapter 3

Early Love "Sets the Standard"

"IT WAS NEVER PUPPY LOVE. IT WAS NEVER INFATUATION," INSISTS Jim Petrausch, who was 10 years old when he met six-year-old Renee (Shipp). They grew up together, went their separate ways, and finally reunited after 34 years apart. Says Jim, "She was always the love of my life."

Alexis Grossman, 29, originally dated her husband, Matt Wheeler, 33, when they were teenagers. She says, "My parents kept calling it puppy love. I told them it was serious, but they didn't understand. We had already fallen deeply in love."

Parents are forever telling teenagers that their first crushes and romances are "just puppy love," the relationship won't last, the feelings will pass quickly, they'll have "dozens" of boyfriends (or girlfriends) before they settle down. But in some cases, even when a couple spends years apart, the feelings last a lifetime.

What determines who attracts us? Or re-attracts us? Powerful psychological forces that begin when we are babies sculpt our vision of the perfect partner. Then our first sweethearts create another surge of impressions about the ideal mate. Contrary to all the pooh-poohing by "adults who know better," sometimes it turns out that young love *is* true love.

One reunited New York couple in their early 30s discovered that during their earlier romance each had become the other's *ideal* partner without realizing it.

Kate and Ron

"HOW DID ANYBODY ELSE STAND A CHANCE?"

Kate Coyne, a pretty 18-year-old blonde with smoky green eyes, was teaching some seven-year-old girls to play volleyball when she first spotted **Ron Martucci** with his classic Roman nose, thick brown hair, and hazel eyes. He and Kate were summer counselors in 1992 at Camp Hillard in Westchester, New York. She instantly fixated on the football linebacker as he descended the bunkhouse stairs, a six-year old boy hanging off each arm.

She quickly concocted a scheme to meet Ron, who was a student from Hamilton College in upstate New York. "I told another counselor to start chasing me, and I ran right toward Ron and pleaded, 'Let me hide behind you. This guy wants to throw water on me.'"

Ron gallantly acted as her shield. "I thought she was beautiful," says Ron. After that they often talked when she was standing by the pool and he was on the upper deck of his bunkhouse. "Little did I realize," says Kate, "that he could completely see down my bathing suit—which was, I think, part of the appeal." Remembering himself as a 19-year-old and grinning mischievously, Ron does not deny it.

"I orchestrated reasons to run into him," Kate recalls. "One time I dragged a camper to the field where Ron was playing soccer under the guise of looking for a lost canteen." This went on for several days. "In teenage years a week of flirting and trying to get someone's attention feels like an eternity." When she summoned up the nerve to ask him what he was doing on the weekend, he was shocked that such an attractive woman might be interested in him, but he finally got the message.

Ron remembers what she wore on their first date: blue jeans, brown cowboy boots, and a white button-down shirt tied at the waist. They both remember that the evening culminated in their first kiss.

At the end of the summer Kate was scheduled to spend six months in Paris before attending Oxford University. Fearful that coeds and cheerleaders would flirt with Ron while she was away at school, she coached him: "When you go back to college, what do you do when a girl comes near you?'"

"I know, I know. I start screaming, 'Back off! I'm taken!'"

Once settled in Paris, Kate felt like a prisoner, making marks on the wall, writing love letters, counting the days before she returned home to her boyfriend. Ron received his first international letter from her, and today when he sees that type of envelope, a thrill still runs through him. Her need to see Ron was so intense that one weekend Kate flew from Paris to upstate New York to see one of his football games. "I was in the stands," she says, "and I felt like standing up and screaming, 'Hey, everybody, that linebacker is my boyfriend!' That was when we went from being a couple to being crazy, madly in love."

Once she was back home, she spent every weekend with Ron at Hamilton. Then it came time to leave for England. "At first I was miserable at Oxford," she says. "But then I decided I was going to be there for three years, so I might as well put down some roots."

Ron's attitude started changing, too. "I got tired of the long distance," he says. And then there was Kate's family. Her mom was an advertising CEO and her dad a retired radio producer. Ron's mom was a school secretary and his dad a general contractor. "Kate never made it an issue," Ron says, "but we grew up in two different worlds." The truth was that Kate cherished Ron's family life, especially because her parents were getting divorced after 24 years of marriage. "His parents were happily married," she says, "and they ate dinner together every night. My family was literally falling apart, so having dinner with Ron was like a scene out of *Leave It to Beaver*. It was so comforting."

Kate was sitting at a little white-painted phone table in her Oxford dorm room when the call came. "I don't think I can do this anymore," Ron said. Kate cried for a week and made a couple of hysterical "you can't really mean it" phone calls. But Ron held firm, and after the summer of '95, they lost touch.

Kate eventually became the entertainment editor at *Good Housekeeping* magazine while Ron became a teacher at The Hackley School in New York. He always compared his girlfriends to Kate, telling his mother they weren't nearly as smart or as pretty. One day his mom spotted Kate on TV, discussing one of the magazine's cover stories on *Entertainment Tonight*. True to her maternal instincts, she also noticed that there was no ring on Kate's finger. She called Ron and said, "Enough! You've gotta stop comparing everyone. Just call Katie already."

Kate was in her office in the year 2000 when she received the call. "Hi, Katie. I don't know if you remember me . . ."

"He had to be kidding," says Kate. "He was the first love of my life! But there was something sweet about his not presuming I would just fall at his feet." They made plans to meet. "I got to John's Pizza Parlor on the Upper West Side early," she says, "and I sat on the bench coaching myself not to fall in love with him, reminding myself that this was all about closure. But when the most handsome man I'd ever met came walking toward me, I swear he could've told me he had done time in prison and I would have said, 'That's nice, but do you have a girlfriend?' When he kissed me, we felt like 18 and 19 again, and we were off like a rocket."

In December 2001, Ron asked Kate to go Christmas shopping with him. She was in a bad mood that night, but Ron insisted on finding a store to buy a gift for her mom. So why did he keep passing stores in which they could have found perfectly acceptable gifts? Pretty soon he pulled onto a side street and said, "Hey, this is the road to Camp Hillard. Let's see if we can get in!"

Kate agreed reluctantly, but when he suggested they get out of the car, she was skeptical. "Did you not see *Friday the 13th*? I'm not running around camp in the dark at night."

"Katie," he said, "please get out of the car."

"All right, Mr. Nostalgia. You want to take a walk down memory lane?" She walked over to where she had first laid eyes on him at the foot of the bunkhouse stairs. "Tell me why this spot is significant."

"Actually, let me ask you a question," Ron said, and he pulled out a ring. "Will you marry me?"

Kate recalls that the first thing she said was, "Oh, I've been such a bitch tonight!" And then she said yes. They had a garden wedding on Nantucket island on July 3, 2003.

Kate and Ron agree that knowing each other when they were teenagers adds depth to their marriage. "We were fortunate," says Ron. "We found the real thing early on. And I think being apart for a while gave us a chance to realize that we had it right the first time. Katie is beautiful and smart, and I respect her confidence and compassion. She's always been my benchmark for what's important in life. Over the years I have found myself asking, 'Is this something Katie would be proud of?'"

Kate describes Ron as "earnest, stand-up, and good-to-the-core." She says, "He became my standard for what a man should be. How did anybody else stand a chance?"

Entwined Identities

Teenage relationships profoundly influence our later vision of the perfect partner, as Kate and Ron discovered, because these connections are forged at a time when we are first developing our adult identities. "An important developmental task in adolescence is to loosen the bonds with our parents," explains New York City psychoanalyst Colleen Konheim, who has been in private practice for more than 15 years. "In that critical period we attach to friends and peers almost as if they were blood relations. Those connections, those friendships made between the ages of 14 and 25, are often the strongest we make in our lives."

It's like climbing a jungle gym, where we loosen the hold on one bar, our parents, and grab hold of the other bar, our friends. Up until our early twenties our "job" in the sense of psychological development is to individuate and differentiate ourselves from our parents. The boyfriends and girlfriends who are with us as we do this are significant on our journey out of childhood into adulthood. In many ways they become permanently entwined in our identities.

First love relationships are the emotional bridges we build away from what psychologists call our "family of origin." During the teen years it is key to our development as adults that we feel attracted to and admired by people outside our family circle. "In adolescence we are drawn to persons who sparkle in response to our sexuality as well as other features of our being—how we look, how we think, how we make them feel, how much room we make for them in our lives," explains Estelle Schecter, who has been a training therapist at New York-Presbyterian Hospital for 25 years, teaching generations of psychiatrists and marriage therapists. "A romantic partner in the initial phase of our sexual development affirms our desirability and is an important influence on identity formation."

Sharing Adolescent Angst

Feelings of love during adolescence are especially intense because they occur at a time when we are full of hopes and dreams but are often lacking in confidence. We are struggling with who we are going to become and how much of ourselves to reveal. In the sweetest of adolescent relationships, the young sweethearts confide in each other about some of their personality quirks, their impossible dreams, and their darkest fears.

"If one partner allows the other to see aspects that are somewhat unfavorable and the other accepts it and does not denigrate it, deny it, or in some way mock it," explains Dr. Herb Barrett, "then one achieves a kind of safety in that person's presence."

Thankfully, the angst and uncertainties of adolescent life recede as we grow up. But sharing those difficult moments as well as youthful pleasures with a sweetheart creates powerful bonds. Our adolescent loves are precious to us, partly because the intensity of those feelings is rarely repeated with new partners later in life. "There is a level of intimacy with your teenage love that you just won't get again with someone else," says Sherry Bush who has counseled hundreds of couples. "You were at a very important phase in your development, growing physically, emotionally, and sexually in a way that you will never experience again but that you shared with this person." Teenage rapture can quickly return, as a Connecticut man and woman who were high school sweethearts discovered years later.

Laurie and Mike

"HE STILL GIVES ME BUTTERFLIES"

Laurie (Curley) and Mike Clinton were married 20 years after they attended his senior prom in Noank, Connecticut. They reconnected after more than 15 years apart when he was listed as a reference on the résumé of someone she was interviewing for a job.

Mike had been dazzled by the cute 14-year-old blonde at parties and basketball games in the fall of 1978, but it wasn't until Christmas that he got the nerve to ask Laurie out. It was her first date with a boy. Soon they were going steady. "My parents trusted him completely," says Laurie. "My mother said she knew Mike would never let anything happen to me." Laurie remembers many nights curling up with the phone at her ear and Mike telling her the next day that he had listened to her breathing after she fell asleep. Mike graduated a year before Laurie and joined the Air Force. She carefully saved every letter and trinket he sent. When he came back to work in the city utilities department, however, she began to feel that she should focus on her college education without tying herself down, and she broke up with him. Although he tried to talk her out of it, she was firm. "I followed my head instead of my heart."

Each went on to marry and have a family. Fifteen years later when Laurie caught Mike's name on the résumé, they had a brief visit and went their separate ways. Laurie had her second baby in 1998, but her marriage was in trouble, and after two years of counseling she divorced. Mike's marriage had also come unraveled. They started spending time together as friends. On weekends they would take all four of the children out for pizza or stay in and play dominos. Soon they were passionately back in love, and Laurie says by that time she had enough experience to realize what a good, loving man he was. Mike says, "I adore her. She's still beautiful and kind, and she encourages my dreams." In fact, they work together on his dry-goods transportation business, and he is supportive of her plan to go back for an MBA.

On July 22, 2001, they married in Waterford, Connecticut's, Harkness Park where they had often walked together as teens. Living with their blended family in East Hampton, Connecticut, Mike is devoted to Laurie and says, "The honeymoon continues."

"I firmly believe that the intense feelings we shared in high school are the foundation that makes our relationship so incredibly close today," says Laurie. "I'm with someone I trust completely and who is truly my best friend. He still gives me the butterflies I felt when we were together in high school."

Who We Choose in Adolescence

While Laurie's parents were quick to recognize Mike's good heart, some mothers and fathers are flummoxed by their children's choice in a love interest. Why on earth, they might wonder, is their son attracted to someone who seems so wild—or, conversely, so ordinary? Why must the object of their daughter's affection be tattooed and pierced in every discernible place? Hard as it is for some parents to believe, we make our early romantic choices based on our experiences growing up. Something about these partners reflects what we found in our families even though they may appear to be the polar opposite of the example provided at home.

Dr. Helen Fisher theorizes that we actually have what she terms a "love map" programmed into our brains. In her book, *Why We Love*, she writes: "We grow up in a sea of moments that slowly sculpt our romantic choices. Your mother's wit and way with words; your father's zest for politics and tennis . . . these and thousands of other subtle forces build our individual interests, values and beliefs. By the teenage years, each of us has constructed a catalogue of aptitudes and mannerisms we are looking for in a mate."

Distinct preferences in the partners we find attractive evolve from this template or blueprint as we grow up, resulting in a subconscious list of qualities and attributes that we seek in a sweetheart. When the time is right, we fall for someone who fits within those parameters.

Ed and I got a kick out of trying to figure out our "love maps" after reading Dr. Fisher's book. Was it his neighborly self-sufficient nature, so like my dad's, that appealed to me? Maybe he was attracted by the dozen things I had going at once in high school. After all, his mom, after being widowed at a young age, managed an entire medical building while raising seven children and never missed church on Sundays. My mother-in-law makes the rest of us look as if we are moving in slow motion.

Now, 30 years later, the parallels are unmistakable. What I saw in my dad as I was growing up—the clearheaded ability to manage large groups of people, a distinct delight in family, and that typical male passion for cars, hardware stores, and tinkering in the garage—are things I adore in my husband.

While Dr. Fisher's "love map" is far more complex and multilayered, even the obvious comparisons are intriguing and fun.

Making the Same Choice as Adults

With psychological forces from adolescence continuing to operate in our adult hearts and minds, it is understandable that we might choose the same partner again. "What you regard as handsome and charming and appropriate behavior and kindness—these basic values don't change," says Dr. Fisher. "The reasons you loved this person are still with you, so it's quite likely if this person comes back, you will find him or her attractive again."

And this time we are doubly drawn because the partner was a trusted confidant while our identities were taking shape. "When you get back together with someone who meant so much during that formative time, it's like going home again," says Dr. Linda Waud, who intensively studied reunited couples and now counsels adolescents and adults for The Community Health Awareness Council in Mountain View, California. Dr. Waud married her own high school sweetheart, Ben, after more than 35 years apart. She says that even after 10 years of marriage to him, she is "ecstatic." Her daughter lovingly calls them "ridiculously happy." Given the psychological underpinnings, it is no surprise.

Reversing a Loss

We have deep fears beginning much earlier than adolescence that may be eased by reuniting with a past sweetheart. Regardless of how much we mature, our childhood feelings stay with us at some level. "Separation anxiety" or the fear of being abandoned occurs in children starting at about one year. For some it is never fully resolved, and the fear of being separated from our mothers is often transferred to people we love later in life. "No matter what age we reach," writes Dr. Nancy Kalish, "we do not like separating from those we love, so the endings of romantic relationships always bring pain. When lost lovers return to rekindle the romance, it can be felt as a tremendous relief."

Breakups are hard on everyone, but adolescents in particular are vulnerable to feeling deeply wounded. Many teenagers don't have enough experience to put the situation in perspective, to truly believe that all will eventually be well. At that age we generally don't have a lot of self-esteem. If we didn't choose to part, we usually blame ourselves, thinking we must have done something wrong or we must be unlovable. The sense of loss may lessen as we grow up, but we're human—some of it remains. Many couples report that reuniting has the unexpected bonus of vanquishing the residual pain. "Reuniting with that person," says Dr. Sherry Bush, "is like the ultimate fantasy of actually reversing the loss." It is a fantasy that came true for a Florida couple who reunited in their early fifties after 26 years apart.

Geraldine and Jimmy

"I WAS CRUSHED"

Geraldine O'Brien and Jimmy Sibilia started dating in 1966 when he asked if he could walk her home from a dance at Kearny High School in New Jersey. After that they had a wonderful romance for two years, often going into New York City and taking long drives to a huge car dealership in Pennsylvania where they would climb the fence at night to look at the Corvettes up close.

They went to his junior prom in 1967, but then he broke up with her one month later. "I was crushed," she remembers. "It was devastating. I had been thinking he was The One. I kept asking myself, 'Did I do something wrong?'" She now feels it was his "youthful hormones" that caused him to look elsewhere.

In any case she went on to a happy marriage and a career in marketing and communications, and then was widowed in 1997. Jimmy moved to Florida, had a marriage that failed, and has worked for many years tracking construction projects for the Miami-Dade school systems.

More than three decades after the breakup Jimmy signed up

with Classmates.com in hopes of finding Geraldine. After she logged on in December 2000, he wrote that he had never forgotten her and that he still loved her. He says, "I realized that I had made a mistake in leaving her." Geraldine is convinced that her dad and her first husband got together in heaven and said, "We need to find someone for Geraldine. We want someone she can trust who will love her. How about Jimmy Sibilia?" When they reunited, Jimmy told her how deeply sorry he was for hurting her. She was just happy to be back together. "We realized we had even more in common than we could have understood in high school," says Geraldine. "We are perfect for each other."

Because they both have terrific jobs and Jimmy is still helping to raise his daughters, they now commute between Geraldine's home in Orlando and his near Miami. "Gerri is considerate and bright, and we've always found it very easy to talk to each other," Jimmy says. "She is my soul mate." Geraldine smiles. "Jimmy is smart and kindhearted. He helps me relax and makes me laugh. I adore him, and I feel young and pretty when I'm with him."

Geraldine and Jimmy's elation is right on course. Therapist Estelle Schecter explains: "Something of oneself was left behind in those original relationships and is recovered by reconnecting with the person who partnered that phase of life." When we reconnect, we reclaim a chunk of the self-esteem that was damaged in the breakup or relieve the guilt that we have felt ever since that time.

Many reunited lovers say that before their return they had fond thoughts of or even longed for each other. Even when they weren't looking for each other per se, they were looking for the *qualities* of each other in the people they dated: generosity, intelligence, humor, kindness, talent, energy, and an affectionate nature. "The relationship with our desired object, in this case the sweetheart, is played out in subsequent relationships," explains Dr. Bush. "If it was our first love or biggest crush at a very impressionable age, it creates expectations, and other potential partners are compared against this benchmark." A summer romance at the beach in the mid '80s led to years of such comparisons for one couple.

Alexis and Matt

"I WAS ALWAYS LOOKING FOR HIM"

Matt Wheeler was 15 in the summer of '85 when he took a job as a carnival barker on the boardwalk at the Jersey Shore. "Hey!" he'd shout to passersby. "Try the game! Win once and get your choice of any gift on the stand!" While spinning the wheel he spotted 12-year-old **Alexis (Grossman)** walking on the boardwalk. "She looked like a sunbeam was lighting her up," he remembers, so he did what a carnie barker should do: He started yelling in her direction, knowing full well that the prizes (mostly small appliances) were nothing a 12-year-old girl would want.

Alexis thought the tall, skinny boy with short, dark curly hair and an earring was "cool and beautiful." They hung out for a magical week. Matt remembers "breathing, eating, drinking, everything was Alexis." He loved her "spiky punk hair." She says he was "sweet and funny." They shared a passion for punk styles and new-wave music.

When the week ended, Alexis went back home to Chester, New Jersey. They kept up their romance for more than a year, persuading older friends to drive the two hours between their homes for a few precious hours together. But the distance was a problem, so they settled into a friendship with occasional calls.

As the years passed, they lost touch. Matt worked in various cities as a collections agent for health-care companies and then became manager of a nightclub in Raleigh, North Carolina. Alexis became a much-in-demand hairstylist at a hip salon called Xena's Beauty Company in New York City. They both had various romantic relationships but never found the energy and kindness in anyone else that they had found in each other.

They hadn't talked in nine years, and then on September 11, 2001, the World Trade Center was destroyed. Matt called from his home in North Carolina to find Alexis and make sure she wasn't hurt. Her apartment was on West Fifteenth Street and, scared at being so close to the center of the attacks, she had cycled to a friend's place 100 blocks north. She says there was a "not knowing what would happen next" kind of feeling in the air. When she checked her messages a few days later, she was touched by Matt's concern. Alexis says that 9/11 was a huge wake-up call for her about "our vulnerability and how precious life is, and how it can end at any second."

Alexis and Matt made many more phone calls, wrote to each other, and visited. They found themselves falling back in love. Alexis explains: "As we talked, we both realized 'Oh, my God, I think you're my person. I think you're my person!'"

Matt moved to New York, and they got married in 2003. For their wedding Alexis wore a red silk halter dress spray-painted with black stars, a style that Matt fondly calls "Armani meets Dr. Seuss."

Matt says that throughout their years apart he compared every girl to his first love. "There were bits and pieces of Alexis in the girls I dated. She was my standard, right down to her coloring—blue eyes, brown hair, and pale skin." He admires her strength, imagination, and generosity.

Alexis says, "I realize that whomever I was with, I was always looking for Matt—not in appearance but in his artistic qualities and personality. In the end we realized that we'd both been searching all along for what we had together."

During their years apart Matt and Alexis did what many people do: They sought the exciting and comforting aspects of each other in a variety of partners. Their personal discovery is one that frequently leads to rekindled love—sometimes the best way to find those valued characteristics in a companion is to reunite with the original.

As Dr. Sherry Bush told me, "That person imprinted on you." Then, speaking on a personal level, she added, "I know that my own boyfriend in high school influenced my dry, sarcastic sense of humor. And I'll sometimes say things that I just know he must have put into my head. Donna, maybe some of your personality or your sense of humor was fueled by Ed way back then." I believe she's right.

Lady or Lizard?

Soon after we started dating as adults, Ed asked me to hike with him to Sandstone Peak, the highest point in the Santa Monica Mountains. Having been a Girl Scout, I felt confident about keeping up, though in truth I had walked more miles selling cookies than hiking the wilderness. We started out early, inhaling the new day. It felt as if we had the whole world to ourselves. Ed extended his hand, helping me climb over rocks and stray branches on the path. Halfway up, spotting a large flat boulder, I grabbed the chance to lie back and soak up some rays, which I clearly enjoyed. In a tender moment Ed looked over at me and said affectionately, "You're just like a lizard, sunning yourself like that."

As compliments go, this was not his best moment. I looked at him skeptically. "You must mean a very *pretty* lizard."

Taking his foot out of his mouth, he said, "Oh, yes, you're Lizzy with a pink bow."

Quick recovery, Ed.

I actually loved his lizard faux pas; it was such a guy thing to say. He still sometimes calls me "Lizzy with a pink bow." Our sweet bantering that day was reminiscent of how we gently joked when we were teenagers, kidding in a way that said, "I completely trust you to laugh with me, not at me. I have faith that you will see me as admirable and desirable. You are the person I have been hoping to find."

Chapter 4

The Lure of Shared Backgrounds

THE LURE OF THE FAMILIAR IS POWERFUL STUFF. WE ARE PASSION-ately and profoundly drawn to people and places that feel comfortable to us. So in the search for love, a shared background is a tremendous magnet. "You have a frame of reference about your childhood that's very similar," explains clinical psychologist Dr. Sherry Bush. "You've grown up in the same environment and seen the world from the same lens. You can reminisce about those things. You have a lot in common."

Reunitees remember living in the same neighborhood, gabbing in homeroom, competing in 4-H, or attending the same church. "This person sees you differently than other people," says Dr. Helen Fisher. "This person knows your mother, knows the house you grew up in. There is a sweetness about being with a human being who knows your life."

The Windex Date

Ed sees in his mind as clearly as I do the street where I lived, the fireplace in my living room, and my family's kitchen table. I remember the tree-lined driveway to his family's home, the auditoriums where he won his debate trophies, and the Chevy Impala he drove. (There's more to come about this memorable car.) We recall that our moms both baked tuna noodle casserole with crumbled potato chips on top and were expert at suspending any number of objects in Jell-O. We also remember fondly "the Windex date."

One Saturday when we were high school seniors, Ed came to pick me up at the house. I hadn't finished my chores and was still vacuuming when he arrived. The rule in our household was firm: You didn't go out until your work was done. Apparently Ed's mom had read the same manual. He didn't flinch when my mom handed him a Windex bottle and said, "If you want to take Donna out sooner, you can clean the back windows." Not one to mess around with his girlfriend's mother, he got to work, winning points with Mom and a permanent job in our married life.

These memories give us some good laughs, but, more important, they recall the common values our families had as we grew up. As for many reunitees, this shared background deepens our bond today.

Choosing Wrong, Choosing Right

Common backgrounds can draw people together even when they expect the opposite. Therapist Vicki Hillman Firstenberg talks about one of her clients: "The last thing she ever wanted was to be with a Jewish guy from New Jersey. She described herself as 'a Jewish girl from New Jersey' who had spent the better part of her life trying to escape what was familiar. Now, here she was in her late fifties, marrying the very kind of man from whom she'd run away. Whatever she was trying to escape, it took courage on her part to recognize that although there were difficult aspects to her childhood, she still needed to embrace and honor it. Once she did, someone who shared her past was exactly what she wanted now."

The question of what makes two people well matched is a big issue as they pair up. What do they need to have in common? Comparable educations? Shared religion? Agreement on lifestyle? A reuniting couple is more likely to be compatible than two people starting from square one, and when it comes to marriage, that's a big plus. "The question of shared backgrounds is really key," says Dr. Bush. "So much data on what makes marriages successful indicates the importance of having grown up in similar social and cultural venues. You have a similar frame of reference about the world."

Unfortunately, sometimes we learn things the hard way. Dr. Nancy Kalish believes that one reason for the epidemic of broken marriages in our society is that too many couples lack shared backgrounds and values. "Today," she muses, "half of first marriages and 60 percent of second ones are breaking up partly because people don't marry partners with similar backgrounds. We have a lot of diversity as we go off to college or graduate school, meeting and marrying people who are very different. In their twenties, people think that doesn't matter, but often they're choosing wrong."

Choosing each other was choosing right for a couple who remembered family vacations together as children. Today Kathy (Ciero) and Jim Johnson share not only vacations but also more than 24 years of reunited bliss.

Kathy and Jim

"IT ALL BLOOMED RIGHT BACK AT ME"

Kathy (Ciero) and Jim Johnson spent summers together in the 1950s in Wisconsin as kids. Kathy's aunt Martha was married to Jim's uncle Floyd, so their families visited often. One time in seventh grade she went for her water pistol. "I was boy crazy and thought he was the cutest thing I'd ever seen," says Kathy, "so I squirted him with my squirt gun." Jim, who was an eighth grader, didn't take it lying down. "He threw me over a log and spanked me. It was all about flirting." Their high schools in Illinois were about 30 miles apart, and they dated occasionally. "As puberty kicked in, I noticed her. She was a cute girl, and she had a magic personality—real sweet, very caring," says Jim. They also dated some when both attended Northern Illinois University. But Jim admits that as time went on he was "moving fast" and didn't want to settle down. "I was a prude," Kathy clarifies with a laugh, "so we went our separate ways."

Still, they always felt a deep fondness for each other. "When I heard she got married, I thought, 'Well, I blew that chance,'" says Jim. A few years later Jim got married, too.

In 1979 they met at a family funeral. They hadn't seen each other for 12 years and enjoyed the chance to catch up. Jim had moved to Arkansas. He learned that Kathy had divorced soon after her children were born. A year after they met at the funeral he called to tell her that he was about to be divorced and that he hoped to see her when he was in town on business. "I need a friend who's been through this," said Jim. He visited several evenings, playing with her kids and talking with Kathy for hours. "Whistles blew," says Jim. "Everything just fit right."

"It was so comfortable," says Kathy, "as if no time had passed." Kathy had been lonely. "I'd done the bar scene and the singles clubs and never met anybody that I would even consider taking home to my children and introducing as someone I was serious about. I thought maybe I was doomed to be alone," she says. "With Jim it was different. I knew immediately he was the one."

He finalized the divorce and soon called. "I don't want to let you get away again. Will you marry me?"

"For as long as I can remember I always had a crush on Jim," says Kathy. "He had such a sparkle in his eye. I was just absolutely crazy about him when I was younger, and the moment I saw him again, it all bloomed right back at me."

She told him yes and married him in the new house he had bought for her in Flippin, Arkansas. He adopted her children, who were three and six at the time. Together Kathy and Jim run a mom-and-pop printing business that has clients around the country. Does working and living together ever cause problems? They've had their share of small tussles, "but nothing where we thought it wouldn't hold together," says Jim. "I already knew what Kathy was like. There was a connection from when we were kids. It was never like getting acquainted with a stranger. She's got that spirit, that twinkle she had when she was 17. And I know I can trust her."

"He's still the young man I fell in love with years ago," smiles Kathy. "I feel flirty and giddy when he holds my hand, just like a teenager."

They prize their common history. Jim's grandpa taught Kathy how to play cribbage; his family gave hers a puppy; they all swam in the lake. "We often talk about our memories—the summer cottage and the dates in high school going to basketball and football games. Those memories help you mesh together," says Jim. "I know how lucky I am to have her."

Shared Backgrounds, Less Conflict

Even blissfully reunited couples like Kathy and Jim have the occasional tiff, but major, irreconcilable disputes are less likely than for couples with disparate upbringings. "Shared backgrounds are an anchor for couples," explains Dr. Iris SanGiuliano who has been a psychotherapist in New York City for 30 years. "If your background and values are similar, there are a lot of things you don't have to negotiate in a marriage, issues on which you can easily agree. You bypass a lot of conflict."

One couple remembers that as teenage sweethearts their personalities were opposite, and their dreams about where to ultimately live and work didn't match, either. But in their early forties Wanda (Hite) and Todd Lista found that because of their early love, common background, and strong friendship, they had few conflicts, and it was fairly easy to resolve the ones they did have. It all began in Aiken, South Carolina.

Wanda and Todd

"THE HOUSE HAD A GARDEN AND A WHITE PICKET FENCE"

Wanda (Hite) and Todd Lista met in the backseat of a white Chevy Vega in 1972. They were in a school carpool, and she was immediately drawn to the boy with the sandy blond hair and blue eyes. "He was cute, honest, and shy," says Wanda. "We lived less than a mile apart, our parents went to the same church, and I wrote him poems. I chased him for two years."

They paired up to go to movies, horse races, and the golf course, where they sneaked onto a hill overlooking one of the greens and kissed under the stars. "I liked her long brown hair and her blue eyes," says Todd. "She was very attractive. I used to help her with math homework." After graduating in 1974, Wanda studied journalism and drama at the University of South Carolina. She and Todd remained good friends, but Wanda soon moved to New York City. "I was a playwright in residence for a small theater," she says. "Then I decided to pursue soap opera writing. Two years later, in 1988, I was a soap writer's assistant filling in for script writers on *Guiding Light*."

Todd stayed in Aiken and went into the family photography business. "I started taking pictures at rock concerts and shot photos for the yearbook," he says. "Then I studied photography for two years at a school in Asheboro, North Carolina, before I came back home to work in my dad's studio."

Wanda recalls that whenever she visited her family, "Todd and I got together to play catch-up. We always remembered one another's birthdays." In 1989 she left New York to pursue a romance that did not last. As she moved around the country, Todd visited and they enjoyed what she calls their "prized but platonic" relationship. "With each other we never pretended to be something we weren't," Wanda says. "It was a wonderful friendship. We talked freely about our failures and successes and were very supportive of each other."

Wanda moved back to New York in 1992 to transcribe interviews for TV shows such as *20/20* and *Biography* on A&E. When she learned that Todd was about to marry a woman named Debbie, Wanda says, "I called him at work to say I was really happy he'd met somebody. And I was."

Four years later, while home for a visit, she heard that Debbie had left Todd. Wanda was about to fly back to Manhattan when she passed Todd's studio and stopped in to see if he was okay. "He had lost about 25 pounds, and the minute he saw me, he burst into tears," says Wanda. "I canceled my flight. I didn't make judgments on Debbie. I just listened to him talk, and I was willing to help him get back with her if that was what he wanted."

Her concern meant everything to him. "She's really here for me," he realized, and he began thinking of her as more than his treasured friend. "I saw her compassion. She and I were raised with the same values. We both had great childhoods with strong families. I realized I'd fallen in love with her a long time ago."

Wanda returned to New York, promising to visit, but even in the era of $99 flights she couldn't afford her annual holiday trip home—until a $100 bill arrived in the mail with a blank card on which someone had sketched an airplane. She recognized Todd's handiwork and flew back home. For Christmas, Todd gave Wanda a beautiful necklace with a 1996 gold coin, commemorating what had become a very good year.

"Even when we lived in different cities, being with Todd was the most natural thing in the world," Wanda says. "He never attempted to change me. He just accepted me, good and bad, everything. He was my first love, and I admired him as a person." On Valentine's Day 1997, in a burst of romantic fervor, Todd managed to overnight Wanda a fresh red camellia from his garden in an art deco vase. The card read, "This is from our house."

He rented a U-Haul and helped Wanda move back to Aiken later that month to live in the kind of house that had literally appeared in her dreams. "It had a garden and a white picket fence." In September 1997 they married in their hometown, and two years later Wanda gave birth to their son, Sam, whom they love raising in Aiken. "Everything just feels so natural," says Todd. "When we do Christmas, Sam gets to see his grandparents on both sides."

"In the seven years we've been together, Todd has always been the best of the best. We're in it for the long haul, and I envy no one." She loves that Todd supports her writing career and the occasional travel it entails. "I have a great life, a great family, a great husband. I think people should give their first sweetheart and that era of their life more importance. It's the start of finding out who you are."

Living the "Travel Afar" Fantasy

Wanda's extensive travel before marrying Todd echoes the story line of Broadway's longest-running show, *The Fantasticks*. A girl goes around the world and ends up with the boy next door. "There's a common fantasy that we can go away but then wind up with the boy from our old neighborhood," comments Dr. Sherry Bush. "Is that a fantasy for the one who traveled or for the one who got left behind? It fulfills both."

A reunited couple from Long Island, New York, separately traveled great distances before fulfilling the fantasy of finding love with the one back home.

Marge and Coty

"MAYBE SOMEDAY"

Marge (Waldman) and **Coty Keller**, both 59, became husband and wife 31 years after their high school prom. They were 16-year-old juniors at South Side High School in Rockville Centre, New York, when they met. She recalls: "I fell in love at first sight. It took me a year to plan a strategy to attract him." She gave him a ride home from a soccer game, and that did the trick. They spent senior year as sweethearts.

After going to different colleges, they lost touch. He served in Vietnam; she moved to California. They both had families and got divorced. More than 28 years after their high school graduation, a mutual friend put them back in contact with each other. By their second date as adults they realized that this time around they were going to get married. Today she is a teacher and he's a professor. They live in Freeport, near where they grew up. A piece of jewelry reveals their youthful hopes. "The coolest thing," Coty says, "is that she still has the gold heart I gave her in 1963 that was engraved 'To Marge, Maybe Someday, Love Coty.'"

Love in Prehistoric Times

Our ancestors found mates in somewhat the same way the Listas and the Kellers did. They simply looked around the neighborhood and selected the most appropriate cave dweller. "This phenomenon of seeking familiarity has roots that go back millions of years," says Dr. Helen Fisher. "Ancient peoples traveled in little hunting and gathering bands and met at permanent watering holes. They knew each other's families—whose father was a great hunter, and so on. There were no artificial introductions to your parents back then."

It was actually her mother's talent as a great seamstress that impressed one girl's beau. Gail Robinson's mom set high standards for her daughter and welcomed Raymond Whitehead into their home. She would have been pleased to know that years later her daughter finally married the respectful young man who spent so many hours visiting.

Gail and Raymond

"SHE LOOKED LIKE A BEAUTIFUL DOLL"

"The movie *Superfly* had just come out," says **Raymond Whitehead,** remembering the first time he met 15-year-old **Gail Robinson** in 1972 at a party in the Bronx where they both lived. "I was a freshman in college. My buddies and I tried to emulate those guys—you know, the big hats and platform shoes. I also had a brand-new 1972 Buick LeSabre. You couldn't tell me anything back then."

Gail was quite impressed when Raymond walked into the room. "He had on a red-and-blue-plaid suit with a long jacket and a black gangster hat. I told my girlfriend I was going to meet him before the night was through."

"When I saw Gail in her flowing white dress, she looked fine, like a beautiful doll," remembers Raymond. They started talking and spent the rest of the party together. Raymond called her soon after, and Gail was thrilled.

He attended college in upstate New York, but he dated Gail on weekends when he came home. "If I didn't have classes on a Friday, I'd shine up the car, wax it up all day. I'd dress myself nicely—"

"He thought he was The Man," interrupts Gail with a grin, "with those wide bell-bottoms. When he picked me up at school, seven or eight of my girlfriends would be right behind me to meet the college man I was dating. But he had to get me straight home because that's what my mother expected."

"Gail's family was tight," says Raymond, "and we had to abide by her mother's rules. When I picked her up on a date, I'd be waiting on the sofa in her living room for a whole hour sometimes, talking to her grandmother and her sister while Gail got ready. Her mother owned a fabric store and sewed clothes for her daughters. When Gail came down that long flight of stairs in a pretty dress her mother had made, it was right out of a movie." After chatting a little longer with the family, they would leave for their date. "Everybody in the neighborhood would see Gail and me walking to my car," remembers Raymond. "She was always the lady, and I tried to treat her with class and respect."

Gail says she always felt Raymond was her protector. On one of their dates he scooped her up off the sidewalk to avoid a puddle, carrying her across the street. "When he put me down," she says, "everybody on the corner started applauding."

After graduating from high school, Gail attended Marymount College in Tarrytown, New York, where Raymond drove to visit on weekends. When Raymond graduated and got a job as a paralegal, he saved his money for six months to buy a ring with a marquise diamond and then he proposed. They had been dating for five years. Gail was delighted and accepted, but two months later he called it off, saying he wasn't ready to settle down. "I was in a funk, sad to the point of devastation," Gail says. "Luckily, after a few weeks my friends got sick of me in a zombie state and dragged me to a club where I met somebody."

When Raymond returned three months later to say he had made a mistake in breaking the engagement, Gail had moved on. He felt terrible but decided to concentrate on work. Interested in contributing to society, he became a corrections officer in the New York prison system and was swiftly promoted to captain. In 1979 he married, but the union was annulled shortly afterward. A second marriage that didn't last, either, left him with a son.

Gail worked in the travel industry and enjoyed many trips to exotic destinations. As for men, she says, "I didn't view the people I dated as potential mates, not long-term anyway. It was just for the moment, and that was it." When Gail's mother died in 1987, Raymond heard the news from a mutual friend and arrived to help her through a tough time, but a reunion was not to be because they were both in other relationships at the time.

Then in June 1999, 20 years after the broken engagement and seven years since they had last seen each other, Gail received a call from Raymond at her American Express office, asking her to dinner.

"It was the most amazing evening," Gail says. "He was sweet, and he wanted to see me every evening that week. We took long walks, we went to a restaurant across from Lincoln Center, and we held hands. It was so romantic. He seemed like the Raymond I'd met back in '72, so honest and open." By September 1999 she had moved into his house. A year later they bought another engagement ring at Tiffany's, and they married on February 6, 2003.

Gail and Raymond feel that their past is part of their strength as a couple. Raymond loved being part of Gail's close family and still treasures their gatherings. He sometimes goes over to talk politics, sports, and cars with her dad when Gail is busy in her new career as a chef. "My dad loves Raymond," says Gail. "And my mom would be so happy to know that we are back together. She always thought he was special."

Raymond says Gail makes him feel whole. "She has qualities that I'd like to have but don't. She has an eye for style. She makes friends easily. She's sensitive and very smart. I'm pretty straightforward, and Gail helps me put things in perspective."

"I've always loved him," admits Gail, "even when I was mad at him. He's my friend and my soul mate, the person I love waking up with. He's very kind, and he treats me with a lot of respect. I can't go to sleep if he's not in the house. And I love his son, Rayvon, as if he were mine."

"When we initially broke up after our engagement," says Raymond, "it felt like a piece of me had been removed. With her I can be 100 percent myself." He says he has always loved just talking with Gail, and that's one reason he finally made a decision to try to win her back. Now he says, "There's nobody else in the world. I'd do anything for her."

For Gail's part, Raymond was always in the back of her mind. "Even though we spent so many years apart," she says, "I still see him as the young guy who chatted for hours with my family and drove me around in his Buick. I feel as if we've always been together."

Reunions such as Gail and Raymond's are possible because we grow in our ability to value and nurture closeness. "The brain stores emotional memories like buried treasure," explains New York therapist Dr. Carolyn Perla who has counseled hundreds of couples in intimacy workshops. "We revisit these recollections later in life with more developed capacities to nurture the bond, hopefully stirring fresh possibilities and rediscovering the treasure."

A Potent Combo

Of course many married-young-and-stayed-married couples also have the joys and benefits of a shared background. Reunitees sometimes envy that long stretch of years. But in some ways we have the best of both worlds: In reuniting we're essentially meeting someone warmly familiar and yet intriguingly unknown. Dr. Helen Fisher believes that the comfort of a shared background coupled with the thrill of discovery makes a potent mixture. "That combination of familiarity and novelty must be extremely stimulating because you have all the joy and ecstasy without all the fears."

It is a fabulous mixture according to Ken Kohn who reunited with his first love, Linda Hart, after not seeing her for 28 years. "We had this very intimate young lovers' experience and then didn't see each other," he says. "Now there's a big part of our lives we're exploring, so the neatest thing is we have both familiarity and newness." (More on Linda and Ken to come).

Delight in the "new and familiar" combo fills the story of a couple who married in their fifties. Marjory Lehrer and Barry Spiro now live near Boston but feel that Brooklyn is part of their glue.

Marjory and Barry

"PEOPLE FROM BROOKLYN BOND IMMEDIATELY"

"He was part of the 'in crowd,' and I had only one foot in it, so when we were seniors and he asked me out for New Year's, I was in absolute heaven!" says Marjory Lehrer. She is recalling the beginning of her romance with Barry Spiro in 1968 at Brooklyn's Erasmus Hall High School.

"I thought she was pretty and smart, and we had a wonderful time. But I wasn't ready to go steady, so I broke it off after two months," remembers Barry. While still friendly, they soon headed off to different colleges.

Both married in their early twenties, had children, moved to the Boston area, and divorced after two decades. In 1992 a woman who knew them both mentioned to Barry that Marjory was living nearby. "I had a longing to bump into her," says Barry. "I looked around every corner in every supermarket." Five years later another friend said, "I think we have a mutual acquaintance, and she's recently been divorced."

"I was ready to burst," Barry says. He called but didn't leave a message because of the deep voice on the answering machine. "I thought I had bad information and that she was still married." The voice, it turned out, was her son's. After several days Marjory finally couldn't stand waiting for the call, so she phoned and left a message: "Is this the Barry that I went out with on New Year's Eve 29 years ago?" He called back and they talked for two hours, until his cell phone battery died. They talked every night after that, and on Friday, April 18, 1997, they went out. "You are so beautiful!" were his first words. They pulled out their high school yearbooks and reminisced late into the evening. They've been together ever since.

Not that there haven't been challenges. Six months after they reunited, Barry was struck with an autoimmune disease that has taken his vision and made it hard to walk. But he still manages his dental practice; she teases that he wooed her with free samples of dental floss. On a more serious note, he appreciates her devotion in the face of the illness.

"We love each other so much," exclaims Marjory. "How many good people do you find? I would have to be crazy to give this up!"

He says because they knew each other long ago, "There is no tension, no pretense. When we started again, we were so linked with each other that anything we said was a hit."

"We're both from Brooklyn," she laughs, "and people from Brooklyn bond together immediately. Our parents shopped at the same Waldbaum's supermarket, we went to the same movie theaters. That really does play into it."

But they aren't living in the past. "When we reconnected, he looked as handsome as before but more professional and distinguished," says Marjory. "And we've both added layers of wisdom."

"There's camaraderie, of course, because of the past," says Barry. "But she is a ravishing, vivacious woman. When our lips meet, the passion is very current."

The Chevy Impala

Ed and I may not have Brooklyn to brag about like Marjory and Barry do, but we'll always have . . . fruit.

We grew up in an area surrounded by orchards. My family made huge quantities of jam from our one apricot tree, and Ed and his siblings earned pocket money cutting "cots," endless trays of apricots on their way to being dried and packaged. And the summer after our senior year, we both needed to earn money for college, so while Ed had a job washing dishes and supervising meal trays at O'Connor's Hospital, I separated peaches on a factory conveyor belt. I was lucky to be earning the union wage of just over $2.00 an hour. But don't offer me cobbler. It was mind-numbing labor that ruined my taste for peaches forever.

Ed tried to make it easier for me. I worked the evening shift, so when the "lunch" bell rang at 10:30 P.M., he'd pull up to the loading dock in his big old '61 Chevy Impala. It was glossy tan with a stripe down the side and white sidewall tires. By no means a cool car, it had one compelling advantage: bench seats. My break lasted an hour, most of which we'd spend smooching in that fine set of wheels.

For Ed and me the ability to visualize places and events like these from our youth helps us feel deeply connected today. Our shared background is a bridge over the time that passed while we were apart, and our lasting memories are far better than gossamer, ethereal fairy tales. Like the other reunited couples we've met, we treasure the gritty, wonderful, real details of our shared experience. Though my Prince Charming saw me wearing a hairnet and covered in peach juice, he still rode to the rescue in his Chevy Impala.

Chapter 5

We Were Friends, Not Sweethearts

PERHAPS YOUR TEENAGE "TRUE LOVE" JUST ISN'T AVAILABLE. OR maybe you didn't really have one. Some reunited partners never actually dated or held hands or even acknowledged the crushes they had on each other when they were younger. Maybe she was a cheerleader and he was a geek. Maybe he was a stud and she was still in her braces-and-oxfords phase. Or perhaps they were pals but never thought it could go anywhere. All of these scenarios have led to passionate adult romances.

Think back to the he-never-gave-me-the-time-of-day dreamboat. Or even the I-never-gave-him-a-second-glance class clown. Might be a future there.

Despite your school-age differences, once you are adults you may find yourselves drawn together because you already know so much about each other. You may not have been sweethearts, but you knew the same kids, had the same teachers, hung out at the same Dairy Queen or pizza place, and knew the unspoken hierarchy in the cafeteria and the school parking lot. You may not remember the same make-out spots (at least not together), but the annual musical, big game nights, and goofing off in the library are memories free for the taking. Remember the principal's voice over the PA system? Food fights in the cafeteria? Clubs and sports and car washes? It's all good material for laughing your way to love.

These are boom times for rekindling relationships, in part because adult matches between people who were friends and classmates tend to ignite at school reunions or on the Internet as we check out a whole group of our compatriots. Suddenly someone stands out.

Friendship, it turns out, is a strong foundation for connecting romantically later in life. Dr. Nancy Kalish says her data show that even reunited couples who were sexual partners in their youth are drawn back primarily by the feelings that came from being true friends. The memory of their kissing or sexual contact is not by itself what makes them feel deeply connected; the enduring attraction between them is much more about the confiding, the laughing, the trust, and the camaraderie that came with the experience. "I think the heart of it is friendship," says Dr. Kalish. "I think that's what the love is. It's caring for the growth and development of that other person." In her survey, people who were friends or classmates rather than actual sweethearts still considered themselves rekindled lovers when they got together as adults.

Couples often stress the importance they attach to the friendship they felt as young people. Sandi (Russell) and Tom Anton, a New Orleans husband and wife, say the fire in their marriage is founded on the companionship they shared long ago. Both 51, Tom and Sandi were buddies during their junior high years in Grosse Pointe, Michigan. "When we were growing up in the late '60s, we were best friends. We never even kissed," says Tom. Sandi, however, would throw a rope out her bedroom window before she went to sleep so that Tom could climb up and wake her to go out pool-hopping with a bunch of their friends in different neighbors' yards. Describing how he feels about Sandi now, Tom says, "She's gorgeous, with a cute little body and long dark hair. It took me 27 years to get that first kiss. And when we fell in love as adults, we also became best friends all over again."

Youthful friendship (and a sense of mischief!) primed Sandi and Tom for love later on. Friendship also led to marriage for Michael Gallagher and Theo Schwabacher, a husband and wife now living in San Francisco.

Theo and Michael

"YOU CAN'T LEAVE. I LOVE YOU"

Theo Schwabacher, 48, and Michael Gallagher, 49, thought of themselves as pals during their college days. In fact, when they were classmates at Skidmore in 1975, Theo consciously chose a friendship over a romance with Michael so she would not be one of the many women chasing her handsome friend. "I felt an attraction," she says, "but I thought he was sort of a bad boy, and I didn't really want to have anything to do with him on a romantic level." Michael recalls being attracted to Theo, especially in her short jean skirt and cowboy boots, but he didn't want to endanger their friendship and the fun they had together hanging out, playing sports, and qualifying to be ski instructors. She was "smart, fun, and bright," he remembers, and he valued her friendship. But then she moved from upstate New York back home to San Francisco, and they went their separate ways.

About three years later, after he moved out to California and she returned from a trip to Europe, they began spending time with the same group of friends. This time Theo was afraid her crush might show, and Michael was startled at how much he looked forward to Theo's company. The romantic charge in their relationship couldn't be denied, but until this point neither of them had considered doing anything about it.

One night they were with some friends playing chess at a bar, and she told him, "I'm leaving." He suddenly feared she meant "for good," caught her wrist, and said, "You can't leave. I love you." She burst into tears, and they finally kissed. In 1984 they married, and both are grateful for the route their relationship took. Michael says, "We were friends first, and that's part of the reason that today we feel so close and so free to be ourselves with each other."

Early friendship gives a couple like Theo and Michael time to know each other without the complications of a boyfriend-girlfriend relationship. When romance enters the picture later, they already have trust and attachment to sustain the heat. "During that earlier close friendship, even if it wasn't sexual, the couple was practicing affection and emotional intimacy," explains Dr. Iris SanGiuliano. "And their history together helps them trust each other." A college-friendship-tinged-with-a-crush made it easier for Anne Zehren and Harvey Anderson to fall in love years later. They remet at a basketball game, but there was no guarding their hearts.

Anne and Harvey

"WE WERE FRIENDS FIRST"

Anne Zehren, 42, and Harvey Anderson, 40, started out as friends at Marquette University in 1980. They would chat, go to church together, and stroll around campus, but they were each dating other people. Harvey does say that he once "made a move" by giving Anne a back rub, but she missed the signal that he was trying to move toward romance. And he didn't try again because he was flat-out afraid of rejection. Both feel that when they remet at an NBA basketball game in San Francisco almost 20 years later, their friendship was the basis for what became love.

"You trust friends you've known for a long time," he says, "so there wasn't as much self-protectiveness because Anne and I didn't have to work through all the different layers to get to know each other. When you meet someone new, there's a lot of information you need about them before you can open up your heart."

Anne feels that because they had been friends before, they didn't have to worry about saying the wrong thing or having some little mistake be perceived as a big one. "You can communicate better right off the bat, with no game-playing and no anxiety," Anne explains.

"Anne and I certainly had to get to know each other again and figure out how we'd changed," says Harvey, "but we were friends first, which gave us a high level of trust with each other."

Such stories show how adult love gets a head start if the young friendship had a subtext of attraction (that is, *the crush*). As teenagers we were perhaps too shy to speak up, afraid of rejection or worried about losing a valued friend. So the sizzling romance comes later, as it did for Deb (Giragosian) and Bob McGarry, two Massachusetts teenagers who loved to sing.

Deb and Bob

"WE HUNG OUT IN THE CHORUS ROOM"

"You've got Elegance" was all the e-mail said. But 28 years melted away, and Deb (Giragosian) zapped back the song's next line, "You can carry it off." She was responding to Bob McGarry, a fellow quartet singer from their days at Silver Lake High School in Kingston, Massachusetts. Bob didn't really think she would remember him, but did she ever! "I had a big crush on him," Deb recalls. "He was cute, and he had a wonderful sense of humor that always kept our group laughing. But I thought he didn't know I existed." For his part, Bob considered Deb "a cut above." Between classes and rehearsals they had hung out in the chorus room, but to Bob she was "the girl I never dared to ask out." The song he e-mailed years later was from the musical *Hello, Dolly!* which they had performed in chamber choir.

Bob joined the Air Force immediately following graduation in 1973, and Deb stayed in Kingston to care for her mother, who died two years later. Deb subsequently married and divorced, raised a daughter, Jen, and was working as a securities financial auditor in Boston. Bob served in the Air Force for 20 years, rising to the rank of captain. He married, divorced, and was raising his daughter, Noël, as a single father while working as a logistics analyst for Boeing in Seattle, Washington.

In the spring of 2001, Deb signed on to Classmates.com. When Bob saw her entry, he says, "Her name went off like a beacon." And he started the correspondence that changed both of their lives dramatically. "We spent the first few weeks catching up," says Deb. "It was funny how many of our goals matched. We had the same interests in high school, and now it was a little more personal."

"Our values came out in our writing. We both believe in the respect people have for each other in New England and the heartwarming, old-fashioned traditional beliefs," says Bob. "There was such a commonality in our upbringing, I thought, 'Where has my life been?'"

On June 10, 2001, Bob flew from his home in Seattle to Boston for a mini-reunion with Deb that was just supposed to be "a quick drink and a little socializing over our yearbooks," says Bob. But it stretched into five days. They sat on the beach listening to the surf and getting to know each other all over again. No sooner did Bob leave Boston than Deb flew to Seattle to visit.

"We kept flying back and forth," says Bob, "until I was in Boston on September 10, 2001. My daughter and I were scheduled to leave on a flight out of Logan Airport on September 11. When planes from Boston were part of the tragedy at New York's World Trade Center, Bob, Noël, and Deb found themselves confined to a hotel room together for a week. Bob says, "It became clear that we had to live for the moment and hold on to the ones we love." A week later Deb quit her job and shipped everything to Seattle.

"She is sincere and dedicated," says Bob, "with a sparkle in her eye and a smile on her face. No one in my life ever put me first the way Deb does." They married on May 25, 2002, less than a year after that first snippet of song arrived in Deb's e-mail. She feels blessed. "It may sound corny, but we don't feel whole unless the other is here. We really do complete each other. Our religious beliefs are similar and strong, and our friendship is very important to us."

The soprano and the baritone still love the music they shared as youngsters and even have a small recording studio in their home. They also have a nickname for each other. Instead of calling out "honey" or "sweetheart," they call each other "loml." It stands for "love of my life."

Though they never dated as young people, Deb and Bob made beautiful music, literally. Some reunited couples, on the other hand, had youthful interactions that were anything but positive. A great "reel life" example is the movie *When Harry Met Sally*. . . . The characters played by Billy Crystal and Meg Ryan start out hostile to each other on their drive from Chicago to New York after college graduation. About every five years they meet accidentally until they eventually become friends and finally fall in love. This hostility-to-love scenario also occurs in real life.

One reunited couple's history actually includes a "diss" in a yearbook.

Robin and Jeff

"I COULDN'T STAND THE BOY"

Robin (Faylor) Lewis came across Jeff Baker's name in 2000 when she was looking for her old best girlfriend on a Web site now called Reunion.com. She remembered that Jeff had dated this friend, Holly, when they all attended North Garland High School near Dallas, Texas, in the early '80s. She also remembered feeling annoyed about all the time Jeff took up in her friend's life and then being furious with him when he finally split from Holly and broke her heart. Robin wrote in her friend's yearbook, "I couldn't stand the boy."

After high school graduation Robin moved to Florida and then to Tennessee, joining the naval reserves. She later became a police officer, got divorced, and by 1999 was raising her two children by herself.

Robin was seeking to reconnect with friends from her school days when she went online to find Holly. After checking out various high school alumni Web sites, she sent e-mails to a few people who were listed, including Jeff, to see if anyone knew Holly's whereabouts. Jeff e-mailed back. They corresponded and talked on the phone, discovering they both had served in the military and had children they adored.

When he planned a trip to Tennessee for business, he asked her out to dinner. "I was terribly nervous to see him again," says Robin, "and when I picked him up at the airport, I was amazed how little his appearance had changed. We talked for hours on end; it was just so comfortable being with him. He was kind, gentle, considerate, and very charming."

"Robin was a tomboy in high school, but she had blossomed into a beautiful woman," Jeff says. During the next seven months they talked constantly. Then she moved back to Texas, and he proposed. They began living together, built a new home in Murphy, Texas, to hold all five of their children comfortably, and, deeply in love, celebrated their wedding on September 26, 2003. "I never thought I'd be living in Texas again," says Robin, who now uses the last name Lewis-Baker, "but even more amazing, I never thought I'd marry the boy I said I hated in high school!"

An insult in the early days didn't prevent a romance later on between schoolmates who were also neighbors. Of course, Mary Lou remembers it differently than Ray does.

Mary Lou and Ray

"I WAS TOO SCARED TO TALK TO HIM"

Ray Smith teases that during junior high when he used to walk past Mary Lou (White) standing outside her house, "she'd snub me." She disputes that. "No! I was just very, very shy. I was too scared to talk to him. Nobody would believe it now!"

For a year Ray lived just one house over; then his family moved to a different part of town. But Mary Lou and Ray knew each other through their high school days in Medford, Oregon. He definitely *wasn't* the shy type. "He played baseball very well," she remembers, "and during football season he was head cheerleader."

After graduation in 1951, Ray married a local girl. The marriage did not last, and he soon found himself living alone in the San Francisco Bay Area, with his son visiting in the summertime. As a lieutenant colonel in the Marines, Ray became a pilot, and when he left active duty and joined the reserves, he flew helicopters.

Mary Lou was happily married, had two children, and was living in Roseburg, Oregon, about 120 miles from her hometown.

Then in 1975 her husband died suddenly of a lung disease. She was 41, her children were 12 and 15, and they adjusted as best they could. The next year she decided to attend her twenty-fifth high school reunion. She went shopping and bought herself something a little out of the ordinary: a lovely yellow barebacked dress.

She went to the reunion feeling pretty, and she had a good time. At the end of the night one fellow asked if she would like to go out for breakfast. She answered that maybe she would, but first he went to the bathroom. Big mistake. At that moment her former neighbor Ray strolled over to say hello and invited her to a party. "Actually, he kind of commandeered me. He said, 'Come on. You can drive me over there,'" she says with a laugh.

Ray was captivated by Mary Lou's beauty and her vitality. "I had realized that there comes a time in life when we need companionship," says Ray. "I thought, 'I'm successful. I can buy anything within reason. But something is missing—someone to share it with.'"

"I was impressed that he was a Marine helicopter pilot," she recalls. "We had a little bit to drink, so there *was* some bragging. I was attracted by his masculinity." They talked through the night.

"I didn't get home until the sun came up." Mary Lou giggles, "I was 42 years old, and my dad was waiting up for me!"

Ray called a few days later. They talked on the phone many hours over the next few months and visited back and forth. "We found we were very much alike," says Mary Lou. "We had the same background. We came from parents who didn't earn an awful lot. My father was a painter. His dad delivered oil. Our ideas were similar, like saving money for a rainy day."

Ray proposed and Mary Lou accepted. Her mother, however,

was suspicious of Ray because Mary Lou had been left with a nice house and some cash. Ray has a dry wit and never missed the opportunity to tease her mom, saying, "I can hardly wait for Mary Lou and me to get married. I love to bet the horses, and I'll make Mary Lou a lot of money."

They were married in March 1977, and Mary Lou moved with her children to California. "Ray and I had lived in the same town and gone to the same schools. I know I was attracted by the familiarity and the stability," says Mary Lou, "but he was also very exciting." Ray, by the way, eventually became a favorite with her mom, as he proved his trustworthiness over time. When Ray was ill a few years ago, Mary Lou's children were there every day, appreciative of Ray's longtime steadiness in their lives.

"We're not perfect," Mary Lou says. "We argue once in a while, but if you agree all the time, it means somebody is always giving in. We were both raised to believe that you stay the course together."

They have done a lot of traveling and enjoy working in their garden. Mary Lou says, "Ray is thoughtful and loving, and he has a droll sense of humor. I really didn't snub him back in junior high!"

Hometown Hearts

Memories associated with hometowns seem to have a particularly powerful impact on reunited couples who were friends rather than sweethearts because those recollections comprise a significant part of their shared history in lieu of romantic times together. The sights and sounds of home, and of each other, pull them back.

WABC-TV sportscaster Scott Clark and his wife, Heather, may even retire in Lima, Ohio, after their years in the Big Apple. And Garden City, New York, has a siren call for *Passions'* TV star Liza Huber and husband Alex Hesterberg. "You have a commonality of experience. You both remember the place where you grew up," explains psychoanalyst Colleen Konheim. "You both understand the attitudes of the people, the beauty of the countryside, the pull of home."

It turns out that for people who were friends or acquaintances long ago, hometowns often hold a magnetic charm, as in the story of Kathie (Beck) and Joe Jensen, who married only 45 days after their high school reunion and moved back to their hometown of Superior, Nebraska.

Kathie and Joe

"THIS IS WHERE WE STARTED OUT"

It took 30 years for Joe Jensen to realize he was actually in love with Kathie Beck. Not that he hadn't noticed her. He'd had a crush on his second grade friend back in 1957 when they were growing up in Superior, a little farming town about three hours southwest of Lincoln, Nebraska. Joe remembers that Kathie "was extremely cute and always laughing, very happy." His crush was so strong that during free play at recess, when Kathie asked Joe to give her his ball, a much-desired prize on the playground, he handed it over.

Kathie has no real memory of Joe until seventh grade when he registered only as "shy and quiet" on her radar. "I was an average student," Joe says, "and I didn't date. I had a passion for finding out how things worked. When we kids watched *Star Trek*, everyone else wanted to be Captain Kirk, but I wanted to be Scotty, the chief engineer."

Kathie, on the other hand, says, "I was loud. I spent probably three-quarters of high school grounded. I think it was my folks' way of keeping me out of trouble." She was never without a boyfriend, dating various football and basketball players, which made her seem even more unattainable to Joe.

When the class of '68 graduated, Joe joined the army and spent the next 20 years in exotic locales like Turkey and Haiti. He married and had a son, but divorced after eight years. He assumed that Kathie had married "a brain surgeon type" and was living happily ever after. The truth was that she had spent a year in business school, until "my parents dragged me kicking and screaming to Oregon where they were moving," she says. "I started working in the insurance industry at 19 years old. I met someone, got married, and had two boys." She stayed at her job for 32 years even though she found it stressful and unfulfilling, as was her marriage. "After 24 years together," she says, "my first husband didn't want to be married anymore, and he left. I felt shock and rage."

Kathie had been divorced for two years in July 1998 when she attended her thirtieth high school reunion back home in Superior. "I saw her right away, sitting by the door," Joe recalls. They didn't speak one-on-one during the event, but at the end of the night Joe asked her to stay and talk. "I didn't know what to think," says Kathie. "I guess I had become more shy and Joe had gotten more outgoing." They chatted for about 45 minutes, giving her lots of time to appreciate Joe's six-foot physique, broad shoulders, blond hair, and blue eyes.

Joe came out with it: "You were the cutest girl in school, the one I was in love with. I had the biggest crush on you."

They spent the second evening of the reunion absorbed in each other. And then he kissed her. When Kathie got back home to Oregon, Joe called daily, and they spent hours getting to know each other on the phone. He visited two weeks later and talked about being together. She said, "Are you asking me to marry you?"

"Yes," Joe answered. "I guess I am."

One month later, 45 days after the reunion, Kathie arrived in Phoenix where Joe was living. There, she and Joe, both 47, bought wedding rings at the shopping mall. She says, "Our engagement period was the time it took to get the rings sized." Later that afternoon, on August 28, 1998, they got married. "This may sound corny," says Kathie, "but after we reunited, the air smelled better, the sun was brighter, and the colors were more vivid. I knew he was the one, and I didn't want to let him go. We just had to convince family and friends that we hadn't lost our minds."

Joe moved back to Superior, Nebraska, soon after the wedding to take advantage of a job opportunity, but Kathie stayed in Oregon to keep her 15- and 17-year-old kids in their school. Joe and Kathie saw each other once every eight weeks for the next two years. "I was so homesick for him," says Kathie. "I'd found love, and now it was 1800 miles away."

Two years later Kathie was finally able to move to Superior, but the bliss of her homecoming was not without its challenges. One night her car got stuck in the mud on her way home. "I'd forgotten how those country roads could get, and there I was, stuck in the muck up to the top of the wheel wells. The mud sucked my shoes off, and I had to walk barefoot to a farmhouse so somebody could pull my car out."

She's happy, however, to be with her husband and living in Superior again. They walk up and down the old familiar streets with no fear. "The air is clean, and there are no sirens at night," she says.

Kathie and Joe both love their hometown. As he points to some folks in front of the grocery store, Joe says, "See these people? I've known them my whole life. See this sidewalk we're walking on? I walked down this sidewalk when I was five. This is where we started out, and it's where we want to end up. You know, this town is so peaceful, it'll add 10 years to your life and take 20 points off your blood pressure."

Kathie creates graphics and writes articles for the town's weekly newspaper. She gets half the pay she got in Oregon, but she likes the job more than twice as much.

Had Kathie and Joe not reunited, she thinks, "my life would have been okay, but I would have missed so many wonderful things—like the times Joe lays his hands on my shoulders or puts his arm around me." Their children are all doing well, and Joe has become the utilities manager of Superior, which owns its own gas, waste, water, and lights. "When he was a little boy," says Kathie, "one of his goals was to own the traffic light in the center of town. Now, in a way, he does."

As Kathie and Joe discovered, we literally can go home again. Or we can get much of what we treasure about home through romance with someone who grew up there with us. Many couples have discovered that a long-ago friendship (and maybe that long-hidden crush!) can be magical, investing adult love with a beautiful history that stretches back into our youth.

Chapter 6

Our Families Pulled Us Apart

WHEN I TOLD MY MOM IN 2002 THAT I WAS AGAIN DATING ED Oster, now a successful attorney, she had a classic "mother" response: "Yes, of course I remember Ed," she said, "but he was going to be a doctor. What happened?"

Actually, both my folks and Ed's mom have been very supportive of our modern-era romance, as they were during our teens, when Ed was welcome in our house (especially when he was washing windows!) and his mom occasionally invited me to dinner at their home. But as we know, not all parents are so approving of their children's choices.

Several couples I interviewed felt that in rekindling their love, they were rectifying a decision that their parents had made for them. In these cases their mothers and fathers were instrumental in ending their early romance. The stories of these couples have a lot in common with the tale of the star-crossed lovers in *Romeo and Juliet*, but happily the finales are more akin to another of Shakespeare's plays, *All's Well That Ends Well*.

One mother's interference with a young romance only came to light many years later. After realizing what had happened during high school, Sandi (Russell) and Tom Anton rekindled their relationship in their early forties, married, and have made a film called *At Last* based on their reuniting story.

Sandi and Tom

"MY MOM HID OUR LETTERS"

Tampering with the U.S. Mail is a federal offense, but Tom Anton's mother didn't see it that way when she put the kibosh on his budding love for Sandi (Russell) back in 1971.

The youngsters met in Grosse Pointe, Michigan, in 1966. They were 13 years old and they became pals. "We bought clocks," says Tom, "and synchronized them. Late at night I'd call, and we'd be on the phone together watching movies like *I Was a Teenage Werewolf* and *The Razor's Edge.*

Tom first spotted Sandi in homeroom. "She was cute and petite, about five-feet-two, with long dark hair," he says. "She wore great little skirts, and I adored the bounce in her walk. But we were not romantic. We just had so much in common that we became best friends, even discussing our 'love problems.'"

Sandi remembers: "Most guys at that age weren't very verbal, but Tom was sensitive and loved to talk. I spent more time on the phone with him than I did with my girlfriends."

In 1968, Tom's family was transferred to New Orleans. "I was in the ninth grade," Tom says, "and I was on football, baseball, tennis, and hockey teams. I was devastated because I was leaving my friends, including Sandi, behind. Sandi and I stole the FOR SALE signs from in front of my parents' house and hid them because I didn't want to leave."

Sandi felt terrible for Tom. "Fifteen was a difficult age to be uprooted," she says, "but we promised to write." The night before Tom left, he tried kissing her, but she wasn't yet ready to move past friendship.

After the move they sent long letters back and forth, creating a diary of sorts. "I lived for the mailbox," says Tom. "She was a lifeline to my past." The letters were long—sometimes as many as 30 pages. They wrote about music, the Vietnam War, politics, everything. After three years of correspondence, Sandi decided she wanted Tom to take her to her prom in Michigan, and she would like that kiss after all. She sent him a letter saying, "I've figured out that I love you, and I want to come visit."

Tom wrote back to say he felt the same way and invited her to visit on her birthday in April 1971. "I bought a plane ticket with my babysitting money," says Sandi, "but he never wrote again. I called once, and his mother answered the phone. It turns out that she never gave him the message. She also hid the last few of our letters, mine to him and his to me. I thought he stopped writing because he got cold feet, so I got angry and stopped writing." It was painful, but Sandi eventually moved on, married, and had three children.

Tom, thinking Sandi had dumped him, also went on with his life, married, and had two children. Decades later his mom cleaned out her attic and sent him a box full of photos, report cards, and souvenirs. Buried inside were the letters he remembered receiving from Sandi. He says, "I sorted them by postmark, starting with 1968. After I'd read a few of the earliest ones, I got Sandi's number from our high school reunion committee."

Their first phone conversation in 1992 lasted for a couple of hours. Tom says, "We discovered so much about each other. She was helping women in a pregnancy crisis center, and after years of working in marketing as an energy consultant, I had become a screenwriter. We found out we'd both named our first child Katherine, drove minivans, and worked in stained glass as a hobby. We even liked the same merlot." At her request he sent her some of the early letters, and they reminisced together.

"We caught up on the last 21 years during that time," says Sandi. "I enjoyed the memories of being 15, the laughter and playfulness." But she felt confused when he said, "Why did you stop writing me?"

"The question is," she said, "why did *you* stop writing *me*?"

One night about six weeks later, Tom opened a dozen old letters from Sandi that he had never seen before. "I love you," she wrote. "I want to marry you, have your children, and be with you forever." Digging deep into the box of mementos, he found another pile of 10 old letters from him to her, without a postmark. At that point he realized his mother had stolen the letters from the mailbox. Sandi's last letter to him said, "I was going to break up with my boyfriend because I don't love him. I love you—but now I hate you."

His last letter to her was tear-stained. "I'm at the Café Dumond," he had written. "I was going to bring you here. It's really romantic, but I hate you. I don't ever want to hear from you again."

With the shock of the discovery, their weekly phone reminiscing became even more important. When the calls had started in August 1992, Sandi says, "It wasn't romantic at all. It was just a connection." By Christmas those feelings had changed. Their marriages were both deeply unhappy, and by 1994 both had divorced. Tom says they are sad and not proud that their reuniting involved dissolving their marriages, but they have no doubt that it was the right course for them. They married each other in 1998. Both are devoted parents, and they spent years commuting between Michigan and Louisiana until their children were raised. They still have both homes but now spend much of their time in New Orleans.

The feature film they teamed up to produce, *At Last,* is based on their personal story. They cowrote the script, changing the leads' names to Mark and Sara, and Sandi calls their movie "the child we never had together."

After six years of marriage to Sandi, Tom says, "She supports me, she believes in me, she challenges and encourages me. I have everything I could dream about and want with somebody. She's gorgeous, with a big smile and freckles. She was my first love, and I still get that spark whenever I look at her."

"Tom is very caring and attentive," says Sandi. "I love being with him because he's so intelligent and funny."

Although Tom is not close to his mother because they have different points of view on many issues, she did attend Tom and Sandi's wedding. As for the "letter lifting," Sandi looks at it philosophically. "I've never had ill feelings toward my mother-in-law," Sandi says. "Things happen for a reason. It's so much more interesting when you have a little bit of life behind you and then come back together again, versus when you're young and you don't know anything. I so much more appreciate Tom and who he is as a 50-year-old than I could have as a 20-year-old. I have three beautiful children, and he has two wonderful children. You just go: 'Well, it happened for a reason that way, and I'm okay with it.'"

While Sandi and Tom were unaware of parental interference until decades later, many rekindled lovers say their parents' objections were very clear during their early romance. Dr. Nancy Kalish explains that in her survey of reunitees, it was often the girl's parents who kept the couple apart. "The unstated thought was usually 'We're afraid this guy's going to have sex with our daughter,'" she says. "Some couples sneaked around for a couple of months, but in general they broke up because the parents told them to."

When parents set difficult rules or forbid a romance entirely, adolescent rebelliousness sometimes kicks in for a while. But ultimately kids usually abide by their parents' rules on dating whether they agree with them or not.

"You feel very much in need of your parents' validation, support, and feedback when you are an adolescent," says Dr. Sherry Bush, explaining why parents' wishes have such a huge impact on young couples. "So while you want to be your own person, you also want their blessing on your romantic relationship." In addition, since teenagers generally live with their parents, it's not as though they have much choice in the matter.

Some reunited lovers recognize that Mom was well meaning when she nixed their early romance, as in the story of Linda and Max.

Linda and Max

"MA, YOU WERE ABSOLUTELY WRONG. HE'S A GOOD GUY"

Linda (Fisher) Rentzer and **Max Blitzer**, now in their sixties and living in Boca Raton, Florida, originally met in 1951 at a party in the basement of their Brooklyn apartment building when she was 11 and he was 14. "Oh, gosh, she's gorgeous," Max thought. Soon he started carrying Linda's books when they walked home from school. He even scraped together enough money from delivering groceries to buy her a gold ankle bracelet.

Then one day, Linda remembers, "A neighbor saw us and ratted me out to my mother." Max was no longer allowed to see her. But Linda's dad said he could come back in three years when Linda was 14—and he did. Max says, "I thought about her all the time while I was waiting."

Finally they were allowed to go to romantic movies like *Brigadoon*, and they spent one magical afternoon at Rockefeller Center in Manhattan. "Her lush brown hair was blowing in the wind," Max remembers. "She wore Shalimar perfume, and she smelled so beautiful."

But by the time Linda was 16, in 1956, her mom was so concerned about the intensity of her young daughter's feelings for Max that she put her foot down and declared, "No more!" She had seen Max with his arm around Linda, who says, "My mom must have realized I was in love with him."

Linda and Max were heartbroken at being forbidden to see each other. "I was upset," Linda says, "but back then you didn't question what your parents said. And I was afraid of my mother. She was a tough lady." Max says most parents at the time were strict, even with boys. "Parents had lots of rules, like always keeping the doors open if girls were visiting so the moms could see what kids were doing," Max recalls. "I was angry about not being able to see Linda, but what could I do? I had no choice but to respect her mother's decision."

The young sweethearts went their separate ways, and after a time they each married other people and ultimately divorced. Three decades after they split up, while mourning the recent deaths of her sister and her mother, Linda searched for Max's phone number and called him. "I was feeling like an orphan," she explains. "I needed to touch base with someone who knew my family from before." After calls back and forth every night, they got together in upstate New York where she was traveling on business. He gave her roses and asked if he could kiss her on the cheek. Linda says, "In the flash of a second I became 16 again."

They began to see each other on weekends, and then about 15 years ago they bought an apartment together. Remembering how much she had liked his teenage gift, Max gave Linda a new gold ankle bracelet. They've been a couple for 15 years now and got married two years ago. Referring to the physical chemistry between them, Linda says, "He winds my watch!"

Six years ago Max nursed Linda through a bout with cancer. She calls him a "good soul" and says with admiration that he is gentle and kind, much like her dad. "A first love is embedded inside you somewhere," she says. "It makes an impression on your brain and your heart, and you judge other people against him." Max agrees: "If it's your first love, it gets into your soul."

As for her mom's influence, Linda sometimes looks up to the sky and whispers, "Ma, you were absolutely wrong! He takes care of me. He's a good guy."

Of course, few parents would believe it possible that their children have the maturity to find life partners while still teenagers. Parents know that all too often the passion their children feel will pass, leaving two bewildered souls wondering what hit them and why no one stopped them.

"Parental objections may not be about the qualities of a specific person," explains Dr. Sherry Bush. "It could just be that they don't want their child getting deeply involved so young." Even Max and

Linda, who waited so many years to be together, realize that Linda's mother was just trying to protect her.

When we become adults, our parents' opinions don't usually have the impact they once did, and sometimes that opens up possibilities for loving companionship. "Adolescents are loosening the bonds with their parents, but it's a conflicted transition," explains Dr. Iris SanGiuliano. "Once they have obeyed the rules and then grown up, they may feel stronger in following their own lights. This can be an important factor in the decision to go back to a past sweetheart." That's what happened to a Vancouver couple who finally overrode their fathers' objections and reunited in their late forties.

Ellen and J.R.

"HE DIDN'T WANT ME IN HIS SON'S LIFE"

Fifteen-year-old **Ellen (Hector)** saw **J. R. Barberie** on her first day as a sophomore at Central High School in Calgary, Canada, in 1957. Ellen had a bandage on her leg when she passed 17-year-old J.R. and his buddies sitting on a fence. One of them called out, "Cut your leg shaving, did you?" She wanted the sidewalk to open up so she could die right there.

Their next meeting was at a big Sadie Hawkins party where the girls asked the boys to dance. "J.R. was a little over six feet tall and had curly black hair and gold-colored eyes," says Ellen. "He was very well built and muscular, a sportsman, and absolutely delicious-looking. I asked him to dance."

"I was doing my own thing," J.R. says, "just sort of watching when this little girl in the tenth grade asked me to dance to a Sam Cooke song, 'You Send Me.' She wore cute, pointy little glasses, she was outgoing, and she was interested in me. All of a sudden I was interested, too." They dated for a couple of years, going to movies and skiing. Ellen still has a picture of them standing on a porch together back then "with my pointy glasses and pointy boobies."

But there was an insurmountable obstacle. "The kicker of our relationship," recalls Ellen, "is that while we dated, half of it was on the sly because I'm Jewish and my father didn't want me going out with a Christian boy. J.R. is Protestant, and his father had an absolute fit that he was taking out a Jewish girl. In those days you did what your dad told you. But we snuck out."

In fact, the first time Ellen encountered any anti-Semitism was the day J.R.'s dad discovered she was Jewish. She had been invited to dinner with J.R.'s family at his parents' golf club. A woman at the club called his father over and whispered to him, "Did you know that your son's girlfriend is a Jewish girl?"

"J.R.'s dad confronted me," says Ellen, "and told me that Jewish people weren't welcome at his golf club. I said, 'Well, then, I guess I'm not, either,' and I got up and walked out." J.R. took her home, feeling terrible about the whole experience. To this day he still comments wryly that his father was the Archie Bunker of Calgary.

"He really didn't want me in his son's life," remembers Ellen. "My parents weren't as virulent about the whole thing." But her father was upset about the relationship. Her mother actually tried to help, reminding her husband that in the Jewish tradition any children born carry on their mother's religion.

"It doesn't matter," he said to Ellen, banging his hand on the table. "He's nothing but a football player. He's not going to be able to provide for you because he'll be going to university on a football scholarship. He's not good enough for you."

"Her parents never said anything to me about having a different religion," J.R. recalls, "but they made it clear that Ellen and I shouldn't see each other."

Ellen's folks sent her to the University of Arizona to separate her from J.R. "I never applied to that school," says Ellen. "My mother applied *for* me. Since we had a winter house in Tucson, they thought it was a good place to send me. J.R. was attending university in British Columbia."

Ellen and J.R. did see each other once when they were both home from college in 1960. "I invited J.R. to what we called a 'stampede party' at my dad's ranch," Ellen remembers, "but he arrived with another woman he was dating. He didn't tell me beforehand on the phone, and he spoiled my party."

They remained apart for the next 27 years, with only a few brief encounters. When she was on her way home from Tucson to get married, she stopped off near Missoula, Montana, where J.R. was in graduate school. He wasn't home, so she left a message with the landlady, but he did not call. "I always wondered," he muses, "if Ellen was giving me one last chance to ask her not to get married." A few years later they happened to meet at a party and chatted for about 10 minutes. "Our old friends were there," says Ellen, "and everybody was watching to see how we would react. I felt bad for my husband at the time, and J.R. felt uncomfortable for his wife."

Throughout their years apart Ellen thought of J.R. as her unspoken dream, her fantasy. J.R. says that he thought of Ellen as "a generous, loving person" and that he always had a longing for her. Then in 1987, 27 years after the stampede party, they ran into each other in the Vancouver airport, about to get on the same flight to Calgary. Ellen says, "The first thing that came out of my mouth was 'You son of a bitch, you look better now than you did when you were 18.' We sat together on the plane. It was a short flight, but the sizzle was there."

At the end of that year they got together and celebrated what she calls "a glorious New Year" Ellen, who was long separated with three teenage children, and J.R., who was divorced with four kids of his own, began traveling to see each other. She eventually moved to Vancouver, where J.R. lived, for a fresh start. They married four years later, on August 31, 1991, at ages 48 and 50. Currently, Ellen owns a stationery store called The Write Place in Vancouver. J.R. works in business as a food broker.

With their fathers both deceased, their different religions are no longer a big problem. When they married, Ellen says, "my mom was absolutely thrilled for me. And J.R.'s mother took me to her heart, too." The children on both sides needed a little time to adjust but soon realized they would not be losing their cherished traditions. Ellen says, "We do the Christian holidays for J.R. because he has his faith, and we do the Jewish ones for me, so we are participating in each of our religions in that way." Ellen admits she went over the top at first. "Basically, I'm a gastronomic Jew because I cook all the good stuff, so I asked my gentile friends for their holiday recipes. J.R. and I laughed at the piles of food and the presents that extended all the way from the front door through the living room on that first Christmas."

"She didn't want me to lose anything," J.R. says, "and I didn't. I haven't lost my Christmas, and she hasn't lost her Hanukkah. We both gained a festivity." She jokes: "I think of it as 'Hanumas.'"

Ellen says, "We have a seder every Passover, and J.R. is right there beside me. J.R. doesn't go to synagogue with me, but he always shares my observances at home. He doesn't follow any specific religion, but he is religious in his heart and in his beliefs."

Their faiths supported them during a tough time in the mid '90s. Ellen was diagnosed with cancer, and J.R. was there for her. "When the doctors thought I was going to die, J.R. was so sorrowful, I was dumbfounded," she says. "But six months later we discovered that my diagnosis was a mistake, and we got our lives back. Now I really know I'm loved, and the passion of our lovemaking reflects that."

Like many couples they have developed some charming traditions. They don't do much card-giving since Ellen is in the stationery business. "But we go to my store on our anniversary, and each of us picks out an anniversary card and hands it to the other. After we read them, we put them back." And after she pouted because he wasn't using enough terms of endearment with her, he started making her smile by calling her "Honey-CookieSweetieDarling."

Ellen says she shivers at the mere thought of being close to J.R. "He's my best friend," she says, "and every time I look at him, I still melt." J.R. says he loves how affectionate Ellen is. In a gentle reference to the parental interference that tore them apart when they were young sweethearts, Ellen confides, "We joke about going out and finding two cemeteries, a Christian one and a Jewish one next door to each other. And we'll each get buried on the fence so we can be together always."

As with Ellen and J.R., reversing the fatherly squelching of a romance can also be a statement that the next generation is overthrowing old attitudes. Dr. Marlene Marko, a psychiatrist on the faculty of Mount Sinai Medical School in Manhattan, explains: "A relationship that breaks up in adolescence often has a parental prohibition aspect, that is, 'she's not right for you.' Reuniting is a chance to get past the rules that prevented you from making that choice."

Occasionally the parental influence affecting young sweethearts is not even intentional. Fran and David Bilon broke up in the late '60s and finally reunited in the late '80s. They say their years apart were caused by her overwhelming need to get away from home.

Fran and David

"I MARRIED TO ESCAPE"

Fran (Conner) and David Bilon dated in 1965 at Baker High School in Columbus, Georgia. He remembers: "She was so pretty, and I loved her sweetness." Fran says, "I noticed him in civics class. He seemed bright and outspoken and smart. He wasn't as shallow as some of the other boys." David's dad was in the Army at Fort Benning, and Fran's mom had a high-ranking civilian job on the base. Fran's parents were pretty strict—even on prom night she had to be home by midnight. "Oh, I was home, let me tell you," she remembers ruefully. But Fran and David still managed to have fun going to movies and taking rides when he was allowed to use his family's car.

After graduation David went away to Cornell University while Fran attended college in the South. They had trouble keeping up the long-distance relationship. To David's despair Fran started dating others and then married in 1968 before she even finished college. "My mother was on her second marriage, and she and her new husband had their own little life going," Fran explains. "I didn't want to stay with them anymore during the summers. I thought, 'What is the easiest way to leave?' My first husband was a nice man, but I married him for the wrong reason. I married to escape."

Fran had children and tried to make a go of the marriage. David had several relationships and an unsuccessful marriage. He contacted Fran 20 years after their high school graduation, finding her in a directory created for their class reunion, but she was married at the time. A few years later, after her divorce, she called David back. His first reaction: "I went into a protective shell, thinking, 'I'm not going to let myself get built up and hurt again.'" But when they got together, David even shaved off his Fu Manchu mustache as a gesture to help Fran feel more comfortable with him. They quickly became a couple. He says he had often thought of her over the years as "the one that got away." He writes poetry for her and still loves her sweetness.

They married in 1991, and both are high school English teachers in Newnan, Georgia. Fran says she regrets that her reaction to living at home with her parents caused her to make a decision that kept them apart so long. "David was definitely The One," says Fran. "He was always The One, this sweet endearing person. David was always my heart of hearts."

For some couples it was not their parents who caused difficulties the first time around but, rather, their children. That's what drove Eva and Harvey,* a married couple who had children from previous marriages, to divorce each other. Therapist Ginny Fleming, who has counseled many couples attempting to blend families, explains what they are up against: "Stepparenting is complicated and difficult. There's no totally graceful way to do it, and it takes years to be successful." Eva and Harvey finally surmounted this obstacle by rekindling their love and remarrying after most of their childrearing was behind them.

*For reasons of privacy some couples have requested to be identified by first names only.

Eva and Harvey

"WE JUST HAD TO WAIT UNTIL MOST OF OUR PARENTING WAS OVER"

"You probably don't remember me, but I saw you on a video," said the man who called 36-year-old Eva in August 1985. "I about died," she says. "I had been dating in the four years since I split from my first husband, and I thought to myself, 'Uh-oh. What did I do? Sure, I went out, danced, and drank a little. But I don't remember getting so drunk I'd have said yes to a video.'"

The teasing ended there when Harvey, 45, chuckled and introduced himself. "You came to my son's bar mitzvah last October—that's the video I'm talking about! It has taken me this long to get your number from the date you came with that day." Harvey was divorced and had one son in college; another son and a daughter lived with him. Eva herself was raising three daughters who were younger than Harvey's kids.

Eva instantly loved Harvey's humor and accepted his invitation to go out. Soon they were seeing each other exclusively. All looked rosy. "We got along really well," Eva says. "Harvey has a good heart. He takes care of his family and parents. He's an all-around good guy."

"I love the way she looks and acts so young. Eva is kind, wise, and generous. She's artistic and very hospitable and the most beautiful lady I've ever seen," says Harvey. They married on March 1,1986.

What Eva did not realize was how seriously parenthood would ultimately affect their relationship. Trouble began almost immediately after the wedding. Eva was strict with her daughters, and

Harvey was much more lenient. Harvey wanted Eva to take charge, but when push came to shove, says Eva, Harvey undercut her authority. It upset Eva terribly, and there were big fights. Eva told her husband, "You have to put your foot down. If we're going to pool together in one house, we must present a united front to the children, or it'll be total chaos."

After two years of marriage, concerned that the children were hearing too much fighting, Eva walked out. There were two more years of attempted reconciliation, as Harvey tried to be more supportive, but it didn't work and they finally divorced.

"When we separated, we both took it hard," says Eva, remembering the sadness. "Neither of us really wanted to separate, but we both wanted the fighting to end.

"I went on with my life. I finished getting my kids through college. I was heartbroken because the problem wasn't him and me. It was very hard, but I got over it." Both Eva and Harvey started dating other people again, but, Eva recalls, "when I got past the anger, I was sorry it ended the way it had. We had family problems, not personal ones. I always felt that the person who had really treated me best and loved me most in life was Harvey."

But reuniting with Harvey was not on her radar. "I never foresaw getting back with him," says Eva. In 1996, eight years after her split from Harvey, she went out to lunch with a girlfriend in Palm Desert, California, and Harvey was in the restaurant. They all ate together, and then he started calling her. On Valentine's Day he sent a bouquet of flowers. They talked often over the next six months. Both concluded other relationships and started dating each other again.

"In my heart I remembered how wonderful it was. So seeing him again stirred up those feelings," says Eva. "And being sexual with him came naturally. That had always worked really well."

Nevertheless, there was some hesitation. "In the beginning stages of reuniting, I thought, 'Whoops, I'm putting my foot back in this water.' But by then the children were all grown up."

Harvey was very persuasive and determined to be supportive of Eva this time around. "I feel passionate about Eva and love her very much. And she's a very good mother." They remarried on June 21, 1997.

"He parents one way and I parent another," says Eva. "We have a really good marriage. We just had to wait until most of our parenting was over."

As Eva and Harvey discovered, an "empty nest" substantially reduces the potential for disputes if issues related to children in the household were the source of conflict the first time around. But even if the specific problems that divided a husband and wife can be resolved, the marriage-divorce-remarriage scenario has unique complications because of the acrimony that usually accompanies divorce. "Divorce brings about a sense of failure," explains Ginny Fleming. "People have generally ripped the fabric of their love and hurt each other badly." If such couples do get past their pain, remarry, and stay together for the long term, she says, "it's a validation of the growth they've had while they were apart."

A common refrain among reunited couples who look back on their families, be it children or parents, as a factor in their split is that they don't want to spend precious time on regrets. They are grateful for the present and the future and for the wisdom they've gained. As Linda (Fisher) Rentzer says of her mom's interference in her romance with Max Blitzer, "I'm not upset with my mother, because it all happened the way it was meant to happen. Everything turned out happy and wonderful."

Chapter 7

Crisis Brought Us Together

WHOM DO WE CALL IN TIMES OF PERSONAL CRISIS? WE TURN TO people we know will care, people we trust will try to help because of our history with them. This dynamic has reunited some grateful sweethearts who definitely weren't thinking about romance when true love came their way.

Most people who refound one another during a personal crisis genuinely needed support and companionship from someone who wouldn't expect them to "perform." They were grateful for someone who could understand their worries, fears, sadness, and despair—certainly not the normal feelings that surround the birth of a new romance.

What they needed was a person who would put shoulder to the wheel on their behalf and act as if "your crisis is my crisis"—someone who would give their needs top priority, someone who wouldn't expect to be coddled or courted. While they would never wish adversity on themselves, difficult circumstances can help couples cut to the chase and discover what matters most.

"When people are in an emotional crisis," says Dr. John Stine, clinical associate professor of psychiatry at New York-Presbyterian

Hospital, "they often long to return to relationships and times in their lives when things seemed simpler."

We don't always know that's what we want. Linda Hart didn't. She knew she was grieving and lonely and that she had to be strong for her children. Who was going to be strong for her? Her first love proved to be exactly the man she needed.

Linda and Ken

"A SHOULDER TO LEAN ON"

Linda Hart's husband, Craig, was killed in 1997 when the plane he was piloting crashed. But even before he died, their lives were full of sorrowful complications.

Linda had dated Craig during the last part of high school, married him after college, and put him through medical school on her teacher's salary. They had two daughters and a lovely home in Short Hills, New Jersey. About 20 years into their marriage, Craig went through what Linda describes as "a big midlife crisis." She says, "He had the girlfriend that was too young, the red sports car, the silk underwear, and the crazy hobby—learning to fly." But shortly before he was killed he told her that he wanted to resume marriage counseling and come back to his family.

Linda was devastated especially because she felt she had been on the verge of saving her marriage. Her two teenage daughters were plunged into deep grief, which was further complicated by one of them requiring repeated hospitalization for pancreatitis. Linda says the combination of crises hit her hard. "It was just an awful time—the worst of my life."

Two months after Craig died, Linda received a call from her first high school sweetheart, **Ken Kohn**, who was unaware of her life's tragic circumstances. He had only heard that she was separated and decided to call her 28 years after they had last seen each other.

Linda and Ken grew up in Fairlawn, New Jersey. "I waited for him to walk past my house each day on his way back from school," she remembers. "I thought he was cute. He had curly light brown hair and little crinkles around his eyes. I wanted him to be my boyfriend."

"She was very pretty, with dark eyes and long dark hair," recalls Ken. "I was just going through my growth spurt, so her being interested in me seemed pretty amazing."

They started dating when she was 15 and he was 16; they soon became inseparable. And then there was that first kiss in his basement den. "We snuck a kiss while his parents were upstairs," Linda remembers. "Wow! I felt lightheaded. I was almost swooning from it. The intensity of everything with him was magnified."

They dated for nearly two years, going to movies and ordering the pupu platter at Chen's Chinese restaurant. They hung out together at the mall in between their part-time jobs selling shoes at different stores. But then Linda met Craig, whom she thought was more sophisticated. She tried dating one boy on Friday nights, the other Saturday nights. Ken remembers his jealousy and "the steam coming out of my ears." Predictably enough, fistfights ensued. One time Craig pulled his car in front of Ken's house, got out, and they both landed some punches. Ken says it ended when "I threw him to the ground and sat on him." Then Craig said, "All right, it's over. C'mon, I'll buy you a beer." Underage or not, that's how they made peace. Ken moved on and started dating someone new.

After graduating from high school, Ken attended a community college and spent a few years in the army. He now runs the printing-services division of a global corporate trading company. Along the way he married, had three children, and divorced. "I sometimes thought about Linda—especially during the last eight years when my marriage was going bad. But I had made a commitment, and I was determined to stick it out—until my wife and I mutually decided to end it."

Then in August 1997, Ken phoned Linda. "I recognized Kenny's voice immediately—after 28 years."

When they met for lunch, Linda says, "He looked just the same, with his happy crinkly eyes. He was just so cute. I brought the blue-flowered diary I'd kept in school, and we read every page together and cracked up for the next three hours."

Neither of them wanted a relationship at the time, particularly since Linda's husband had so recently passed away. "At the beginning it wasn't a romantic thing with Kenny," says Linda. "I would just talk to him and tell him everything I was going through." He remembers: "We said, 'Hey, this is great. Let's be friends, a shoulder to lean on for both of us.'" But it quickly changed. One day Linda blurted out, "I love being with you. I don't want to be without you." Ken felt like the luckiest guy in the world.

But life wasn't easy. "This is how our relationship started—with the death of my husband and with my daughter very ill," says Linda. "I was in such crisis, I didn't know which end was up." Ken helped Linda through her daughter's hospitalizations. Linda calls Ken her "angel" and says, "He was just everything—my support, my outlet, my joy, my love."

Ken moved in for good about two years after his first call. Since then they have comforted his three children through the death of their mom. And when Linda was diagnosed with breast cancer and underwent a double mastectomy, Ken went with her to every single chemo treatment. They've helped each other at each turn. "I'm always impressed by him," she says. "He's just so sincere and honest and up front."

Ken says, "She even thanked me a couple of times, and I looked at her and said, 'What are you thanking me for? This is our life. This is what we both chose.' She was the first love of my life. She is my soul mate."

"Young love is a very powerful thing," says Linda. "We had something special to begin with, and it lasted in our hearts through all the years."

Linda's openness to reconnecting with a past sweetheart is not surprising to therapists and grief counselors. "If a loved one has died, going back to someone from our past helps us recapture a certain level of safety, stability, and innocence," explains therapist Ginny Fleming. "The vulnerability of one partner helps the other person feel tender and protective." Sometimes both people offer empathy and compassion, as when Elisa Albert talked with Joel Farkas. They never expected that tragedy would lead to love.

Elisa and Joel

"IF THIS IS INTRUSIVE, I'M SORRY"

Elisa and Joel grew up in the same Los Angeles community, but at 10 years her senior, he was closer to her brothers. Their moms were friends, and Elisa loved the hand-me-down clothes she received occasionally from Joel's sister.

In 1998, while Elisa was a student at Brandeis University, tragedy struck. Her older brother, David, died of a brain tumor. She found comfort in the arms of her family. In spite of her grief, she returned to school and ultimately moved to New York City to pursue a graduate degree in creative writing at Columbia University.

Joel was also living in New York, preparing to study at Fordham Law School, but they had no reason to see each other. Then in 2001, Joel's brother, Jordan, committed suicide. Joel flew home to spend five weeks with his family as they all tried to make sense of the terrible situation. When Joel returned to law school, his mom and Elisa's mom decided their children might be a comfort to each other while so far from home. But Elisa resisted making the call. "I thought, 'I don't know this guy very well. I don't know that he would want to talk to me in the aftermath of this horrible event.'"

Several weeks later her mom brought it up again, so Elisa dialed and left Joel a cryptic message. "If this is intrusive, I'm sorry. Our mothers are meddling. If you don't want to talk to me, don't worry about it."

Joel was actually pleased to hear a hometown voice and called her back the next day. They met for coffee and talked about their brothers. A week later he invited her to go hear some music, and they were together every day for the next three months. "I felt an immediate warmth and connection with her," says Joel. "My brother was my best friend, and I could either talk about him with her or just know that she remembered him."

"We shared a profoundly broken family experience," explains

Elisa. "He was still reeling from it because his loss was so recent. And because it was suicide, he was wracked with guilt, wondering if there was anything he could have done. We didn't have anything practical to give each other. What mattered was our common experience and our interwoven pasts."

From the sadness grew something beautiful. "She has a passion for living that makes even mundane events exciting," explains Joel. "He's expansive and interested in the world," says Elisa of Joel. "I love him like crazy."

They became engaged in December 2002 and married in August 2003. They still grieve for their brothers, but, Joel says, "I had to find some good in this or I would have been destroyed. My relationship with Elisa did arise out of it. That allows me to look at the universe as not just a terrible pain-inflicting place but one that can bring joy, too."

Elisa agrees. "We marvel that something so awful gave way to something so positive."

Joel says their moms were truly hoping to find comfort for their children, not looking to make a match. "But they *are* happy they made one."

Tragedy sometimes tears couples apart as each partner attempts to deal with and make sense of the pain. "Loss can be a disorganizing crisis for many people," explains therapist Estelle Schecter. Grief, obligation, and confusion were certainly factors that overwhelmed Tom Cahill and Kim Caris, a young couple living in Ohio. The death of his beloved older brother drove a wedge between them, but, ironically, other family tragedies brought them back together more than 20 years later.

Kim and Tom

"I WAS TRYING TO LIVE MY BROTHER'S LIFE"

Kim Caris and Tom Cahill met in geometry class in 1976 at Galion High School, 70 miles south of Cleveland.

"I was intrigued with her beauty," says Tom. "We were seated alphabetically, and she was right behind me. I was shy, but I finally got up the nerve to ask her out. She watched some of my basketball scrimmages after school, and she was intelligent and witty. I always felt proud to be with her."

"We were best friends as well as sweethearts," says Kim. "He was kind and thoughtful; he always remembered birthdays and holidays. We had so much in common. We both loved sports, animals, and being outdoors."

They went to basketball games and movies, and in the summer it was drive-ins, picnicking, and canoeing. Then in the late summer of 1978, Tom's 28-year-old brother, Jeff, was diagnosed with cancer. "It went fast," says Tom, "and he died within six months, in March 1979. I was so sad for my nephew, Nate, whom I adored. He was only a year and a half old. Jeff's wife was seven years my senior, and I started spending a lot of time with them to provide a kind of father figure for Nate."

"Tom and his brother had been best friends," Kim remembers. "At 19 years old Tom didn't know how to deal with the loss, and neither did I. I only knew that I never got to see Tom alone anymore, and I asked him to make a choice—me or his family."

Tom tried including Kim in the time he spent with his brother's son, but it wasn't enough and she eventually broke up with him. "I was too young to understand grief and his feeling of obligation," she says.

Kim was devastated when she later learned that Tom was marrying his sister-in-law and they were having a baby together. Kim had a series of failed relationships and never married. "Tom was too hard a guy to replace," she says. She concentrated on her studies but kept up on where Tom was living through her mother.

When Kim's aunt died a painful death from cancer about five years later, she finally understood what Tom must have felt with his brother's death. She hoped to run into him again, to let him know she finally understood what had happened, but their separation lasted more than 22 years.

In March 2003, Kim was home from her job as a middle school teacher in Las Vegas when her mom mentioned that Tom's mother had died. Kim planned to write a note but was distracted by her own father's grave illness. After he died in April, she spotted a sympathy card from Tom at her mother's house. Embarrassed that she had not sent condolences about Tom's mother, she wrote to Tom's dad, hoping he would show his son the letter. But she used her Las Vegas home as the return address.

Tom, whose marriage had long been unhappy, immediately wrote to Kim in Nevada. "If you ever want to communicate with me, here's my e-mail address. I would love to hear from you, but I'll leave that up to you."

Seven long weeks went by before Kim received his letter because she was still in Ohio helping her mother. Finally home, she was thrilled to read it and she e-mailed him right away. On her next trip to Ohio a month later, Kim and Tom got together. "When I saw him for the first time in more than 20 years, I felt like I was struck by lightning! My first impulse was to run up and hug him. It was like the years had vanished!"

"She went back to Vegas, and I waited for her e-mails," recalls Tom. "Each time one came, I was ecstatic, in seventh heaven!"

At first their correspondence was platonic. Then she signed an e-mail "Love and Peace." His next one started with "Hey Babe," which broke the ice between them. Their relationship took off.

"I've thought about you for 25 years," Kim soon wrote. "I care for you now. I loved you back then and I may still love you."

"I had all these nice things that people use to measure success: the car, the house, the big-screen TV," says Tom. "But the only time I was ever really happy was with Kim. I see now that I was trying to live my brother's life." Separated in October 2003, Tom says, "My children are grown, and I want my own life now. I want the chance to be with Kim again."

They feel some sorrow about the road they have traveled because of the pain it has caused his children. And there is another factor: "He is the love of my life," says Kim, "but we do feel some guilt because it seems that if his mother and my father hadn't died, we wouldn't have each other. It's a bittersweet irony that in death our parents pulled us together."

Most lovers who reunite as a result of tragedy do recognize the irony in the situation, but they come to accept that whatever conditions brought love their way, it's welcome and, many of them believe, "meant to be." Death or serious illness is not a circumstance anyone would choose as the basis for a romantic reunion, but sometimes these events make people focus on the important things in life. At such times we need dependability and strength, and the companionship of someone who already cares gives us great comfort.

"When we're threatened, we want to go back to the nest,"

explains Dr. Sherry Bush. "We want to go back to someone familiar so that we feel safe and grounded. We associate that person with home." Such was the experience of one New York woman who reached out to someone from her past at a critical moment in her life.

Jane and Mark

"I NEEDED SOMEONE I COULD TRUST"

Her mother's heart attack in 1988 was a shock for Jane Waldman, who was 30 years old at the time. "My mother was my best friend," she explains. "I lost my dad in high school, so Mom and I became war buddies. We had been very wealthy, and then all of a sudden he was gone. At 16 I had to work, and we couldn't afford my fancy private school anymore. She took care of me, and I took care of her. She was everything in the world to me."

Jane was working as a reporter at an all-news radio station in Austin, Texas, when she received the call about her mom. She says, "When I hung up, I had to go on the air and sound chipper." But the minute she finished the assignment, she rushed to the news director and said, "I'm going home to New York."

Jane mentally flipped through the list of people she could phone for comfort and help. Mark Braverman's name came to mind. Though they hadn't talked for almost three years, he was the one she called.

Jane had met Mark in 1984 when he was her instructor for a video project at a university in Long Island, New York. She was 25 and he was 38, but in spite of the age difference he had an immediate reaction to the dynamic redhead. "She was spe-

124

cial, very intelligent, and self-assured. I felt she was the person for me as soon as I saw her."

Jane had a different reaction. "I was clueless." They started going out occasionally, but Jane did not share the depth of Mark's feelings. She was focused on her career and wanted freedom to travel. Nevertheless, she had fun with Mark, who understood the crazy time demands of Jane's broadcasting profession because he was also a freelance network cameraman.

"I don't know if you would call what we had 'dates,'" says Mark. "Basically, I would drive an hour to the radio station where she was doing newscasts. I'd hang out while she did on-air reports and put tapes together. Then maybe we'd get something to eat." But Jane had been clear that she didn't want to settle down, and when the job opportunity in Texas came up, she jumped at it. Mark was sad when she moved away but realized there was nothing he could do.

When the crisis occurred, why did Jane call Mark of all people? "I knew he really cared about me. I called him to help me as a friend, not as a sweetheart. But I guess deep down I knew he loved me, and I needed someone I could trust to be with me through something so important."

Mark had thought of Jane often. "I'd always kept her picture, so I guess some part of me never gave up."

When Jane phoned from Texas, the first thing Mark said was "I never stopped loving you." He volunteered to pick her up at the airport, arrived with flowers, and was at her side every day for the next three weeks as she saw her mom through dangerous bypass surgery. Of course, while any daughter would be concerned about her mother, Jane's fears were especially intense. She envisioned the worst. "I was afraid she was going to die because my dad had died in that same hospital."

Jane remembers: "Mark held my hand and calmed me down during the eight-hour operation." The surgery was a success. And then Jane and Mark began to help with the slow process of recovery.

"I don't think her mom particularly cared for me," Mark says with a chuckle. "She thought maybe I wasn't good enough for her daughter. But I was there and willing to help."

Mark's devotion was not lost on Jane. "He helped when Mom was confused by the medicines. He was very patient and kind, and it told me that he was a solid, good guy and that he really loved me." Given the situation, Jane couldn't help but compare him to a doctor she had dated. She had become ill, and the doc had dropped her off at an emergency room with $10 for cab fare home. Mark was definitely looking good by comparison.

Three weeks after the surgery Jane flew back to Texas to wrap up some assignments and resign from her job. Mark went there to help her pack and drive home to New York. On the trip Jane finally let down her guard. She smiles, "That's when it got serious between us."

They dated for several years and married in her mom's backyard in 1990. Nowadays, Jane's mom still lives in her own house, and Mark helps with repairs or takes her to the doctor when Jane is on assignment for AP Radio. "Mark is the son Mom never had," says Jane. "He is caring, supportive, and generous. I love Mark, and marrying him is the best thing I ever did."

"Jane is the love of my life," says Mark. "When she called, I was sorry that she was scared but happy that she reached out for me."

Like Jane and Mark, most of the couples who refound each other in a time of personal crisis focused first on getting through the moment. Their pain, sorrow, and anxiety were intense. Their needs were different from those in the normal course of life. Romance was the last thing on their minds, but help with practical issues or emotional hurts was so welcome that their hearts opened. Then, as worry and grief receded, the effervescence of loving companionship helped them feel joy again.

Chapter 8

The Chance to Do It Right

MOST OF US WOULD LOVE A "DO-OVER" IN SOME PARTS OF OUR lives; we may wish we had made a stronger point in an argument, or had chosen a different career, or taken an opportunity we passed up. When it comes to the heart, reunited love gives us that second chance. While we can't exactly climb into a time machine and, *presto*, alter our personal history as in those *Back to the Future* movies, we do have the opportunity to change the *ending* of a love story.

If one or both partners caused the early rift in a hurtful way, the chance to add a new conclusion is particularly welcome. Some people regret not just that a relationship ended but *how* it ended. Some are sorry about the way they acted; perhaps they embarrassed or wounded their former sweetheart. Some were like ships passing in the night, missing each other's signals about their feelings. And there are those who messed up that iconic moment, The Prom. Years later they want to set things right. Reuniting with a past sweetheart is an exhilarating way to take care of unfinished business and find not only a happy ending but a new beginning.

Runaway Bride

In our story of a runaway bride—not to be confused with the Julia Roberts movie!—both partners confess that they made mistakes. Michael made his error early. Jeanne's came when a stranger's flippant remark in Las Vegas sent her running from her groom. It wasn't until years later that this Los Angeles couple's wedding bells rang for real.

Jeanne and Michael

"I DON'T WANT TO GET MARRIED!"

Jeanne (Trattner) was 20 when Michael Harris, 26, knocked at her door in Westwood, California, to pick her up for a blind date in 1961. "We both had big smiles on our faces after we saw each other," she says, "because we liked what we saw. He was tall, about five feet eleven inches, with sandy brown hair. He had boyish good looks, and I liked his personality. I also was physically attracted to him."

"She was about five feet one, with brunette hair and an hourglass figure," Michael recalls. "Bells rang. There was chemistry, and we dated for the next six months."

Jeanne planned to go into real estate, while Michael was a young lawyer working with Mirisch, a successful independent film company that made *West Side Story* and *The Magnificent Seven*. It seemed that all was going well when Michael invited Jeanne to The Luau, a popular Beverly Hills restaurant on Rodeo Drive. "I always loved being with him," Jeanne remembers, "but that night out of the blue he said, 'I don't think we should see each other as often for a while.'

"It felt like a knife went through me," recalls Jeanne, "and I said, 'Well, Michael, I've got one better. I don't think we should see each other at all.'"

Michael explains now that he was about to strike out on his own careerwise, and he feared the responsibility of a committed relationship. He says, "I just wasn't ready."

But from that day on Michael couldn't get Jeanne out of his mind. She, on the other hand, worked him right out of her system and started dating other guys. "He called after three months and said he'd made a big mistake. He wanted to see me again," she says, "but I felt nothing—even when he said he loved me and was ready for marriage."

Over the next six years Michael continued to call Jeanne and they went out a few times, but she wasn't that interested. When she turned 25, she planned an open-ended trip to Europe. "I'd never been away from my family," she says, "and it was time. But Michael begged me not to go."

"Cancel the trip and marry me," he pleaded. "I've been devoted to you for six years. Doesn't that mean anything?"

Jeanne went anyway and had the time of her life. "Attracting men was never difficult for me, but I realized they were a fly-by-night thing," she says. "I thought, 'Here is Michael, this wonderful man who has valued me for all these years. Maybe I should marry him if he asks again.'" She called him when she got home and made a date. "He took me to the big round restaurant at the LA airport, and he flashed two tickets to Las Vegas. He still wanted us to get married. 'Yes,' I told him, and we were off."

They turned in the tickets and drove because Jeanne doesn't

like flying and they wanted the car available for use after the wedding. Meanwhile, Jeanne's mom, who was already in Vegas celebrating her anniversary, started making calls to gather the relatives. It was all going fine until Michael went off to play a few hands of blackjack and Jeanne stood beside a gorgeous hunk at the craps table. She says, "When this stranger asked why I was there and I said I was getting married, he said, 'Gee, that's a shame.' I suddenly thought to myself, 'He's right! I don't want to get married.'" Jeanne makes it perfectly clear that she never had a 'thing' with the stranger. "I never even knew his name, but he planted this idea in my head that I shouldn't get married."

After obtaining the marriage license, she had a major anxiety attack. "Don't you think we're rushing this?" she asked Michael. "Can't we just get engaged first?" Finally she just blurted out: "I can't do this. I don't want to do this." She became the runaway bride.

Her mom had the job of calling the relatives to cancel their trips. She got the same telephone company long-distance operator who had put through the invitation calls, and even she commiserated with Jeanne's mom: "Oh, you poor darling."

"I was more sad than embarrassed," remembers Michael. "I thought, 'Well, that's the way the cookie crumbles.' I did myself in at the Luau that night, and I'll never be able to climb out of that hole." They had what Michael, in a huge understatement, calls "a very awkward drive" back to Los Angeles. That was the end of that, or so they both thought.

Michael married a year and a half later, in 1970, and had two children. In 1972, Jeanne married a man who, unlike Michael, had never wavered in his relationship with her. Though she and Michael once ran into each other at a restaurant on the Sunset Strip and spoke politely, they had no other contact. It was a good 28 years after the runaway bride fiasco that a friend of Jeanne's told Michael his old flame was divorced and living in Irvine, California.

"I'd thought a lot about her during our years apart," Michael says, "and I was separated after 22 years of marriage. I called and used her given name. 'Rosa Jean,' I said, 'I'd like to see you.' We met, but she still wasn't interested." Then one day Jeanne watched an Oscar-winning short film called *The Line and the Dot*, narrated by Robert Morely. The story went like this:

A straight line loved a little dot, but the dot thought the straight line was stiff and dull. The squigglies bouncing around were much more interesting. The straight line was very sad until suddenly it realized that it could bend into some very interesting shapes such as a triangle and a parallelogram, which the squigglies couldn't do. With its new confident attitude the straight line won over the little dot, and together they became an exclamation point!

"Gosh," thought Jeanne, "that's just like Michael and me. I could never be an exclamation point without him!" Her therapist encouraged her to call him. "But not just to see him once or twice," he said. "You need to get involved with him—even if you don't feel it inside. And marry him. If you can't stand it, you can get a divorce."

"I thought his advice was bizarre," she recalls, "but I also thought he might be right. I decided to follow an old Jewish tradition for arranged marriages, requiring the couple to see each other seven times. If it still wasn't there, I'd move on. We started dating in July 2002 and, sure enough, after five dates I fell madly in love with Michael again." They married on April 24, 2003, at the Peninsula Hotel in Beverly Hills.

"I had to grow up a little, even at 60," Jeanne says. And she is "ecstatically" happy now. "Michael is a man of such principle, integrity, and fairness. He treats me beautifully. He's a loving husband who wants to make me happy, and I want to make him happy. I adore him more every day. We have a great companionship, our personalities still meld well, and he has a cute sense of humor. You know, what's not to love? Apart from his being a vegetarian, but I've adapted."

Michael calls their being together *B'shaert,* a Yiddish word for something that is meant to be. He says, "Others might see Jeanne as a 60-year-old, but in my mind's eye she is still that 20-year-old girl who was very, very sweet, giving, and understanding. And attractive. I feel as if we're still 20 and 26 with the same vitality." Jeanne may have been a runaway bride, but Michael feels that now "she is everything you would want in a wife."

Michael's explanation for his misstep at the Luau—wanting to concentrate on a career—wasn't especially cruel, according to therapists. It was developmentally reasonable for a young man. "For males, their early needs are the three M's: medals, money, and mastery," explains Dr. Iris SanGiuliano. "Their focus isn't necessarily making whatever woman they have in their lives happy. But the needs are not immature. It's the level of maturity young men are supposed to have at that time. What happens later is that they start to tap into other aspects of themselves. It's a softer side."

Alas, sometimes the damage has been done. Jeanne wouldn't allow herself to be interested again. Why was it so hard for Jeanne to be open to Michael a second time? Why did she keep running? "So much of who we are—more for women than men—really depends on how we were treated by our early loves, how we were dumped or how we broke up," explains Dr. Sherry Bush. "We remember that, and it really impacts our self-esteem."

Michael clearly regretted the initial breakup and repeatedly tried to apologize for the upset he had caused. Luckily, he was able to renew his pursuit, and Jeanne overcame her reluctance. They feel they finally got it right. As it turns out, an apology is often the cata-lyst that helps rekindle a relationship.

Apologies

"We have the need to right wrongs," explains therapist Ginny Fleming. "Carrying guilt is like shouldering a bag of rocks all the time: When we lighten our load, our journey becomes easier. We also want to save face by saying, 'I am not that person anymore.' In a way, apologizing tells someone who you are today. An apology accepted from an old sweetheart restores innocence to that relationship."

Ed's apology as we took our first walk was significant in helping me open up to him and reignite our relationship. I felt he had made his heart vulnerable to me, and that was most endearing. When they heard the story, some of my women friends joked about the long list of men who owed them apologies. I agree that it's best not to sit around waiting for one! But don't be startled if someday it happens, as it did to Leslie, an anthropologist at a university in New York.

Leslie and Russell

"I NEEDED TO ASK HER FORGIVENESS"

Nine years after their split, Leslie and her graduate school sweetheart, Russell, rekindled the love they had begun on an archeological dig out West. Their reunion started with an apology. "I needed to ask her forgiveness," he says. "I realized that I had bungled a number of things. I didn't think I would necessarily have a future with her, but I wanted her to know how important she was to me and how wonderful our time together had been."

He regretted hurting Leslie with a choice he had made back then to spend time with a different woman. "It was youthful foolishness that left me feeling I was not the person I wanted to be. Leslie is a beautiful person inside, in all those great human ways of true kindness and caring. I knew I had hurt her badly, and the best thing to do was to write and tell her everything that was in my heart," he explains.

Leslie says that when they split up, she'd felt profound loneliness and had "hated him right out of my life. I totally let him go. I didn't pine after him. But it was evident through his letters, e-mails, and phone calls that he had markedly changed. I've certainly had enough of my own travails, and I respect another human being who can change and grow."

She remembered with excitement the time they had originally spent getting to know each other. "It was a summer of living in a tent camp in a remote location, making dinner and drinking beer together. I loved his blue eyes and his slender hands. We had an intense flirtation."

She says of his apology, "He sang my accolades in a sweet

and profound way." In response she wrote back, "I don't know if this is an opening or a closing. Are you trying to court me, or are you trying to say you're sorry and move on?"

They began to talk on the phone, and Russell says, "We spoke very intimately about a great variety of things. There was a 'coming home' kind of feeling. Neither of us wanted a fling. We wanted something with a future. I told her, 'I'm here because I want something deep and promising.'" They are now husband and wife.

"We have found more than we ever imagined in being together again," says Russell. "We are incredibly attracted to each other, and we are very fortunate that our profession has wonderful opportunities to be adventurous beyond our wildest imaginations. One of the reasons we love being with each other is that we don't hesitate. If the choice is adventure or thinking about adventure, we pack our bags and go!"

When Russell looks at Leslie, he still sees that outdoorsy girl from their days in Utah. "Always, always we are the same two tanned, sweaty people, barely wearing any clothes, running across the valley in Arches National Park. We are still those people who said so much without speaking, without sex. We communicated through pure affection and the physical joy of just being with each other."

An apology like Russell's can be self-healing as well as therapeutic for the person receiving it. Asking for forgiveness has several motives: It alleviates guilt, clears up misunderstandings, and sometimes kick-starts the relationship again. It lets both people feel better about the past. "An apology might protect one's own sense of worth," says Dr. Herb Barrett, "and at the same time allow the other person to feel safe again."

Looking back, some couples say neither of them committed an egregious wrong. It was simply a case of crossed signals. Failure to be clear and lack of patience cost one Arizona couple 34 years before they had the chance to make things right.

Renee and Jim

"FOR 34 YEARS I NEVER KNEW THAT RENEE LOVED ME"

Renee (Shipp) Petrausch, 58, is madly in love with her husband, 62-year-old **Jim Petrausch.** They have settled near Phoenix, Arizona, but their story began when he was ten, living in Thermopolis, Wyoming, and six-year-old Renee moved across the street. As they got a little older, Jim made a point of running into "Shipper," his nickname for her. He would carry her books home from school, and they would lie in the grass, looking for four-leaf clovers and blowing dandelion parachutes. If Jim came to the door when Renee wasn't home, her mom would invite him in for tuna sandwiches and Kool-Aid. Renee remembers, "He was so handsome. He looked like Dr. Kildare. And he was always a perfect gentleman."

As a freshman in high school "I was already in love with Shipper," Jim recalls. "We'd go to the movies as friends. She'd be wearing a light, cotton, summery dress, and when I happened to brush the little wispy hairs at the back of her neck, I thought to myself, 'She's so beautiful.' When I was a lifeguard at our neighborhood pool and she came over and said, 'Hi, Jim,' it made my day."

He never expressed his true feelings for Renee because his mom forbade him to date a girl who was that much younger. However, as DJ for a local radio station he would dedicate the song "Only You" by the Platters to Renee "from a secret admirer," hoping she was listening. All the while he feared that his love was one-sided. "I was afraid that if I asked her to be my girl, she'd say she didn't think about me like that." He never spoke up for fear of losing his best friend.

To complicate matters, Renee's mother told her that the boy should make all the moves, so Renee never told Jim that she loved him, either. She was waiting for him to speak first. Their feelings remained unexpressed when Jim joined the U.S. Navy in the fall of 1959. Whenever he came home, he brought Shipper gifts: perfume from France, cashmere sweaters from Naples, a wall tapestry from Saudi Arabia, and a hand-carved mahogany elephant from Ethiopia. He desperately wanted to tell her, "I've always loved you, Renee, and I'll always be faithful to you. Will you please be my girlfriend?" But he never said a word.

"Everywhere I went, to the Parthenon in Athens or the Colosseum in Rome," he said, "I would always turn around and imagine saying, 'Wow, look at that, Renee.'"

In 1964 when Jim was 22 and back in the United States on leave, he visited Renee in Denver where she was working as a secretary. They had a wonderful Valentine's Day and a weekend trip home to Wyoming. That Sunday night Jim finally got up the nerve to ask Renee to marry him. Renee wanted to answer yes but felt she should talk to her mom first, so she said, "I think we should wait."

"I've been waiting for five years," he replied, crushed at her answer. Renee, who didn't realize Jim was quite so upset, spoke to her mother and decided she *would* marry Jim, but she had to return to Denver early in the morning. She waited for a chance to tell him yes in person.

But Jim made a huge mistake. Devastated that Renee hadn't accepted his proposal, he turned around and married a local girl who saw him as her ticket out of town. Jim takes the blame. "It was *stupid*," he says. "Marriage no longer meant anything to me because I thought my fate was sealed. Renee didn't want me."

When Renee found out that Jim had gotten married, "I bawled and I bawled," she says. "I was in hysterics. 'He can't marry her,' I cried to my friends. 'He loves me!'" As a result Renee and Jim were estranged for the next 34 years.

Renee eventually moved on, marrying, having children, and working as an office administrator. But she always hoped to see Jim again. Jim, who ultimately rose to the rank of senior chief petty officer, carried a high school photo of Shipper wherever he went. Even though he was married and he loved his kids, "I sealed up my heart when Renee refused my proposal," he says. "I encased it in lead and never again allowed a woman to get truly close to me."

One night in 1973 while in Rome with the navy, nine years after the fateful Valentine's weekend, Jim popped open a bottle of wine and toasted Renee, "wherever you are." It was 2 A.M. on a starlit night, and there he sat, tears running down his face, thinking he would never see her again.

In 1998, in spite of all the missed signals, the miracle happened. Jim was in the middle of a divorce, living in Florida and taking care of his elderly mother, when he picked up a copy of the hometown newspaper his mom subscribed to. The issue was dated months before and featured a picture from a high school reunion. Jim gasped when he saw Renee's name in the caption.

He called the reunion coordinator for her address and got up the courage to send a Christmas card. "Hi, Shipper," he wrote. "How's this for a voice from the past?"

Renee, who was divorced, picked up her mail a few days later, and one red card stood out. Before she even opened it, she knew it was from Jim because, to her astonishment, she recognized his handwriting after 34 years!

She called him the next day. When they talked on the phone the day after that, Renee spoke the words that Jim had wanted to hear since he was young: "You've always been the love of my life."

They reunited seven weeks later for Valentine's Day. "She looked just as she always did," said Jim, "absolutely gorgeous, the most attractive girl I ever met in my life. The contagious giggle and that smile! It was all still there."

And she sees him through youthful eyes as well. "He looked the same," Renee says, "except for the mustache that I'd never seen before. But I liked it. He looked so handsome, just like a movie star."

Jim says, "We both feel in our hearts and minds that we're still 18 and 22. To us, our early time together seems like it was just yesterday."

Jim gave Renee 34 red sweetheart roses and one white rose with a card that read, "A red rose for each year that we missed, with one white rose for the light of my life and our future happiness." Jim feels that he made a huge mistake by not proclaiming his love for Renee when they were young and missing the signals that she loved him, too. His advice to other guys: "If you love a girl, tell her. If she says she doesn't love you back, then you can move on. I never knew for 34 years that Renee loved me, and I was heartbroken all that time."

For Renee's part, "I feel as if we were betrothed from birth," she says, "because Jim always was my true love."

Crossed wires have tormented a lot of people looking back on the one that got away. Ed and I had our own less critical episode of bad timing and missed signals in our youth. It may sound silly, but we are sad to this day that we didn't attend our high school senior proms together. By the time we started dating back then, each of us had committed to attending our proms with other people. I remember my mother saying, "Honey, if you say yes to one boy, you can't go back on your word just because you get a better offer." But even now Ed and I have wistful feelings about it. Sure, we kept our word to our dates, but what a memory to miss!

To continue on a sore subject, it turns out that many reunited couples remember The Prom as a defining moment.

The Prom

However they handled it at the time, for many young couples The Prom was a big deal. Rekindled lovers often spontaneously mentioned their twist on this major event when I spoke with them. Some, like Carol Pedersen and Gary Puetz, actually used their prom picture on their wedding invitations.

Some couples split up right after the prom. Geraldine O'Brien was crushed when Jimmy Sibilia took her to his junior prom and then broke up with her one month later.

Dr. Hilly Dubin, whom we'll meet in the next chapter, says that because his now-wife, Cheryl Kagan, turned him down for his senior prom, he didn't go at all.

Wanda (Hite) and Todd Lista went to their prom with different dates but snuck away together for part of the evening. "I wasn't getting anywhere with Todd because he was worried about my being two years older," Wanda explains. And in a twist worthy of one of the soap operas that she has written, "I had suggested he take my best girlfriend to the prom instead."

Todd says, "We didn't exactly ditch our dates, but we spent more time with each other than with them."

Beverly (Hancock) "borrowed" a friend's boyfriend, Burl Howard, in his Marine uniform for the junior prom because she wanted the handsomest date she could find. Beverly made her "eat your heart out" point to her ex-boyfriend that night and then married Burl 48 years later.

David Bilon says he and Fran thought the prom was okay, "but the bowling afterward was more fun."

Laurie Clinton still remembers that when they went to Mike's senior prom in 1981 before he joined the Air Force, he not only brought her a corsage but also gave her a dozen red roses.

The fact that these happy reunited adult couples recall their prom experience so vividly is significant. "The prom is a rite of passage," says Dr. John Stine, "and it has powerful symbolic meanings for teenagers. For a girl it can mean, 'Look, I am now a woman who can present herself as sexually desirable. I may not even want to act on it, but by spending so much time and money getting beautiful, I can now announce my entry into womanhood.'"

Today there are even magazines like *Teen Prom*, *Your Prom*, and *Seventeen Prom* that feature such articles as "How to Find Your Dream Prom Date," "Prom Makeovers," and "Your Prom Horoscope Revealed." (In 1968, Ed's must have said that Sagittarius would go to the prom with the wrong girl!)

And it's not just a female thing. "Renting a tuxedo, arranging for a limo, asking a girl out on this most special type of date," adds Dr. Stine, "all carry the meaning that a boy is entering into a more adult world."

Years ago a young man and woman often announced to the world simply by going to the dance together that they were a couple. It was a do-or-die kind of moment with lots of expectations, hopes, and fantasies. The prom is a little less "coupled" these days, with kids sometimes going stag or in groups. Still, for kids who do go in pairs, it's often a big moment. "It can solidify the fact that you and your date are a couple," explains Dr. Sherry Bush. "This night can be a platform on which sweethearts tell each other, 'This is how I see us after we leave school.'"

Given the importance of the prom, it is not surprising that some of the wrongs people want to rectify when they rekindle their love are actually prom related. That is what happened for Janet Jacobson and Mark Davis, who now live in Somerset, New Jersey. During high school they were best friends—until he invited her to the prom.

Janet and Mark

"WE MADE OUR OWN PROM"

Janet Jacobson and Mark Davis were very close friends at Madison Central High School in Old Bridge, New Jersey. Their love of music had brought them together. "I was a drummer," says Mark. "Janet played guitar, and I'd wander into the record store where she worked. She was six feet tall and thin, and she wore peasant skirts."

Janet recalls, "Mark was shorter than me, and he had the most beautiful blue eyes. He was my first close 'guy' friend, and I loved our bantering back and forth when we discussed books, music, and art."

Just before graduation in 1979, Mark stopped Janet in the school hallway, and their close friendship took an unexpected turn. "I invited her to the prom," he says, "but she turned me down. In the end neither of us went."

"I turned him down because my close friend, Sheila, kept saying that she hoped Mark Davis would ask her to the prom," remembers Janet. "When he asked me instead of her, I was torn. I didn't want to hurt my girlfriend. But it takes so much for a high school guy to get up the nerve to ask a girl to the prom. He really put himself out there, and he was very hurt when I said no."

Their friendship was so damaged by Janet's rejection that they didn't stay in touch after graduation and went their separate ways for 20 years. During that time Mark attended Shenandoah Conservatory in Virginia. He had relationships but never married, and went to work doing job placement for the disabled. Janet got married, moved to Boston, and worked as a director of design for Reebok. She was divorced by 1992. Her career involved a great deal of international travel, which she loved, but when she turned 35, she'd had enough. Quitting her job, she decided to visit relatives in Israel and think about what to do next. But first she attended her high school reunion. "I was so busy packing for the trip that I didn't plan a special outfit; I wore a trouser suit to the reunion as if I were going to a meeting," Janet laughs. "I saw Mark right away, and we were inseparable for the next two and a half hours."

Mark recalls, "When Janet arrived fashionably late, I'd already been to the bar twice and was feeling nostalgic. I remembered

Donna, 1968

Ed, 1968

Donna and Ed's wedding, 2003

Suzanne Pleshette and
Tom Poston, then (Chapter 2)

Tom and Suzanne, now

Raymond Whitehead
and Gail Robinson,
then (Chapter 4)

Courtesy of Gail Robinson and Raymond Whitehead

Gail and Raymond, now

Courtesy of Gail Robinson and Raymond Whitehead

Courtesy of Bob Williamson

Bob Williamson, then (Chapter 11)

Courtesy of Lois Elser-Williamson

Lois (Kenreich) Elser-Williamson, then (Chapter 11)

Bob and Lois, now

Courtesy of Lois Elser-Williamson and Bob Williamson

Alexis (Grossman) and
Matt Wheeler, then
(Chapter 3)

Alexis and Matt, now

Cheryl J. Kagan and Dr. Hilly Dubin, then (Chapter 9)

Hilly and Cheryl, now, with daughter Brooke

Harry Kullijian and Carol Channing, then
(Chapter 2)

Harry and Carol, now

Beverly (Gordon) Hodder,
then (Chapter 10)

Riley Hodder, then (Chapter 10)

Beverly and Riley, now

Max Blitzer and Linda (Fisher) Rentzer, then (Chapter 6)

Max and Linda, now

Ellen (Hector) and J. R. Barberie, then (Chapter 6)

Ellen and J. R., now

Dr. Mike Sperber, then
(Chapter 11)

Mary (Gibbon) Clarke, then
(Chapter 11)

Mike and Mary, now

Marge (Waldman) and
Coty Keller, then
(Chapter 4)

Marge and Coty, now

Sam Nichols, then
(Chapter 10)

Joy (Jemison)
Nichols, then
(Chapter 10)

Joy and Sam, now

Alex Hesterberg and Liza Huber, then
(Chapter 2)

Liza and Alex, now

Millie (Penn) Spitz, then
(Chapter 11)

Arnold Spitz, then (Chapter 11)

Millie and Arnold, now

Ron Martucci and Kate Coyne, then
(Chapter 3)

Ron and Kate, now

Ken Kohn and Linda Hart, then
(Chapter 7)

Linda and Ken, now

Jim Petrausch, then (Chapter 8)

Renee (Shipp) Petrausch, then (Chapter 8)

Jim and Renee, now

Oster brothers Ron, Ed, and Dave invite wives Diana, Donna, and Jeannette to rough it with them in Yosemite

Donna with her children, Caroline and Andrew

her with long hair and those peasant skirts, but that night she looked so adult and professional. We spent most of the evening together. It was terrific, but she was leaving for Israel the next day."

It was hard for Janet to leave after that night. By the time she got to Israel, Mark was mailing her CDs of his favorite music. But he wanted something more immediate. "I had been convinced," he says, "that the computer signaled the death of Western civilization, so I didn't own one. But I realized fairly quickly that if I wanted to communicate with Janet in a timely way, I needed to use e-mail. I got a computer, and pretty soon I was sending three e-mails a day."

"We did some old-fashioned letter-writing as well," Janet recalls. "I also drew him pictures, and he sent me recordings of music that was full of longing."

Janet headed home after six months, flying into Newark Airport. Mark drove to pick her up in the middle of an ice storm. "I was afraid I wouldn't make it in time to meet her. At the arrival gate I jumped in the air to see over people's heads. When I spotted her, I was so excited." They had their first kiss at Newark Airport in the midst of hundreds of people. She says, "I don't remember letting go of his hand. We're still holding hands today."

A few days later they reread the e-mails they had saved. "My romantic side had been buried for years," says Mark. "It was wonderful to get it back with Janet."

Living together was everything they hoped for, but Mark kept teasing Janet that she had made a mistake in turning him down for the prom. "Okay," she said. "I can't keep hearing about this forever. We're going to make our own prom."

In the year 2000, 21 years after the ill-fated prom invitation, Janet ordered a floral centerpiece in their high school colors.

They put up a mirrored disco ball and hung stars in the living room. She bought a prom dress. "I also went to an old-style beauty parlor," she says, "and I got the up-do thing." Mark shaved his beard and mustache (he was clean-shaven in 1979) and gave Janet a corsage. "I got him a boutonniere," she recalls, "and he bought some CDs with hits from the seventies. After dinner we danced all night. We made our own prom. There was a dramatic, pounding rainstorm, which we could see through our picture windows. We had a few bottles of champagne, and it was fantastic!"

"Perfect!" agrees Mark.

"We always have a lot of fun," says Janet, who now teaches and does occasional freelance designing. "Mark is the most amazing person, so good, honest, and loving. He supports me completely. I got home one night with a new haircut and a rinse to cover the gray. 'What do you think?' I asked him. He said, 'You were beautiful this morning, and you're beautiful now.' And he meant it. I'm passionately in love with him, and he is still my best friend."

After four years together they married on May 9, 2004. "We are tremendously thankful to have found each other," says Mark. "She's every bit as lovely, if not more so, than she was in high school. Every day I'm blown away by her. Our relationship deepens the more time we spend together. We have these mini-epiphanies when we think about how lucky we are. I'm tremendously thankful for having found her again."

Janet and Mark's charming story of recreating their prom reflects the humor and attentiveness in their life as a reunited couple. Janet wishes she had responded differently to Mark's first invitation, treading more gently when he was vulnerable. The second time around they have promised to be tender with each other's feelings. They feel the same way Ed does about reuniting: "How many times in life do you get a chance to do something so important over again and this time do it right?"

Our Thirtieth Reunion

Having missed our chance at a prom in the early days, Ed and I found it that much sweeter to attend our thirtieth college reunion in October 2002 as a couple. The moment we set foot on campus, we were teenagers again. We walked the grounds together, taking in the beauty of the Spanish-style architecture and red-tile roofs. We inhaled the familiar scent of the towering eucalyptus trees that grace the campus.

At Ed's freshman dormitory we headed down the hallway and stopped at his old room. The door was open; we peeked in and then burst out laughing. Nothing had changed. The decor was "teenage chaos"—pretty much the same as when Ed lived there. At my freshman dorm, Paloma, in Florence Moore Hall (Flo Mo), we bumped into the girls who had my old room. I told them that I had lived there 34 years ago and that Ed had been my boyfriend back then. They loved the story, said, "Wow, that's so cool!" and invited us in. Standing there together we were flooded with memories: Friday night dates, bicycle rides, studying together, good-night kisses.

Everywhere we walked there were reminders: the old student union, the bookstore, the Quad. Passing Frost Amphitheater, we remembered the day during our senior year in high school when we had driven to Stanford. We were feeling rich, and Ed had sprung for tickets to hear Sergio Mendes and Brasil 66 in concert performing their hits, "The Look of Love" and "Up, Up and Away."

"It couldn't have been more romantic," Ed recalled as we strolled the campus. "Remember how we sat in the natural grass bowl of the ampitheater? It was spring and we thought, 'This campus is where we're going to live in just a few months. Wow, this is really uptown.'"

During the reunion we went to a football game, something we had never done together. Stanford played Arizona, and I'm happy to report that our team won. But a loss wouldn't have mattered to us—we were having a new experience in a dear, familiar place, and we were in love.

That entire glorious weekend we were thrilled to be reliving part of our youth together, and over the next few weeks it became clear that we both wanted to make "us" a permanent thing.

Proposal Day

Although Ed and I blew The Prom, one romantic mistake does not have to beget another. Ed was determined that his proposal of marriage would be memorable. I knew it was coming. (I might have casually pointed out a diamond solitaire or two in a pass through the mall.) I knew *when* it was coming, generally anyway. He informed me that during the second weekend in March he needed a full, uninterrupted day of my time. I offhandedly mentioned that "if anybody was ever going to propose to me, it would be important to make sure I had a chance to blow-dry my hair first."

"Got it," he said.

We rose early the morning of March 8, 2003, threw on comfy old clothes, and drove to Sandstone Peak to reenact our first romantic hike. A few hours later, all sweated up, we drove to Point Dume Beach in Malibu. With a bright sun overhead, we got sweatier still, descending the cliffs to the water. A breathtaking moment had taken place there a few months earlier when Ed suddenly turned to me and said, "I can feel myself falling in love with you." It was sweet indeed to revisit this beach.

I imagined that later we would shower at a hotel, dress up in our fancy attire, and end the night at a lovely romantic restaurant where I would be ready to say yes.

Suddenly Ed pulled a blue box out of his pocket. He went down on his knee in the gentle surf, and I thought, "Oh no, my hair!" It was up in a ponytail, with straggly strays.

Speaking some of the most beautiful words I have ever heard, my high school love asked me at last to marry him. I cried. I said, "I would be honored to be your wife." And in case he had missed it, I added, "Yes!"

We embraced and enjoyed a moment sublimely precious and dear. And then I said to him, "You know, my shirt has a hole in it."

"What?" he asked.

"You asked me to marry you while I'm wearing a shirt with a hole in it."

"That doesn't nix the deal, does it?" he asked with concern.

"No. And, by the way, do you think this is my best look hairwise?"

"You are exquisitely beautiful."

I guess he was going to stonewall on the ponytail. And I guess he made the right decision, proposing to me on the very beach where he had first realized that he was back in love with his high school sweetheart.

PART TWO

Why So Many People Are Rekindling Love Now

Chapter 9

Dating Fatigue

THE POPULATION BUBBLE OF SINGLE WOMEN FROM THEIR MID-thirties through their early fifties is one major factor propelling the rekindled-love phenomenon. I have at least a dozen girlfriends who would be fantastic catches for the right guy, but these women are still waiting. They have given Mr. Right every imaginable opportunity to show up. They have tried blind dates, singles events, setups by friends, wine-tasting classes, flash dating, bowling leagues, golf lessons, and church mixers. They have dating fatigue—they are weary of continually starting over, trying to impress new people, looking for love. They're ready to find it.

This group includes women who have put their personal lives on hold to work full blast at a career. Some have had a long relationship or two—even one they thought might lead to marriage, until it didn't. Others married Mr. Wrong and ended up divorced. These terrific women want to settle down, but they can't find partners.

They bravely put themselves out on the dating market with an open heart and an open mind, only to end up going out with guys who turn out to be insensitive, crude, looking only for sex, forgetful (that's putting it mildly; some were so forgetful they "forgot" to mention that they were already married!), unkind, thoughtless, too attatched to Mama, too ambitious, not ambitious enough.

It's no wonder that many women say they would rather stay home in their snuggly jammies on the weekends. It's challenging to find a guy to have fun with, much less marry.

There is a whole industry catering to this group of women. Magazine headlines plead: "Will I Ever Find Love Again?" and announce "One Thousand Women Tell How They Found Love Online." Internet dating services, such as match.com and eHarmony.com, are increasingly popular. So are old-fashioned matchmaking services that offer personalized, updated approaches to finding a mate. Many of their intended clients are women in their thirties, forties, and fifties who have built substantial, admirable, even brilliant careers. And many of them have had a good time along the way, but, as Los Angeles therapist Ginny Fleming explains, "When you're in your twenties, especially if you're a beautiful, ambitious, well-educated woman, opportunities seem limitless. You think the perfect person might be right around the corner, so why settle now? There might be somebody better. But the older we get, 'the slimmer the pickins,' or so it seems."

In fact, the pickins *are* slimmer. The U.S. Census Bureau's annual list of Valentine's Day–related statistics released in January 2003 was straightforward with the bad news: "There are more single women than single men in the United States. After age 40, the discrepancy between single men and single women becomes even greater." The data show that by age 45 to 64, for every 100 single women there are only 72 unmarried men. The odds aren't good.

Not willing to let statistics defeat them, these women still strive for a more balanced life—one that includes someone to snuggle with at night, someone to confide in, someone to count on when things go wrong. They want a partner to love.

The good news is that many women find reconnecting with someone from their past circumvents all these problems. It matches them up with someone their own age rather than a man substantially older, as often happens in the general dating market. And the male partners in rekindled romances seem to freely speak and truly mean the passionate, tender words many women have longed to hear.

Russell, the archaeologist who met Leslie on a dig in Utah and reunited with her nine years after their breakup, says, "The way she walks is beautiful, and so are her eyes. Leslie is terrifically interesting and smart, and that's such an aphrodisiac."

Jim Johnson of Flippin, Arkansas, reconnected with Kathy (Ciero) when both were in their thirties. He remembers with a smile the summers their families spent together when they were kids and says, "I adore her. She's caring, loving, and giving. When she agreed to marry me, I felt incredibly lucky to have won her heart."

Need I say more?

There is good counsel to be had from a woman who knows what it's like to have a successful career *and* find the man of her dreams. Nicole Miller, one of the best-known names in fashion, says: "I always tell my girlfriends to go through their Rolodexes. Rather than try to find a fantasy Mr. Perfect who probably doesn't exist, think about the people you know, people you went to college with. Even if it's somebody you didn't date—maybe it's somebody who was a friend or that you knew in some way in the past. Odds are if you're 40, you have a better shot of reconnecting with somebody that you know a little bit already rather than with a total stranger." Nicole herself reunited with former sweetheart Kim Taipale and married him in 1996.

Cheryl J. Kagan, a public relations professional in Los Angeles, tried the Rolodex approach in her early forties. Using the same drive, organization, and dedication she had devoted to her career, she found that looking back for love was the answer.

Cheryl and Hilly

"SHE WAS TOO IMMERSED IN HER WORK"

In 1991, **Cheryl J. Kagan,** who was 41 and a highly successful career woman, finally decided she wanted a personal life, too. She gave herself an assignment: to find a relationship with someone not in show business. "I took it on as I would a client," says Cheryl. "I put an ad in *LA Magazine*, and I joined dating clubs. I went on dates and to dances. And I looked up old boyfriends. I knew that **Hilly Dubin**, my old sweetheart at James Madison High School in Brooklyn in the 1960s, had become an optometrist, but I didn't know where he practiced."

Her mom soon got into the act. "Luckily," says Cheryl, "a Jewish mother never gives up hope." Mrs. Kagan made an entirely unnecessary appointment with her own optometrist in hopes of obtaining a directory of others across the country. Score. When her mom presented her with a phone number for Dr. Hilly Dubin in Tulsa, Oklahoma, Cheryl decided to make the call on her birthday, which was three weeks later, "for good luck."

She and Hilly had met during high school and spent summers at the Palm Shore Club in Sheepshead Bay, Brooklyn. At 16, while Hilly played guitar and sang with a band, THE CROWNS, he noticed Cheryl on the dance floor. "It was 1966, and she had shoulder-length hair," Hilly recalls, "a little teased in front, with a headband. She was wearing pink and green flowered culottes and white sandals, and she was doing 'the jerk.' She caught my eye instantly. She was the most beautiful thing in the world. I felt inferior, that she was way beyond my reach."

Cheryl saw it differently. "He looked like Paul McCartney, about five feet ten, slender, with dark hair. A real babe magnet."

They started dating, taking the bus to King's Highway to see the shops and restaurants. "We bought ice cream sundaes and we kissed," remembers Cheryl. "But that was all we did because Hilly respected my conservative family."

"Cheryl was so beautiful," he says, "the kind of girl you put on a pedestal. We kissed and held hands, but beyond that I couldn't bear to touch her. She was too pure and innocent."

He did, however, find an outlet for his more daring impulses. "The times we weren't together, he'd hang out with a wild crowd and go to parties with lots of girls," says Cheryl. "I got aggravated. We had dated nine months and two days when I told him we needed to go our separate ways."

Hilly doesn't deny his "running around" back then, but the breakup came as a shock because, he says, "I didn't actually care about anyone but Cheryl."

Cheryl and her family had also been significant in helping Hilly focus on his schoolwork. "I never paid attention to academics," he says, "but education was so important to Cheryl and her family, I applied myself one semester in high school and got straight A's." After graduating in 1967, he attended

Northwestern State University in Oklahoma. "Because of Cheryl's earlier influence, I ultimately got a graduate degree at the Southern College of Optometry in Memphis, Tennessee, in 1976."

Cheryl graduated from Syracuse University and became an NBC tour guide in New York City in 1972, then a secretary in the local news division, and finally manager of talent casting for prime time and late night. Hilly visited her once in New York in 1974, six years after her high school graduation. "But he loved the suburban lifestyle," says Cheryl, "golfing and fishing. I loved Manhattan and the constant stimulation. We were going in different directions, and I didn't think we had much in common. We lost touch for the next 17 years."

"I'd always wanted to end up with her," says Hilly, "but when I was finally ready in the mid '70s, she was too immersed in her work. I went back to the Midwest, got married, and settled down in Tulsa." Hilly adopted his new wife's youngest child and raised her older one, but as much as he tried to take his father's advice, "You make your bed, you lie in it," the marriage ended in a bitter divorce in 1990. "I didn't date anyone for a while," says Hilly. "I figured I'd stay single—except for Cheryl, if I ever saw her again. There wasn't a better girl in the entire world. Period. She was second to none."

In 1991 he was sitting in his office when his receptionist announced he had a call from someone named Cheryl Kagan. It was February 25, which Hilly remembered was Cheryl's birthday. "I felt like Roger Rabbit," he says, laughing. "My heart pounded right out of my chest as I stared at the flashing red phone light that looked like a strobe." He closed the door to his office. "A minute felt like a year while I tried to gain my composure. I wanted to sound calm so Cheryl wouldn't think I was a total idiot."

They talked for a long time, discovered they were both single, and decided to get together. She was in a hurry, secretly wanting to know whether to cross him off or keep him on her list, so three weeks later she flew to Tulsa. She says, "I was nervous on the plane, but I thought, 'When that door opens, you'll be seeing an old friend who shares your history.' "

Hilly spotted Cheryl getting off the plane and felt stunned by how beautiful she was. "We held hands the minute we saw each other, and in a sense that day has never ended," Hilly says. "She's wonderful." Cheryl felt as though they had never been apart, as if 17 years had not passed. "He was adorable, as handsome as ever."

They dated for the next year and a half, but when Hilly actually started talking about marriage, Cheryl felt terrified. "I had never married, and we both had successful businesses in different cities. I couldn't imagine it would work, so when he started professing his love for me in the car one day, my hands froze on the wheel. I was 41, but I asked him if he could just get me an ID bracelet and go steady."

One Sunday morning in 1992 when Cheryl was in Tulsa staying with Hilly, she wandered into the master bedroom in her flannel pajamas, hair rollers, and no makeup. "I saw two full champagne glasses on the table, and I was surprised." Hilly handed her one and said, "Sip slowly." When she looked into the glass, beneath the bubbles was a sparkling diamond engagement ring. "I was so stunned," she says, "I couldn't hear a word he was saying. It finally occurred to me that he was proposing, but all I could say was 'Oh, its pretty.' "

"Take three days," he said. "If you haven't decided by then, I'll let you propose to me next time."

Three days later she told Hilly that her answer was yes. "I

was proud of what he had done with his life and what a good man he was," she says, "a guy who would be there if times got hard. I knew he would be supportive if we had a family. I love Hilly, and he has always loved the real me."

They were married at the Four Seasons Hotel in Beverly Hills, California, on November 27, 1993. "I wasn't ready to marry when I was in my twenties and thirties because my priorities were different," says Cheryl. "But I love being with someone who knew me when I was young. I know his core and substance as well as his values, ethics, and the way he feels about family and friends—the important things."

Today they are both 54 and the parents of a beautiful daughter, six-year-old Brooke Madison, named for their shared background: James Madison High School in Brooklyn. They live in Tulsa, and they also have an apartment in Los Angeles because Cheryl's work takes her to the West Coast for about a week each month. Hilly is supportive and respects her independence, and she believes that in some ways the marriage has helped her career. "He calms me down," she says. "We can talk about anything. We really complement each other since I'm a type A personality and he's laid-back. He gives me great advice."

"Sure, it's tough to have Cheryl traveling between cities," says Hilly, "but having her part-time is better than no time. I've always been in love with her, and when you find the best person in the world, you go with the flow. I figure I lost her once, and I don't want to lose her again."

The population segment of women who waited, like Cheryl, has expanded rapidly. According to a U.S. Census Bureau press release in March 2000, that year the number of women aged 30 to 34 who had never married was *triple* the number in 1970. Careerwise, these hardworking women are now at the top or close, and some are bailing out of schedules that demand every ounce of their energy and every minute of their time. Some long to go through the world two by two.

These women often feel safer connecting with someone who knew them when they were younger, believing, as Nicole Miller suggests, that a familiar person will be more appreciative of them than a new man might be. Dr. Helen Fisher confirms, "A reunited lover has those memories of you as a young person. No question about it, that can be tremendously exciting to him."

The high divorce rate in our country also makes many people who qualify as someone's former sweetheart, like Dr. Hilly Dubin, available for reuniting. Once we find the right person, we are often willing to make extraordinary changes, such as switching careers, so that a valued relationship can work. That was the case for Anne Zehren who had climbed to the top in the publishing world and then started over for love.

Anne and Harvey

"I WOULDN'T TRADE THIS FOR ANYTHING"

At 36 years of age Anne Zehren was publisher of *Teen People*. She had one of the premier jobs in the magazine world, having completed stints as director of employee communications at NBC, director of marketing for *Newsweek* magazine, and associate publisher for *Glamour* magazine.

On the personal front, Anne had divorced in 1992 after five

years of marriage. For the next ten years she dated a lot, went out, and had fun. She even encouraged friends who were sitting home in New York City on Saturday nights to do what she did. She says, "Some of my girlfriends were out of practice. They'd forgotten how to flirt after not having a date for a couple of months. I told them, 'Once you get in a rut and stay home, it just perpetuates itself. It's better to go out even with someone you don't like all that much. Just get yourself out there, and good things will happen.'"

But no one Anne herself dated seemed exactly right. "I was looking for a guy with a really kind heart and eclectic tastes. I'm sort of a downtown girl who lives uptown. I like music and sports, and I'm family-oriented because I'm one of six kids. But I couldn't find the right person, partly because my job was demanding and I was on the road a lot."

Then in early 2001, Anne went to an NBA basketball game that changed her life. She was in San Francisco on a business trip, and a sportswriter she was casually dating took her to watch the Warriors play the San Antonio Spurs. At the ending buzzer one of his buddies came over. Anne couldn't believe her eyes. It was Harvey Anderson, who had been a good friend of hers 18 years earlier when they both attended Marquette University in Wisconsin.

Harvey didn't recognize Anne, and he's still trying to explain why. "She was all dolled up in tight suede pants, and she was so *hot*. I was trying not to look at her directly because I thought my friend was dating her. I didn't want to be rude and stare."

When she said, "Harvey, it's Annie Zehren!" he threw his arms around her in a big bear hug. They talked and laughed about the old days.

They had met in 1981 in their freshman year when he was dating a girl who lived on her dorm floor. After that relationship ended, Harvey and Anne hung out—walking to class, going to church, or eating lunch together.

"He had beautiful green eyes," she says, "with lashes half an inch long. He was about six feet four. Harvey was in the engineering school and ran track, but his first love was swimming. I'd go over with a girlfriend and watch him in the pool."

"Annie was five feet five and had curly blond-streaked hair," says Harvey. "Real skinny and stylish, she had an inner joy and a glowing spirituality. Everyone loved her." Harvey recalls, "One Valentine's Day a whole group of us went dancing as friends. When I dropped her at her dorm room, there was a pile of red roses (a Marquette tradition) in front of her door that different guys had left anonymously as a sign that she had secret admirers. She scattered them outside the doors of girls who had no roses. She was good like that, so unpretentious and generous. But the thought of competition from all those guys made me afraid of rejection, so I didn't ask her out."

But one evening Harvey finally made his move while he was giving Anne a friendly back rub. He recalls: "She was on her stomach, and my hands wandered a little bit past the waist of her slacks, but she didn't respond. That was my big overture, and she acted as if nothing had happened, so I figured she just wanted to be friends."

Anne definitely remembers what they now laughingly call "the rub," but she didn't get the message at the time. "I was clueless," she says. "He claims I should have known he was making a move, but when a guy doesn't ask you out, you just think he's not interested."

They continued to be friendly but didn't spend as much time together. When they graduated, they went in different directions. Harvey was a senatorial aide in Washington, D.C., and then he worked in Los Angeles as an engineer in telecommunications. He moved to San Francisco and went to law school at night, became in-house counsel for a hugely successful Internet company, and went to work in technology as an attorney and an executive. He married and had a son named Luke.

Following the basketball game where they reconnected, Anne and Harvey e-mailed and talked occasionally as friends. Almost two years later, after Harvey's marriage failed, he and Anne started traveling to see each other. Their relationship quickly became serious, and that triggered some decisions on Anne's part. "I was 41 and disenchanted with the dating scene. I spent a few days at a retreat in a silent monastery to take a look at my life." She realized she had never forgotten Harvey over the years. "I would occasionally tell my girlfriends about this cute school friend named Harvey. I found ways to weave him into our conversations because he was always in my heart and mind.

"I suddenly realized that I had loved Harvey since college. We were kindred spirits. My company was generous enough to grant me a three-month leave of absence from my job to spend time with Harvey in San Francisco."

Harvey was willing to move to New York City if he had to, but his first choice was to stay close to his son, Luke. "I prayed and became at peace with the idea of leaving my job and close friends to move permanently to San Francisco," says Anne. "I basically did it for Harvey's son. It was a heart-wrenching decision to leave a great job that I loved and had worked so hard to attain. Ten years prior, even five years prior, I don't know whether I would have quit. By the time I found Harvey, though, the level of what I was willing to give up for love was much greater." Her bosses and coworkers were shocked because she had always been so career-oriented. "But they were wonderfully supportive." Anne and Harvey married on March 7, 2003.

Anne is Caucasian and Harvey is African American, and they have occasionally encountered disapproval at their pairing. But both sets of parents were completely in favor of their marriage. Anne says, "Harvey even kids me that I'm a black woman in white skin because back in college I loved listening to R&B and soul, and now I enjoy hip-hop. In romantic moments we love dancing to Stevie Wonder's song "There's Something About Your Love."

After their wedding Anne quickly became pregnant, was terribly sick for the entire nine months, and almost lost the baby because of a blood-clotting disorder. Fortunately, both she and their baby boy, Cole, survived.

The fact that Anne sacrificed a fabulous job to be with the man she loves and to have a family with him is not lost on Harvey. "I admire her ability to make a decision about what's really important," he says. "It took tremendous courage." He also believes that having known each other from before helped a great deal. "There was a lot of ground we didn't have to cover because we already knew each other in a pure, innocent way. We'd made an assessment a long time ago, a heart imprint."

Anne feels she's lucky because she knows a lot of fantastic women who have not found love. "At my wedding shower, 35 of my girlfriends were there, one more phenomenal than the next. More than half of them were not married or in a relationship."

She wishes they could have the same thing she has found. "When you're with someone you already know, you don't engage in the game playing that's part of a new relationship. It's very authentic right away."

Anne now has a media-consulting company with several big clients, a business that she was able to set up on the West Coast. She says, "When Harvey and I started seeing each other, I felt immediate trust and a deep bond. I suddenly knew what I wanted, and I wouldn't trade it for anything."

A common refrain among 40-something career women is that they look back for love because they can no longer stand the agony of "first dates." Please, not one more evening of trying to impress a guy in three hours! Dating definitely has its downside. Having "been there, done that," many of us prefer the pleasure of being with someone who already cares for us or at least knows something about us. As Dr. Carolyn Perla, who counsels clients and teaches classes on emotional openness and intimacy in New York City, explains, "By their mid-thirties, many women hate the whole dating game. They are tired of the exhaustion and pressure. They are longing to settle down and to have somebody share their lives. These women don't want to be out dating and looking."

One Los Angeles woman who could no longer tolerate playing the field was happy to get the call that her friend and sweetheart from the old days was living in California, too.

Saryl and Roz

"I WAS SICK OF THAT FIRST-DATE SYNDROME"

Saryl Radwin is a TV producer and researcher who has always been a "people person." Friends describe her as warm and open. By 1995 she was in her mid-forties and had been living in Los Angeles for eight years. In spite of her humor and friendliness, the longest relationships she'd had during that time lasted "three months here, three months there." Saryl says, "It was a drought. I was sick of that first-date syndrome where you always have to start all over and introduce yourself and go through who you are and what you've been through. Deep down I always wanted somebody who knew me, maybe somebody from my past or at least somebody who understood me. And then all of a sudden Roz came back into my life. There was an instant connection and friendship."

Roz is Robert Rosenthal, an optician she had dated years before. Saryl and Roz met in the '70s in Brooklyn's Park Slope neighborhood and were part of a large circle of friends. She was 21 and recalls it as a scene filled with people playing volleyball, doing sing-alongs, arguing politics, and protesting the Vietnam War. She and Roz both remember the adrenaline pumping, feeling as though they were doing something important when they led an antiwar demonstration down the main street.

Roz was an elementary school teacher when they first met. He says, "Saryl was cute and fun, with a wonderful smile." Saryl worked in a publishing house and remembers 26-year-old Roz as very attractive. "He was good-looking with strong features, a twinkle in his eye, and a nicely shaped beard. We had

167

fun flirting, but even though we had a sexual vibe, it was completely innocent."

A few years later, in 1981, a mutual friend invited them both for dinner. Saryl says the friend "believed that Roz and I had a sparkle and that we belonged together." They dated for a few months, enjoying each other's company and humor, but then, Roz says, "I wanted to move forward and eventually have kids. I told her we were looking for different things in life."

"It was hard," recalls Saryl, "when he used the words 'You are not my ideal.' I thought he was talking about our physical relationship. I never felt bad about my looks, but I'd recently had ostomy surgery and thought he was rejecting me because I was damaged goods." Roz is deeply sorry about hurting her with his choice of words. "I was too literal. I didn't mean she wasn't perfect the way she was. She wanted to stay single, and I was referring to an ideal mate for having a family."

A couple of years after the breakup Saryl visited him at his business, but then she headed west and they had no contact for 11 years. In the interim Roz met someone and got married.

By 1995, Saryl had made a name for herself in Los Angeles. She was on the team of producers that won an Oscar in 1993 for their documentary *The Panama Deception*. In addition, she helped produce *Television's Christmas Classics* and various network specials, blooper shows, and awards programs for TV.

By the mid '90s, Roz had moved with his family from New York to San Diego, and he was going through a divorce. After their mutual friend made sure they had each other's phone numbers, Roz called Saryl several times. Then he invited her to visit. They dated occasionally. By the spring of '96 they realized their feelings had become serious.

"Relationships have been hard for me," says Saryl, "because my career always came first. But age, wisdom, and experience are helping me get there. I love Roz more than I've ever loved a man, but it took me until 1997 to tell him 'I love you.' Now I know that loving somebody and being loved is realistic, important, and special." Nine years after reconnecting they are still together, and Roz says, "Saryl is very giving and supportive. I love her warmth and openness."

They see each other on weekends because she has her work and doesn't want to leave her elderly mother alone in Los Angeles, and Roz wants to remain near his children in San Diego. Saryl says, "I've given myself more to Roz than anybody, and I wouldn't want to live without him. We came back full circle to a place where we're absolutely perfect for each other."

Women go full-tilt at a career, as Saryl did, for different reasons. Some prefer to concentrate intently on a profession. Others want both a career and marriage but find that their chosen partners can't commit. It's a tale we women know all too well: She wants to settle down. He doesn't.

It turns out that as time goes by, many guys change their perspective. They've achieved some of what Dr. Iris SanGiuliano referred to as "the three M's": medals, money, and mastery. She says, "These men were very busy developing a career and having a good time, and suddenly there is a shift that takes place. Forty is often a transition period. A man starts to look at facets of his personality that he has neglected. It opens floodgates to a new potential."

So when a woman returns to her past to search for companionship and love, she may find that while he couldn't commit then, he can now!

Alan and Suzanne

"AND I'M NOT WITH HER BECAUSE . . . ?"

Alan Stevens, a professional webmaster, first obtained Suzanne Parkinson's phone number 25 years ago when he was 27 years old. He saw her at a party. "I was initially attracted to her beautiful body," he says, "but she also had a great smile and baby blue eyes that were warm and inviting." But he didn't make the call. Twelve years later, when he was 39 and she was 42, they met again. This time they had a brief, intense affair that ended partly because of what Alan calls his "fear of commitment." Their relationship evolved into a friendship in which they shared a sense of humor and an interest in metaphysics and spirituality. "We had similar philosophies, and we became close friends," he says.

A few years later Suzanne's marriage to a younger man was a wake-up call for Alan. "I was invited to her wedding, but I couldn't get out the door. I hadn't realized I was in love with Suzanne. I thought, 'There must be something wrong with me.' I mean, here was this perfectly lovely woman who cared about me, and she was marrying somebody else. What the hell was I doing? Her marriage was a borderline crisis for me, and I couldn't bear to watch her take vows with someone else."

Over the next four years Alan dated other women but grew tired of always starting over. When Suzanne divorced, he thought to himself, 'And I'm not with her because . . . ?' "

One evening Suzanne and Alan met at a friend's birthday party. "I can still see her," says Alan. "She had just gotten a sassy short haircut, she was wearing a sexy black dress, and she was sitting on the arm of the couch with a glowing smile. She looked free and easy, like the kind of woman anybody would be lucky to have in his life. I thought, 'God, she's gorgeous.'"

How could he transform this friendship back into a romance? What if Suzanne didn't trust him because of his earlier reticence? "In the earlier days I just didn't have the maturity," Alan says. "I didn't know what a healthy relationship was. I only knew about the buzz, the infatuation stage. It's absorbing, druglike, when you see somebody across the room and your heart skips a beat. You think you're in love. But with Suzanne I learned there could also be substance. We were friends with common interests and attraction. It was not a hot, high-end, superficial kind of relationship with nothing underneath it."

Alan recalls, "When I finally got up the nerve to kiss her in the car, all the old wonderful feelings were back." At first she wasn't ready for more. Then one night she came over to his house and said, "I don't want to talk about it anymore. I just want to go ahead and make love." She had realized that he was putting her peace of mind before his own. They both saw how much he had changed. "Hurting her again was unacceptable to me," he recalls, proclaiming a date they had on the Fourth of July as the beginning of their new phase as lovers. "I felt as if I was in junior high school again, and at 50 years of age, I bought her an ID bracelet with my name on it."

Alan says, "Knowing her from before makes this love more compelling than meeting someone new and falling in love for the first time. I wasn't ready when we were younger, but now we feel a 'rightness' to our relationship." Alan goes so far as to say that his commitment to Suzanne has "the sanctity of pure love."

Now you might ask how inspiring an ID bracelet is as an initial sign of devotion. More than one set of reunited lovers has used this teenage emblem of love to express their feelings as adults. It has the appeal of humor and reflects the rekindled aspect of their love. It paves the way for more adult symbols as they move toward a new stage of life and love.

When dating fatigue kicks in, reunited love can be tremendously attractive. People think: Wouldn't it be nice to have a relationship with someone who is mature but who also looks at you as if you were still 18? How sweet it is to be with someone you trust now because you were friends or sweethearts back before either of you had money, fame, or success. It is comforting to spend time with someone who knows your old neighborhood, shares your values, and treasures your common memories. It is healing to go back, repair some of the mistakes we made, and perhaps pick up where we left off.

Reuniting is especially appealing to people who are a decade or two or three beyond adolescent feelings of immortality. Many of us at this age realize that we won't have endless chances and are finally ready to commit; or we are divorced and want to try again. These realizations are a powerful factor propelling the rekindled-love phenomenon.

So is the growth of the Internet and its ability to put us in touch.

Chapter 10

The Internet Impact

"I would never have found Cathy again or learned that I had a son without the Internet," Bob Edinger recounts, explaining how he reconnected with the woman who was his high school sweetheart—and, unbeknownst to him, the mother of his child. Cathy (Rosania) had become pregnant the last time they saw each other, in 1991. But after that week, he went on the road as a horse trainer, and she couldn't reach him to share the news that they were having a baby boy. When she heard from one of his former neighbors that Bob had been killed in a car accident, she was heartbroken and stopped looking for him. As we'll see, thanks to the Internet, 13 years later they finally got the once-impossible chance to become a family.

For Cathy and Bob rediscovering each other via the Net was serendipity, a lucky break, since she didn't even know he was alive. For other couples it involves a bit of sleuthing. But up until about 10 years ago, reuniting happened the old-fashioned way: You went to the school reunion, you contacted mutual friends, you called his mother—or it didn't happen at all. In a nation of

258 million people, it was often like hunting for the proverbial needle in a haystack. But the Internet has had a monumental impact on our ability to reconnect. Even though our population has grown by more than 35 million in the last decade, it is now easier than ever to find people—they are literally a few clicks away.

Anthropologists say that the Internet is having a huge effect on lost-love reunions. "I think we are going to see more and more marriages between reunited couples," predicts Dr. Helen Fisher. "One reason is that we have the Internet, so people can be found. People have a mechanism to find old sweethearts."

Internet search engines such as Google, AltaVista, and Lycos, browsers such as Internet Explorer and Netscape, and Web sites specifically designed to help people find one another have created myriad new possibilities for would-be reunitees. The percentage of households with a personal computer in the United States jumped from only 8.2 percent in 1984 to 51 percent in 2000 according to the U.S. Census Bureau. The virtual explosion of people using the Internet means that activities long performed by phone, fax, and regular mail are now happening on the Web. There are new ways to handle shopping, bill paying, stock purchases, research, vacation planning, and finding people from the past. Thousands of couples have been able to reconnect through the Net.

The ability to find people through the Internet isn't limited to hip computer whizzes. People of all generations and even novice-level skills have discovered the vast reach and instant nature of finding former sweethearts via the Web.

Mimi and Jerry

"I DON'T KNOW HOW I WOULD HAVE FOUND HIM WITHOUT THE INTERNET"

Mimi and Jerry, now in their seventies, got back together in 2002 when she Googled him 50 years after their whirlwind three-week romance at the University of Chicago. Mimi's beloved husband had died in 2001, and after a year of terrible grief she decided she "wanted to live again." In March 2002 she found her old college sweetheart, Jerry, on the Web and learned that he had just retired from his job as a professor at a university in Texas.

Via e-mail they shared happy memories of their brief 1952 romance, which had ended when Mimi returned to school at Antioch College. They exchanged long cyber missives about all that had happened to them in their years apart.

Six weeks after receiving Mimi's first e-mail, Jerry visited her in New York and within months moved up to be with her. Mimi sold her house in Westchester County, and together they found a place on Manhattan's Upper West Side that gave them a fresh start. Both say their romance is more passionate than they ever thought possible, and they are thankful that the Internet helped them reunite.

Mimi says, "I don't know how I would have found Jerry without the Internet. And then e-mail allowed us to explore possibilities. It led to the beautiful relationship and the wonderful closeness between us."

"I could write my thoughts and then edit them so I didn't say too much too soon," says Jerry gratefully. "And the speed of the turnaround meant we got feedback quickly on the feelings we shared with each other. E-mail helped us find love, caring, and intimacy. It transformed our lives."

Google, the Internet search engine that Mimi used to find Jerry, gives users access to an unlimited database of information: the World Wide Web. However, search engines are designed to locate everything from swap meets to lawn furniture, so when you type in a name, they may spit out thousands of leads, and none of them may turn up the person you're seeking. Even sites geared to helping you locate a specific person, such as info.com or yahoo.com, need you to provide the precise name and often other information about the person.

Some enterprising minds created Web sites specifically tailored to aid people in connecting with others from their past. Many of these sites are jammed with advertisements for various products and services, but the help they offer can be very beneficial. The most popular of the reconnecting Web sites is Classmates.com, which claims more than 40 million people in its database, among them Cathy (Rosania) and Bob Edinger.

Cathy, Bob, and Christopher

"IT WAS LIKE 30 YEARS HAD GONE BY IN A SECOND"

Cathy (Rosania) became best friends with Bob Edinger when she was seven years old and he was eight. She would ride her horse around the local baseball field in Whitehouse Station, New

Jersey, right across from Bob's house. He had a passion for horses (although his parents couldn't afford one for him), and he loved to watch Cathy ride. He thought she had "gorgeous eyes and a great smile." Bob was an introvert, playing guitar in his room until Cathy would convince him to come out and socialize. He says, "She could melt me in a heartbeat."

"He was handsome—blond with blue eyes," smiles Cathy. They shared their first kiss in eighth grade and became high school sweethearts. But shortly after high school started, his family moved to a different town, and there were no more fun afternoons hanging out in the neighborhood. Bob left school entirely at the end of his junior year in 1974 to escape a difficult stepfather and joined the army.

Bob and Cathy lost touch, and both eventually married other people, although Cathy says her marriage turned out to be abusive. She continued to ride horses and became a veterinary technician. When he left the army, Bob became a horse trainer and breeder. In 1991, much to their mutual surprise, they ran into each other at a horse show in Allentown, Pennsylvania. Seventeen years had passed since high school, and Bob could hardly believe his eyes when he saw her. "She looked beautiful, breathtaking."

"I gave him a big hug and kiss," she says. "All the feelings I had for him came back." Bob, who had been divorced for two years, took Cathy out to dinner. "One thing led to another," she says, "and I found out two months later that I was pregnant." She gave birth to Christopher, and two years later, concerned about her son's safety, she left her marriage. She had tried to contact Bob, but his former neighbor gave her the terrible news that he had been killed in a car crash.

Sad but determined to be a good mother, Cathy did her best

to make a life for herself and her son. Then on March 1, 2004, she saw the banner for Classmates.com on a computer at work and had fun using the site to contact old girlfriends. She soon got the alert that four new people from her high school had joined. One of them was Robert Edinger. "My heart started pounding," she says. "I thought, 'It can't be.'" She wrote to him, asking if he was the person she had grown up with. Within an hour he e-mailed her back, writing, "Of course I remember you." It turned out that Bob's cousin was the one who had died in the crash. Technology that was unimaginable when they were youngsters had brought Cathy and Bob back together. They exchanged more e-mails and then talked on the phone. He says, "It was like 30 years had gone by in a second."

Bob filled Cathy in on his life; he was divorced with two daughters in their twenties. He visited her in Califon, New Jersey, 13 years after their night in Allentown. A few days into his stay Cathy said, "I have something to tell you."

"Chris is my son, isn't he?" Bob interrupted. When she confirmed the news, he says, "I felt grateful, blessed by God."

Within a month Bob closed down his horse farm in Maryland, feeling he had accomplished enough with two international championships. Cathy had been willing to move, but Bob didn't want Chris to experience the same dislocation he had felt as a youngster when he'd had to move. He says that 12-year-old Chris has many of his mannerisms. "And just like me, he likes ice cream and salts his food too much."

What does Chris think about finding his real father? "It's cool," says Chris. They share a love of motorcycles and motocross, and Cathy likes to watch the two of them working together on Chris's bike.

Cathy and Bob were married on June 12, 2004. "I'm so thankful for the Internet. It's fantastic," she says. "Without it I would never have found Bob, and Chris would never have found his father."

The Web site that helped Cathy, Bob, and their son, Chris, become a family, Classmates.com, is organized so that members can register under their grammar schools, junior highs, high schools, colleges, workplaces, and military units. Often, former students peruse their own class lists and those of classes that graduated in other years. Sometimes these cyber journeys trigger long-buried feelings. The site even features stories of couples who have reunited through the service.

At first Classmates.com members don't use their personal e-mail addresses to communicate. They leave messages for one another at the Web site and are alerted on their private e-mail addresses by the company when there is mail for them on the Web site. They can decide later to exchange personal e-mail addresses and cut out the middleman if they so desire. This double-blind procedure allows members to maintain their privacy. There is no charge to sign up, see who else has joined, or receive and respond to messages. But people who want to initiate contact with others on the site do pay a membership fee. The Web site also has a service that helps members organize their school reunions.

The company (its formal name is Classmates Online, Inc.) was started in 1995 by Randy Conrads, a Boeing engineer who came from a military family and wanted to get in touch with some of his old high school friends. He observed some of the romance-related results of that tinkering as a guest at the recent wedding of a former employee. She found her junior high crush while demonstrating the site and, soon after, moved to Reno to marry him.

Brenda and John

"I SAT NEXT TO YOU IN EIGHTH GRADE HISTORY"

In February 2003, 29-year-old Brenda (Elliott) was showing a friend the Classmates.com Web site, demonstrating that people can look up schools other than their own. She explained that people who went to public school can find friends who attended parochial school and that it's even handy for folks who want to jog their memories about old acquaintances or competitors by looking at whole class lists from rival schools. Brenda's family had moved in 1987 when she was in eighth grade, so she logged on to the high school she *would* have attended in Santa Barbara, California. There she ran across the name John McNamara. She'd had a small crush on him in junior high, and he had been crazy for her. She sent him a message via the Web site: "Not sure if you remember me. Sat next to you in eighth grade history. Work for Classmates.com. Doing a demo for the site. No need to respond."

Well, he didn't respond—for two whole months, but only because he had accidentally deleted the notification that he had a message waiting at Classmates.com. When he received notice that another person had left him a message on the Web site, he checked in and found Brenda's as well. He certainly did remember thinking she was cute and passing her notes during class to make her laugh. "She was a cool girl," he recalled, and he typed back right away that he wondered how she was doing. It was a platonic exchange for a few weeks.

A bachelor, John was living in Reno, Nevada, and working as a firefighter. "It was just me and my dog." He didn't even have a computer, but he used one at the firehouse to communicate with Brenda. Then they started talking on the phone, and things heated up. "We racked up some crazy phone bills, talking sometimes 10 hours a day," says Brenda with a laugh. John soon went to Seattle for a visit and, Brenda says, "when he got off that plane, I knew that I would spend the rest of my life with him. There was not a single doubt in my mind."

Even before that trip, John says, he realized he had fallen in love with her. "It was like getting hit upside the head with a frying pan— I got real clarity. This is what I was missing. I love her more than anything."

Brenda and her two daughters moved to Reno, switching to a decidedly low-tech life: living on three acres with a barn and a pick-up truck. They all love the lifestyle, but they remember that it was high tech that allowed the romance to bloom. John says, "The simple, great idea of a Web site that helps people reunite changed my life 100 percent."

Some other Web sites that people use to reconnect with persons from their past are MyFamily.com, Switchboard.com, People Search.com, friendster.com, militarybrats.com, and Reunion.com. One database will sometimes yield results that another will not, so it can be useful to try more than one site.

Occasionally the business of facilitating reunited relationships is inspired by personal experience. The CEO of Reunion.com, Jeff Tinsley, was in his late twenties in 2001 when he attended his own

10-year reunion at Granada Hills High School in California. There Jeff reconnected with Kim (Firment), the former cheerleading captain who during their teen years had spoken only casually to the studious boy with a crush on her. Jeff went to the reunion as a prosperous entrepreneur, arriving in a limo, flush from selling his successful dot-com business. Kim was worried that he might be "a player, just looking to have fun," while she was looking for someone who wanted to settle down. But Jeff won her over, and they married two years later. Kim says of her husband, "He has a Ferrari now, but he's also very humble. This is a guy who lived on ketchup and started his business in his mom's garage. He's a self-made man."

After his reunion with Kim, Jeff and a group of investors acquired a couple of sites, including highschoolalumni.com (started in 1998), and merged them into Reunion.com. The Web site advertises more than 21 million members who can search for each other by high school or by individual name and also use the site to plan reunions. One couple who used the Web site to reunite are Stacy and Mark Heidelberg, both in their thirties. There was a glitch, though. The vagaries of cyberspace caused a two-year delay in their fairy tale ending.

Stacy and Mark

"LET THAT PERSON KNOW YOU HAVEN'T FORGOTTEN"

Stacy (Scott) came across Mark Heidelberg's name in 2000 while looking through highschoolalumni.com, now known as Reunion.com. She'd had a major crush on Mark in high school, and they had actually dated a bit, so she sent him an e-mail but didn't hear back. It turns out that his personal e-mail service was two years late in delivering the notification that he had a message! So when Stacy received a response on Valentine's Day 2002, she almost fell out of her chair. Mark had just returned to Texas after serving six years in the U.S. Navy. He phoned, and they spoke to each other, he recalls, "as though no time had passed instead of 12 years."

Their story began in 1989. Stacy, a sophomore, was on the diving team of her high school in San Angelo, Texas, and she remembers being "blown away" by one of the juniors on the team. "Mark was not only a phenomenal diver, he was gorgeous!" But "except for some subtle flirting here and there," she says with a smile, she kept her admiration to herself.

As time went by, she sometimes visited Mark at the driving range where he worked. She remembers, "Once he even kissed me!" They had a few dates, she says, "but he was very shy, and I thought that meant he wasn't really interested." They both moved away after graduation. During the following years they each married and divorced twice and had sons who were born only nine days apart.

When they reunited after more than a decade, Mark's shyness was gone. He told Stacy he had thought about her many times. She says, "After two weeks I was in love with him—the kind of love I thought existed only in movies."

They now live in Colorado Springs where Mark works for a large computer company, supplying products and services to small businesses. They married on January 3, 2003, less than a year after Mark's e-mail. He cherishes her. "Stacy is both strong and softhearted," he says. "We are more in love than ever." As for the cyberspace delay in their reconnection, Stacy and Mark both feel their reunion happened exactly as it was "meant to be." They feel that since Mark got home to Texas right as Stacy's message was delivered, the timing was actually perfect. She encourages others: "E-mail an old friend. Let that person know you haven't forgotten. You just might make all your dreams come true, like we did!"

For Ed and me, technology was a significant factor in blending our lives. Let me confess here that I had a "mini-byte" level of experience with computers when we started to date. Ed is a natural-born techie. In fact, his daughters often moaned when Saturday errands involved stopping at an electronics store "for a few minutes" that could easily extend into hours. His skill was a lucky break for me because my kids were working on "dinosaurs" and needed new computers in order to keep up with their schoolwork and, admittedly, their social lives.

Ed and Caroline went online together to order the new ones—speaking "computerese" that a nontechie like me can only envy. They comfortably communicated in a language complete with words like gigabytes, scanners, downloading, burning CDs, firewalls, and USB ports. They did teach me that "IT" is cool talk for "information technology" and that burning a CD does not involve arson. And then they went back to their indecipherable verbal hieroglyphics. When the computers arrived, Ed installed them, crawling under desks and hooking up tangles of wire. His effort was a way of reassuring Andrew and Caroline that whatever we needed, he would be there to help.

"IT" is actually big in our life for another reason. Ed and I have a living situation that is not unusual for reunited couples. We are bicoastal; every weekend one of us flies across the country so we can be together. During the week, e-mail is a godsend. It gives us an option besides the phone for staying in close contact throughout the day.

If e-mail had existed 20 years ago, one Massachusetts couple feels, they never would have gone their separate ways. And it took the Internet to bring them back together in their forties.

Beverly and Riley

"I HAPPENED TO COME ACROSS YOUR NAME"

Riley Hodder was sitting at his desk on the slow morning of New Year's Eve in 2001. He logged on to Classmates.com and looked through his high school graduating class, 1974, and several others to check out the new people who had signed up. Though he had joined several years before, he had never sent a message to anyone. When he got to the class of '72, he stopped dead at **Beverly Gordon**'s name. "Beverly was special to me. She was two years ahead of me and moved away from our hometown of Belmont, Massachusetts, to Rockport after her graduation. Twice I drove there in the middle of the night to see her. I never forgot her."

Riley composed an innocuous e-mail, something like "I happened to come across your name. . . ." Actually, he admits, "my heart was racing 100 miles per hour."

Riley remembers that in high school Beverly was "adorable." She remembers first seeing him in the parking lot next to their school during a paper drive. A girlfriend warned her to steer clear of him because he had a reputation as a terrible flirt. But she didn't listen. When their school put on the musical *South*

Pacific, she was in the crew, while Riley played Lieutenant Joe Cable. They spent time together and had crushes on each other, although they were never technically boyfriend and girlfriend. Beverly says, "I was madly in love with him. But I was afraid it would scare him away, so I only said I liked him."

She does remember his arriving unexpectedly, right outside her bedroom window, in the middle of the night back in '73. "I opened my eyes when I heard him whispering as loudly as he could, 'Beverly, wake up!'" She snuck out through the basement so she wouldn't wake the dog or her parents, and they sat out on the rocks by the ocean to talk. "It was very romantic."

But during the school year she was off at college, and he still had high school to finish. She did come back in 1976 to tell Riley that she was engaged, hoping he would say something to keep her from going through with the wedding. "I was crestfallen, a lot crestfallen," says Riley, "but I was 20 and didn't realize she wanted me to stop her."

In the following years they each married, had three children, and divorced. Then in 2001, Beverly was stunned to receive his e-mail. "I couldn't catch my breath," she said. She stared at his message for 10 minutes and took another 20 minutes to respond, rewriting her e-mail several times before it sounded lighthearted enough to send.

They got together within 24 hours, on New Year's Day 2002. Her first words were "You were the one I wanted to marry." Before two hours had gone by, he had proposed. They were married on June 23 that year.

They are deeply in love. Beverly says Riley is "sweet and generous," and he describes her as "full of energy and life."

Riley says ruefully, "If e-mail had existed 30 years ago, we never would have drifted apart. When we were teenagers, letters involved at least a three-day delay, and long-distance calls were very expensive."

They had both been through a lot in their years apart. Beverly had a daughter who died of cancer at age 11, right around the time Riley started helping the Jimmy Fund, which assists the families of children with cancer. Several times they were in fairly close proximity without realizing it. He had been in her town, for example, for his singing performances; Beverly says she would have gone to find him if she had known. Riley says, "We were like ships passing in the night, and we think we might not have refound each other at all if not for the Internet."

They both understand and appreciate technology at a professional level because Beverly works as an e-commerce manager for a relocation company, and Riley has a software business. But they didn't realize it would have such a profound impact on their romantic lives, offering them a second chance at happily ever after.

E-mail is actually a terrific development on the romantic front. Even when former sweethearts reconnect through more conventional avenues, they often do their courting online. While there may be nothing more romantic than an old-fashioned letter, when time is of the essence, who says heartfelt love poetry can't be delivered in bits and bytes?

Seniors are among those who have discovered the power of the Internet to reunite them. The number of seniors using the Web has jumped at an astounding rate. A study by the Pew Internet & American Life Project released by Princeton Survey Research Associates on March 25, 2004, reveals that the number of Americans age 65 or older who go online has increased almost 50 percent in only four years. And fully 94 percent of wired seniors have sent or received e-mail. Well into his seventies, that's how Sam Nichols pursued Joy (Jemison). Split apart by World War II, they reunited more than 50 years later, and both feel grateful about the role this thoroughly modern medium played in their rekindled romance.

Joy and Sam

"YOU WERE MY FIRST LOVE"

"E-mail is an amazing gift," enthuses **Joy (Jemison).** "It's like sharing the tapestry of one's life while you're still weaving it. Getting a letter back that quickly is remarkable. It's one in a series of serendipities that reconnected Sam and me after all this time."

They have fond memories of a decidedly low-tech, magical summer in the early '40s after Joy's family had moved to an antebellum home in the countryside outside Memphis, Tennessee. Joy was just 13, and often the neighborhood kids would gather for games on balmy summer evenings. During a turn at "spin the bottle," **Sam Nichols** gave Joy her first kiss.

They remember the glow of fireflies as they walked in the moonlight holding hands, with the heady scent of gardenias and honeysuckle perfuming the air. "I'd rather hold your hand than kiss any other girl," Sam told her. Each had a tremendous crush on the other. Joy thought Sam looked like William Holden, with his broad shoulders and curly, sandy hair. Sam says he had no idea Joy was so young; she was a beauty in both face and figure.

Then came the attack on the U.S. fleet at Pearl Harbor, and their whole world changed. Upon graduation from high school, Sam enlisted in the navy. For a while he and Joy corresponded, but then they gradually lost touch. After the war Sam remained on the West Coast, pursuing his dream of becoming a commercial artist by attending the famed Art Center of Los Angeles. His talent for creativity and design was soon recognized, and he eventually became the art and creative director of the Jantzen Corporation in Portland, Oregon. Meanwhile, he had fallen in love with a girl from Oregon, married, and had two children.

Joy pursued her dream of becoming an opera and concert singer, attending Juilliard in New York and singing in Austria and Italy. She, too, married and had two children. Many years later, in 1995, when her husband became terminally ill, he insisted that they move from Colorado Springs back to Memphis so that she could be near her family. At the funeral someone from the old neighborhood told Joy he had heard that Sam was dead. Strangely enough, Sam had been told the same thing about Joy.

They feel that a miracle occurred next. Sam's sister, Millie, happened to call one of Joy's relatives with a question and discovered that Joy was not only alive but again living in the Memphis area. When Joy heard from Millie that Sam was very much alive and living in Arizona, she was stunned. She longed to hear what his life had been like. What kind of person had he turned out to be? But Joy also learned that his wife was still living, though she was terminally ill in a nursing home. Millie had given her Sam's e-mail address and encouraged her to write, but Joy hesitated several days. When she finally did compose a message in January 2000 and punched the SEND button, the response was almost immediate. "Let's be completely honest with each other," Sam wrote, and gradually the childhood sweethearts began to catch up on their lives and adventures of the last half century.

Once again fate intervened. One morning Sam typed a brief, sad note that his wife had died, and Joy heard nothing more from him for many days. Since she had been through a similar situation a few years before, she understood his grief. Soon the e-mails resumed, becoming a new breath of life each day for both of them.

As they shared their deepest thoughts, concerns, and delights, they realized that they were falling in love all over again, but this time it was much deeper than what they had felt in their teens. Still, they didn't know how they would feel in person.

"Sam, do come for a visit to your sister in early April," Joy wrote, reminding him that "then, with the colorful azalea and lacey dogwood in full bloom, Memphis becomes a virtual fairyland." He did, and when he went to see Joy, they were as excited as teenagers and found themselves more in love than ever before.

Each visited the other's home, meeting and liking each other's families. They had occasional tiffs, each wanting to express a certain independence, but quickly got past those issues. They took trips together and found their devotion growing until they were ready to turn their romance into a lasting commitment. On July 28, 2001, they were married in the lovely Oregon rose garden belonging to Sam's daughter and son-in-law.

Both Joy and Sam credit the Internet in part for the seamless way in which they were able to catch up on each other's lives and eventually marry. Joy says, "Our volumes of e-mail correspondence created a firm foundation for that giddy feeling of falling in love."

Today they still occasionally e-mail each other—Sam from his studio upstairs to Joy in her downstairs study. Joy recently wrote, "When I'm around you, I feel safe and loved. We joke and play a lot, almost like teenagers. Whenever you touch me, I absolutely know that all is well." And Sam responded, "You were my first love, and I know that we will never part. I am forever grateful for having found you a second time."

Joy and Sam discovered, as many couples do, that e-mail is a new way to pursue something as classic as courtship. Several people I spoke with commented that over their years of separation from a sweetheart they had thought of writing a letter or leaving a telephone message. But they hesitated, not knowing who else might see or hear it. Despite their curiosity, they didn't want to cause trouble for their former friend or sweetheart. Beverly (Gordon), for example, says she actually called Riley's parents one time and got his number in Florida, but she decided not to leave a message. E-mail fuels romance not only because of the comparative privacy but because it is more casual than posting a letter or meeting face-to-face. As Riley explains, "People will say a lot more in an e-mail than they will in person or in a letter. There's something freeing about it. You can hide behind the computer."

E-mail does seem to reduce inhibitions. You don't have to look someone in the eye, afraid of rejection. You don't have time to reconsider as you would if you had to put your message into an envelope, stamp it, and take it to the mailbox. As Riley says, "You just hit the 'send' button and sometimes ask yourself, 'Did I really do that?'"

There is no way to measure precisely the impact that e-mail, Web sites designed for reconnecting, and the Internet as a whole have had on the number of couples who reunite. But anecdotal evidence makes it clear that the Web has given people an incredibly useful and efficient tool, one they are using to find their lost loves.

Joy and Sam were in their seventies when they took command of modern technology to advance their romance. They are part of a tidal wave of seniors discovering that looking back can be a wonderful way to find love.

Chapter 11

"More Wonderful Love"

"I'd already had the best of everything," says 73-year-old Mary (Gibbon) Clarke who was widowed in 2000 after 45 years of marriage. "But suddenly I got all this extra joy, which just amazed me. The phenomenon you're writing about includes people like me who had found their true love already and are lucky enough to find more wonderful love with someone from their past."

When Mary's first husband passed away, she experienced a terrible emptiness. "I felt as if I'd been amputated," she says, vividly describing her grief. In reuniting with Dr. Mike Sperber, Mary learned what many seniors discover: There can be a second chance at love with a long-ago sweetheart, and it doesn't diminish the memory of the dear one who has been lost.

Mary and Mike are among the flood of retirees driving the rekindled love phenomenon, and Dr. Helen Fisher predicts that even more seniors will try it. "We are going to see more and more of this kind of marriage," she says. "Why? There's an extension of middle age—40 percent of the people aged 76 to 85 are basically healthy. There's also a very high divorce rate. And seniors can reconnect with each other through the Internet. In the past they moved in with their kids to take care of the grandchildren, but now they live alone. They're available for love."

The percentage of seniors (defined as people aged 65 and over) who are divorced nearly doubled, from 3.5 percent in 1980 to 6.7 percent in 2000, according to the U.S. *Census Bureau 2001 Statistical Abstract.* Census figures also show that between 1990 and 2000, the total number of single seniors in the United States rose by almost a million to over 15.3 million. Even factoring out those who have no interest, it's a big dating pool.

Meanwhile, medical breakthroughs in the field of intimacy have benefited many of these seniors. "Technologies have changed, enabling many seniors to pursue courtship very actively," says Dr. Fisher. "Viagra for men, estrogen replacement for women, and testosterone creams and patches and injections are some of the developments helping people to sustain a courtship later in life without much anxiety. Today's seniors are a viable force in the dating market."

Why would seniors opt for rekindled love as the most desirable route to companionship? Since reunitees often see each other as the teenagers they once were, both partners luxuriate in feelings of youth and vitality. Because time is of the essence, seniors want to know and trust a partner quickly, which happens more easily when there is a shared past. And, in addition, the comfort found with someone familiar is invaluable.

"When we're seniors, we really don't want to seek out adventure even though all the commercials make you think that way," explains Dr. Sherry Bush. "As we age, we feel safer with someone who knew us from childhood or adolescence. This is the type of person we can trust and with whom we want to build a future."

Recall some of the couples we've met who reconnected in their sixties or later. Broadway superstar Carol Channing reunited with her junior high sweetheart, Harry Kullijian. "We had not seen each other in 70 years," he says, "but the moment I laid eyes on her, I thought, 'This is it. I want to marry her.'" Carol remembers, "When he hugged me after all those years, I thought, 'Oh, I'm safe.' And there was chemistry, too!" Joy (Jemison) and Sam Nichols, who were split apart by World War II, reunited and married in their seventies after more than 50 years apart. Jeanne (Trattner) kicked the runaway bride syndrome and finally married Michael Harris in their mid-sixties. Mary (Gibbon) Clarke and Mike Sperber are in good company. Their story begins in the late 1940s in Ohio.

Mary and Mike

"SEEING HER AGAIN BROUGHT IT ALL BACK"

Mike Sperber first spotted **Mary (Gibbon)** in May Cottage, a coed dining hall at Oberlin College. Both in the class of '53. He immediately thought she was the woman for him.

"I thought Schatzie was very sexy at 17," he says, using her childhood nickname that means "treasure." "She was flirtatious, debonair, and intelligent. I loved it when the sun shown through her light brown hair." Mary was impressed by Mike as well. "He was good-looking, six feet tall, and had brown hair, and he had already spent a summer in Europe. I was charmed

195

by his laugh, which is the same today. We used to laugh like crazy and act like kids, which was unusual for me. Being the oldest in my family of four children, I wasn't very good at play."

"We'd skip through the center of the campus," says Mike. "I was filled with joy to meet my soul mate. She melted my frosty exterior." They strolled through the arboretum at Oberlin and read each other romantic poetry by Walt Whitman and Edna St. Vincent Millay. Mike brought Mary a gardenia corsage for the prom.

"But after the first year Mike just seemed to back off," recalls Mary. "There wasn't really a breakup."

Mike explains that when he was 15, his father had died in his arms, and he now believes it caused post-traumatic stress syndrome, freezing his ability to move forward with meaningful relationships. But also, he was just inexperienced. "I didn't know how to evolve what we had into a physical relationship," he says.

"One night during sophomore year Mike barged into my co-op house," Mary remembers, "and said he wanted us to be more than platonic friends." She felt bad about it but told him she was already seriously dating an upperclassman.

Then about a year later Mary met John Clarke, a student at Harvard. They fell in love, married after graduation, and had four children. Mary also got her master's degree in social work at Boston University. Because of John's adventurous spirit, the family lived in such far-flung, exotic places as Greece and Afghanistan, where John taught biology and chemistry, and Mary found herself teaching English to nurses and midwives. They came back to the United States in the late '60s to start an alternative school and run a ski lodge in New Hampshire.

For the last 20 years of John's life they operated a bed-and-breakfast on Martha's Vineyard and a sailing charter business.

Meanwhile, Mike married, divorced, and raised his two kids alone. He practiced psychiatry at McLean Hospital, taught at Harvard, and at one point worked as a medical missionary on a Navajo reservation. In the late 1990s when Mike was living in Newton, Massachusetts, a young man visiting Mike's daughter mentioned that his grandfather was John Gibbon. Mike immediately recognized the name as Mary's father, got her number, and placed a call to her just to say hello.

Mary's husband was already seriously ill when Mike left the message on her answering machine. It would be three years before she returned the call. For two of those years she nursed her husband; the third was a time to grieve. When she began to emerge from her grief, she telephoned Mike. "My little excuse was an Oberlin alumni meeting happening right in Cambridge that I invited him to attend. Instead of going, we spent hours talking, and when I cried about my husband, Mike was so comforting, he opened my heart."

"She looked like she'd been hit by a Mack truck, with her face so full of pain and grief," Mike says. "I wanted to protect her."

"I felt devastated after John died," Mary recalls, "but when I saw Mike, I had stirrings of strange feelings I hadn't felt for a while." Their romance grew gradually. She calls herself "the country mouse," used to gardening, sailing, and playing tennis, and Mike "the city mouse," who introduced her to the symphony and the theater. "I trusted him because I knew him from college," she says. "He was down to earth, not overlaid with false sophistication, a generous, open soul."

Mary says, "I'd already had a fantastic marriage with John, so this wasn't about finding love for the first time. I didn't deserve it, but I suddenly got all this extra joy and love with Mike."

They write love poems to each other that are beautiful, poignant, and sensual. These were the words he found on his pillow when he got home one night:

> To find each other
> So late in life
> Seems still early—
> Time for Bach in bed,
> Sun warm on the rocks,
> Diamonds sharp on the sea,
> Dulcet poetry.
> So late in life, but
> Early for eternity.

Mike loves her words and her spirit. "In the puzzle of my life, there was a big piece missing. Schatzie filled that piece, and now my life is complete."

When they discussed marriage, neither of them wanted to give up their homes, so Mary answered Mike's proposal with her own question: "Would you marry me and accept my house at the same time?" They kept both houses, one in Gloucester, Massachusetts, and one in Cambridge, and feel they have the best of both worlds. Mary volunteers for a hospice, helping other families who are facing the death of a loved one. She describes Mike as an intellectual who spends 80 percent of his daylight time working with words. He recently published a book titled

Henry David Thoreau: Cycles and Psyche. He also works with inmates at the Middlesex jail.

"When I first knew Schatzie," Mike says, "we shared an incredible energy. Seeing her again brought it all back. She encourages our passion because she knows what's important. Thank heavens for Viagra!" adds the 70-year-old man who sees their reconnection as a miracle. "Sometimes our self-esteem and confidence flag as we get older. Being accepted by Schatzie enhances my feelings about myself. At a certain age people can feel futility, pessimism, or despair. I strongly suggest that if you are unmarried, divorced, or widowed, think about others whose lives touched yours in the early years and reach out to them."

"Just do it," encourages Mary with a twinkle in her eye. She and Mike celebrated their wedding on August 8, 2004.

Mike often proposes the following toast when they go out:

> *To love is to admire with the heart.*
> *And to admire is to love with the mind.*

"I've loved people," he says, "and I've admired people. But it's rare to encounter someone whom I love and admire at the same time. And I can say that about Schatzie."

As a psychiatrist, Mike believes that his and Mary's modern-day love is rooted in their early attraction. "Neurochemicals in the brain create positive circuitry. I loved Schatzie when we were young. And I always will."

A school alumni gathering was Mary's "excuse" to return Mike's call three years after his original message. While they never actually got to the meeting, it gave them a framework and impetus for contact. Many seniors find that a school reunion is the ideal ground for love to bloom.

"Especially if you're widowed or divorced and you're an older person, where do you meet people? You can go to reunions or get in contact with people you know from back home," encourages Dr. Sherry Bush. "That was your initial network, and it makes sense to go back to it." Lois (Kenreich) and Bob Williamson, an Ohio couple who were high school sweethearts, went the reunion route and remet in their seventies.

Lois and Bob

"SOMETHING BETWEEN US HUNG ON"

Bob Williamson thought **Lois (Kenreich)** would always be his girl when they dated at Greenford High School in the mid-1930s. They were both farm kids who grew up about a mile apart and really connected at orchestra practice where she played clarinet. "He was my first boyfriend, and he gave me my first kiss," says Lois. "He had dark hazel eyes, and he could play the trumpet better than anybody!"

Bob was attracted by Lois's black hair and blue eyes. "I thought she looked like movie star Norma Shearer in *The Divorcee*," he says. Bob was allowed to drive his dad's Model A Ford to take Lois to square dances.

After two years Lois broke it off, according to Bob. "I didn't like it, but she wanted to look around and see what other guys were like." Lois doesn't deny his teasing account of their breakup but puts it more diplomatically: "I was young and not ready to settle down!"

A few years after graduation Lois *was* ready and married Donald Elser, her high school English teacher, who ultimately became a university professor. Lois began teaching English and art herself at the high school, they had four daughters, and the whole family got heavily involved in community theater. Bob married Becky Luplow, a girl from a nearby town, and they, too, had four kids. Bob became a licensed operator at the local AM radio station, working for 15 years in the technical end of broadcasting as it moved into the era of color TV. He then switched to electrical engineering at the forefront of automated machinery.

Both had happy marriages. Bob kept track of Lois as her theater and community activities showed up in the newspaper now and then. They ran into each other only once or twice even though both lived in the area where they had grown up.

Many years later their spouses passed away. One of Bob's neighbors, an old classmate, started looking after him, making sure he ate well. "The first thing I knew, I was going out with her." He started seeing a second woman as well and says, "They were both lovely girls."

In the spring of 1994, the former classmate took Bob to their yearly school reunion lunch at a restaurant in Salem, and who should arrive? Lois. More than 50 years had passed since their last drive in the Model A. "I left my poor date sitting there," admits Bob, "and spent the whole luncheon with Lois. I regret that because my date was a nice person, but I couldn't help it." As for Lois's reaction, she says, "I thought, 'Wow, he's great!' I still had 'that feeling' for him."

They started spending time together, and Lois got Bob

involved in the theater, first as a carpenter and then as an actor. The last time they had acted together was in their first grade production of *Goldilocks* when he played Papa Bear and she shone as Mama Bear.

But Bob was still seeing his other two girlfriends as well. "I didn't want to dump them because they were nice. And I wasn't sure about Lois because she had quit me once before." He felt she might be "a cut above him" with her education and vacation travel experience to Europe and the Far East. But his daughter, Cheryl, who had been a student in Lois's class, knew her former teacher was special. "She introduced us to Andy Warhol and Picasso, and encouraged our creativity. She was youthful in her thinking." Cheryl advised her dad to choose Lois.

Finally, around Christmas 1994, Bob cut the other girlfriends loose, and in May 1995, he and Lois took a cruise to the Greek islands to tie the knot. Just to lock it in, they had a second wedding in August under a tree on her farm. Her four daughters were her attendants, and his four children escorted him. Both feel they have been doubly blessed. "I've been married to two fantastic guys," says Lois. "I couldn't get any luckier." She uses the name Elser-Williamson to honor both of her happy marriages.

Today Lois and Bob live on his hardwood tree farm. She watches NASCAR racing on TV with him, and they are still active in the theater. They have even tried playing the clarinet and trumpet again although they are "pretty rusty." Bob found a woolen scarf Lois had given him during their dating days. "I'd stashed it in an old suitcase in the attic because I thought 'How'm I going to explain this?'" Bob admits. "I guess there was a dormant spark smoldering all those years. Something between us hung on."

When they speak of each other, their eyes sparkle. "Bob is the most wonderful guy," says Lois. "He's intelligent, kind, and caring. You name it, he's got it." Lois loves the natural curls in Bob's hair, so he's found "a lady barber who makes me look like an accountant in front and leaves the curls in back.

"Lois still has the sunniest disposition," he says. "I saw that right away at the reunion. She's happy and energetic. She's the kind of woman who makes life wonderful regardless of the ups and downs."

When Lois's daughter Patricia wrote and directed a documentary about their love story, she dared to ask the Big Question: How is sex when you marry your long-ago sweetheart after age 70? They both blushed but came out with it. "I feel 20 again," exclaims Bob. "It's so diverse and exciting, I can't believe it," Lois echoes. "I feel like a teenager. It's fantastic."

Lois and Bob live a healthy lifestyle and fully expect many happy years together. But seniors are very aware that if they remarry, they may be committing themselves to caring for another elderly person through a difficult illness. The "in sickness and in health" vow is right in the forefront of their minds.

"Some people want companionship but not the responsibility of caring for another elderly person who may become ill," acknowledges Dr. Carolyn Perla who has counseled many senior couples on issues of intimacy. "But I do see people who are willing to take that on. Whatever time they can get to spend together, they want."

"Whatever time they could get" is what Beverly (Hancock) and Burl Howard went for when they married in their mid-sixties. Reunited through Classmates.com, their time together turned out to be only 30 months, but how precious that time was.

Beverly and Burl

"I'D HAVE MARRIED HIM ANYWAY"

Beverly (Hancock), 17, invited Burl Howard, 19, to the prom at Raytown High School in 1953 even though he was dating one of her girlfriends. "I'd had an argument with my boyfriend," she says, "and being a hardheaded Missouri mule, I decided to take the best-looking boy I could find."

That was Burl Howard, who, with her girlfriend's blessing, accompanied Beverly to her prom in military uniform. It turned out that he and his girlfriend had had an argument, too. It also turned out that Beverly and Burl immediately fell in love.

They quickly decided that after she graduated, Beverly would leave Independence, Missouri, and join Burl in California where he was stationed. She found a wedding dress, prepared her luggage, and was ready to take off, but at the last minute her mother intervened. "He's in the service," her mom objected, "and you don't know anyone in California. What happens to you when he ships out? You'll be left with no one."

Beverly sent him back the ring and broke his heart. Burl ended up marrying his original girlfriend—Beverly's friend—and had a family, but they divorced in 1978. Beverly also married, divorced in 1968, and then married again; she lived in Phoenix and then Banning, California, until her husband died in 1994.

She joined Classmates.com in 2001 to see what her old friends were doing. Burl, who lived in Oregon, was already a member and received notification that a former classmate had signed on. When Burl saw Beverly's name, he eagerly sent her an e-mail, "I've finally found you! If you had the feeling over the years that someone was thinking about you, it's because I was."

Beverly remembers, "My heart went pitty-pat, just as it did in 1953 when we first met." He sent additional e-mails telling her he had loved her since he first laid eyes on her. "How could I not love a guy like that?" Beverly says. Sight unseen for almost 50 years, they once again decided to marry at ages 65 and 67. This time her mom, now in her late eighties, was worried that Burl might reject Beverly when he saw her because of her weight gain.

His response to Beverly's mom was "I fell in love with her for her heart, not her body."

Beverly's mother was there when they married in Redmond, Oregon, on June 20, 2001. The next year they settled in California where, in August 2002, Burl was diagnosed with esophageal cancer. Beverly was by his side for radiation and various rounds of chemotherapy, feeding him malts and helping him deal with the disease. He died on December 31, 2003, after 30 months of marriage. Still, Beverly feels fortunate.

"If I'd known how ill he was, I'd have married him anyway," she says. "I thank God every day that I was able to rekindle a great love for Burl and have many months of marriage with him. Together we knew a happiness beyond description, and when love is the real thing, like ours was, it never goes away."

Beverly and Burl followed their hearts and, however short their time together, they felt like winners in the lottery of life. They had the kind of positive approach that opens people up for reunited love. "In seeking out a sweetheart from the past, there is some sense that there are still possibilities," reflects Dr. Herb Barrett, who is himself in his early eighties and has counseled hundreds of seniors.

"It means things aren't over yet." Dr. Barrett has some personal experience with people reuniting in their later years. His mother married her former brother-in-law after both of their spouses passed away. They had known each other as teenagers in Russia before emigrating to the United States. It was a union that Dr. Barrett says extended their lives and helped them feel joy again, and was therefore welcomed by their children.

Joy was clearly in the air when the vivacious 73-year-old Millie (Penn) walked down the aisle to marry 89-year-old Arnold Spitz. They had hoped to wed more than 50 years before, but fate took them separate ways.

Millie and Arnold

"THE HEART POUNDS THE SAME AT 73 AS IT DOES AT 17"

Millie (Penn) and **Arnold Spitz** initially met on a blind date in the Newark area of New Jersey when she was 17 and he was 33. "We had a wonderful time, and he was a perfect gentleman," recalls Millie. "But when he asked me for a kiss, I said, 'No! What did you ever do for me, buy me dinner?'" Arnold was captivated. No girl had ever turned him down that way.

He kept asking her out, and they fell for each other quickly. "The age difference didn't matter to me or my mother," says Millie, "because I had always looked and thought a little older than I was and because Arnold was so gracious and had a young attitude."

"She was a lovely girl," he says. "I liked her outgoing personality, and she was intelligent." But Arnold's first wife refused to give him a divorce for many years. "After two years of dating, Arnold released me because he couldn't offer me a future," recalls Millie. "It was difficult, but life went on." She married and had children. Years later Arnold was finally divorced, and he married again. These marriages were both loving unions. Over the years Arnold passed Millie's dress shop in West Orange, New Jersey, called simply "Millie's," and sometimes told his kids, "See that store? I used to know that girl when we were young."

Eleven years ago Millie suffered a tragic loss when one of her sons died of a heart attack at 41. She was devastated. "I used to believe in God a lot, but when I lost my son, I didn't believe in anything anymore. He had never hurt anyone, and he was a man to be proud of." When her husband died as well, Millie felt that her life had stopped. Meanwhile, Arnold's second wife passed away after a long struggle with Alzheimer's. Millie saw the obituary in the newspaper, located his son's telephone number, and called. "Give your father my sympathy," she said. "I know what it is to lose." When Arnold got home, there was a phone number left by his son and a message that said quite simply, "Call Millie."

They arranged to meet. When Arnold picked Millie up at her home, he says, "She looked like she was still 17. So beautiful."

"I went mostly out of curiosity," says Millie. "But when I saw him, the years just melted away. We weren't stupid; I knew I wasn't really 17, but I also knew immediately that we would be together. I'd lost half a family, and although I know life is a gamble, I didn't want to lose any more."

Millie finally became Mrs. Arnold Spitz on November 9,

2003, at a ceremony in Maplewood, New Jersey. Arnold feels as if they've never been apart. "She makes me feel young again."

Millie says, "After my husband died, I wouldn't go out with anyone. Everyone brought suggestions of men to date—their uncles, brothers, fathers-in-law. The answer was always no because the concept of taking care of another man was not appealing. But knowing Arnold and remembering him, I felt very much at ease with him. I never pretended, I never had to fake it, and I trusted him in every way. Marrying him was a natural thing."

At times they feel as if they have always been together. "We may have only a few years left," says Millie, "but Arnold taught me that you have to live each day. As my 95-year-old mother says, 'You're never too old to love. The heart pounds the same at 73 as it does at 17.'"

The zest for living and loving that these senior rekindled pairs exhibit is exciting and contagious. Our culture seems to focus on the deficits of aging. We do lose some of our sharpness, strength, and flexibility as we age and may not always be able to do some of the things that previously made life pleasurable. But we don't age out of reunited love. We can age right into it.

Rekindled love can be a reality regardless of our time of life, circumstances, or locale. First, you have to go for it, and it helps to learn how from couples who have succeeded.

PART THREE

How to Find Rekindled Love

Chapter 12

How to Reunite

IS REUNITED LOVE IN YOUR FUTURE?

After hearing one or two stories of rekindled love, much less 20 or 30, someone who has been wondering how to find companionship might ask, "Could this happen for me? Or maybe my daughter, friend, or parent?" People in the know deliver a resounding "Go for it!"

Michael Harris, who finally won over his runaway bride, Jeanne (Trattner), says: "Do it. Keep at it. If the timing and the situation are right, you can't beat it."

Barry Spiro, recently married to his reunited love, Marjory Lehrer, whom he dated at Brooklyn's Erasmus High School in 1968, gives a big thumbs-up. "I recommend it. We've been back together six years and it's still magical."

Dr. Mike Sperber, who wed his Oberlin College sweetheart, Mary (Gibbon) Clarke, after almost 50 years apart, says, "Get the word out. This could bring happiness to a lot of people."

Kate Coyne, who reunited with her fellow camp counselor Ron Martucci and then married him, sums up: "Do it. Do it!"

211

And the experts, while waving a flag of caution, are also on board:

Therapist Ginny Fleming declares: "I say go for it. When you look to reconnect with a past love, you will reconnect with yourself at a deeper level no matter how it turns out."

Dr. Helen Fisher recommends: "Try it. Absolutely. It's one of the safest places you can go because you have a lot in common with people from your youth."

Dr. Linda Waud advises: "I think you should give it a shot. What can happen to you if you take the risk and the person doesn't want to talk to you? It would be sad, maybe, but I think you'd want to find out."

How They Did It

First of all, it is clear by now that you may reconnect when you least expect it. But it's more likely to happen if you are out in the world moving, doing, *living*. And, by the way, it doesn't hurt to be in good shape and look your best while you're out there! Anne Zehren and Harvey Anderson reconnected when they were both spectators at an NBA basketball game; four years later he still mentions how great she looked in her "hot" suede pants. More than 25 years after their parents split them up, Ellen (Hector) and J. R. Barberie remet in the Vancouver Airport. She wins the award for best unplanned reuniting line with "You son of a bitch, you look better now than you did at 18."

Feeling proactive? Definitely consider the Internet. Someone may already be looking for you. When Beverly (Hancock) signed up on Classmates.com, she got a message from her prom date of

48 years before, Burl Howard, who wrote, "I've finally found you." Checking the class lists on such Web sites can jog your memory about people you once found interesting. (See chapter 10 on the impact of the Internet.) It's not a bad idea to get back into the network of your old classmates and friends because even if *they* aren't of romantic interest, as matchmakers know, people know people who might be The One.

Whether you use the Internet or not, staying in touch with old friends ups your game. In fact, mutual friends are often cited as the "angels" that helped couples reunite. Broadway star Carol Channing and Harry Kullijian were reunited in their eighties when Merv Morris read what Carol had written about her junior high love in her autobiography. Merv happened to know them both very well and, bless him, called Harry to give him Carol's number. (I suppose another lesson here is that if you are writing your autobiography, it doesn't hurt to mention in glowing terms the one who got away!)

A subset of "mutual friends" is "mutual friends' weddings." No doubt about it: Romance breeds rekindled romance. "Weddings remind us all of our first love," explains therapist Ginny Fleming. "You hear the vows, and you want to believe in them again. That's why so many people fall for each other at weddings. Their hearts are open." Designer Nicole Miller reconnected with Kim Taipale, her sweetheart from three years before, at a friend's wedding in 1992. They married four years later.

While you're at the wedding, don't be surprised if you have feelings reminiscent of adolescence! TV sportscaster Scott Clark rediscovered his junior high crush, Heather (Lynn), when they both attended a mutual friend's wedding back home in Lima, Ohio. At the ceremony Heather noticed that "the short boy in eighth grade had turned into a tall, handsome prince." They sat at the same table during the reception and, Scott says, "I couldn't take my eyes off her." They talked late into the night, but the next day as part of the celebration a few guests went golfing, and she rode with some of the guys who had been in her class. He remembers being "miffed." She whispers, "Oversensitive." But she made peace by giving him her card. "All of a sudden," Scott recalls, "I was rejuvenated. It was 'Hoohah, here we go!'"

Attending events to catch up on the talents of old neighbors or classmates is a promising approach because you never know who else from your past might be there. Liza Huber was an elementary school goddess to Alex Hesterberg. More than 15 years later she went with girlfriends and he went with buddies to hear a band that included a musician from their hometown of Garden City, New York. Liza, who had become a star of daytime TV's *Passions*, and Alex, who had become a computer software executive, discovered that they loved the same music and ultimately that they loved each other.

Reach out if you're sorry. Some couples reunite when one of the former partners decides it is high time to apologize. Russell, who got to know Leslie on an archaeological dig, wrote her a letter many years later apologizing for actions that broke up the relationship. She gave it a second chance, and they married 16 years after that sensual summer.

The occasional visit home has also led to reunited love. Twenty-eight years after their young romance, Carol Gregory remet high school sweetheart Mike Howell at the local American Legion hall during the Belding, Michigan, town carnival in 1988 when she was back visiting family. Mike admits he was once again "smitten" and called her for a date two days later. They are now married and live in Ocala, Florida. Carol says thankfully, "I don't have to look in the mirror all the time, checking how I look, because I'm not with someone who loves me superficially. We have a history together. Mike loves me for who I am inside."

Subscribe to the hometown newspaper. That's how Jim Petrausch, living in Florida, got information about Renee (Shipp), who had been back to their school in Wyoming for a reunion. They reunited after 34 years.

Listen to Mom! (This is one of my favorites since I've been known to tell my kids that I have garnered wisdom from which they can benefit.) Yes, moms often hear that painful phrase, "You just don't understand." But we can be pretty savvy when the chips are down. Cheryl Kagan's mom went for an eye appointment so she could look at a national optometrist directory in search of her daughter's former sweetheart. Well done, Mrs. Kagan. Cheryl and Hilly married two years later and now have a daughter of their own.

Listen to Mom and her posse! When Debbie Johnson's mom saw her daughter's old sweetheart home for a visit in Virginia, she called Debbie in New York right away, urging her to phone him. Then came reminder calls from her aunt, grandma, and mom again. Debbie and Maurice Skates reconnected. A good thing about moms: They don't give up.

Finally, one of the biggies: reunions. As you might imagine, a lot of emotions grab people when they lay eyes on each other in the company of old classmates, with golden oldies spun by a DJ in the background, and the air permeated by nostalgia.

Reconnecting at Reunions

Bari Belosa, a professional reunion planner who has supervised more than 5,000 of them during her 21 years in the business, says it's not unusual for former classmates to connect romantically at these events. "You're touching a time that was incredibly special in your life. You weren't worried about feeding a family, taking a kid to the doctor, or making the car payment. Everything was intensely magnified emotionally, and the people you shared that time with are absolutely unique to you. Because you had common experiences in your youth, you're more likely to strike up a relationship later. A lot of times you can pick up where you left off."

Janet Jacobson and Mark Davis pretty much monopolized each other at their twentieth reunion. Mark acknowledges that "Janet definitely had the lead spot on my 'top five people I hope to run into' list." As for their conversation marathon, "It wasn't only reminiscing," Janet explains. "We needed to catch up with who we'd become." They married five years later.

Dr. Linda Waud's romance with her former sweetheart, Ben, reignited at their thirty-fifth high school reunion in Waukegan, Illinois. When they broke up during college, he did not tell her why. "I felt that I wasn't good enough for him anymore," says Linda. "He was very cool, a big fraternity man at Duke, and I was just a small-town girlfriend." When they saw each other that reunion night after more than 30 years apart, the first thing he said was "I guess it's time for us to talk." They corresponded for two years. She moved to California to be with him and then wrote her dissertation on rekindled love. Three years after the reunion, they married.

If you still live in the same town where you went to school, do bother to go to your class reunion. Don't brush it off thinking you've already seen everyone who is likely to be there at the local mall or the PTA. The truth is, the people who most enthusiastically attend reunions are those who have moved away, and this is a great opportunity to see them again. "A very high percentage of people who moved away come back for reunions because they're the ones who are most nostalgic," confirms reunion planner Bari Belosa. "So you have a good chance of meeting a sweetheart who left the area." This is a time when I-stayed-in-my-hometown types can check out I-moved-away types to see if there's any chemistry. If you can't attend your reunion, at least send in your contact information. Other people from the school may use it to reach you.

Reunions can also trigger romantic feelings between people who were in the same class but never had much interaction. Bari Belosa explains, "Time is a great equalizer. In high school there are cliques—you're in this group, he's in another group. But people come to the reunion as adults, and a lot of those artificial barriers just fade away." That's what Joe Jensen discovered when he went back for his thirtieth reunion in Superior, Nebraska. Kathie (Beck) had been the popular cheerleader, and he had been a quiet boy who didn't travel in her crowd. By the end of the festivity's second night he finally kissed her, and six weeks later they married. That's what I'd call making up for lost time.

Kim (Firment) and Jeff Tinsley also bridged the status gulf. She was captain of the cheerleading squad, and he was the studious type—with what she describes as "flock of seagulls hair." At their tenth high school reunion, she says, "he was taller, poised, articulate, and savvy—Prince Charming with a much better haircut." She also says that some of the jocks had "ridden off their looks" and didn't look so great anymore. Jeff was thrilled that Kim was still single. "I couldn't believe someone hadn't married her because she is just spectacular."

Speaking of looking great at the reunion, it is definitely worth the effort. Mary Lou (White) was widowed for about a year when she went back home to Medford, Oregon, for her twenty-fifth high school reunion. She had never thought of herself as sexy. But you may remember, she went shopping for a special reunion outfit and bought one she wouldn't have considered before: a beautiful yellow barebacked dress. She won the heart of the Marine lieutenant colonel who had been the boy next door (actually two doors away). She still has the dress, and she has been married to Ray Smith for more than 25 years.

An important piece of advice is to get involved with planning the reunion if it is at all possible. Ed used that excuse to contact me. He had volunteered to make calls encouraging people to attend. Not a bad idea. "If you want to meet people, it does help to be in on the planning," says Bari Belosa. "You get on the phone and speak to former classmates—there's a very social element there." Don't just stuff envelopes. Either put yourself in a position to call someone specific, or call a wide circle of people so you'll know them better at the reunion itself. Be the one who phones interesting grads to convince them that they are panel discussion material. As Ms. Belosa notes, "the reunion itself lasts only a weekend at most, but if you're planning it, you are greatly expanding the hours you're involved to several months or even a year."

Help your class do a "virtual reunion" online ahead of time, or create an actual book containing everyone's bios that can be distributed so that everyone gets to know each other better beforehand.

Suggest strongly that your reunion include multiple years to expand the group of people you'll see. Gary Puetz gratefully remembers, "Because ours was such a little town, when they did the reunion, they included two years prior and two years post. You don't have a 32-year reunion, so I wouldn't have been there if they hadn't invited all those classes. It was a miracle, the chance to see Carol again."

Another example of a multiyear reunion that had positive romantic consequences was the Greenford High School (Ohio) reunion luncheon that Lois (Kenreich) attended in 1994. She was in the class of '39, but since the group included classes on both sides, she ran into her first sweetheart, Bob Williamson, who had been a year ahead of her. Bob actually came with another classmate. Lois says, "He was sitting with a good-looking girl across the table from me." Bob remembers, "The light turned on in my mind. I thought, 'Hey, Lois is single, and so am I.'" They got together and married a year later. The "good-looking girl," 73-year-old Dorothy, was heard to mutter, "I made a mistake bringing you to that luncheon."

Consider gently crashing the reunion of another class. Chris Burgart graduated a year ahead of the Orange High School, California, class that was having a thirtieth reunion in 2001. But he was invited by a friend from that year to join the party and ended up remeeting Kathy (Grant). As one of the reunion planners, she sneaked him into the second evening, and they've been a couple ever since.

It's not just *high school* reunions that are hotbeds of romance. Colleges, junior highs, and elementary schools have reunions that sometimes lead to love. Larry Sasso went to his twenty-fifth reunion from Holy Rosary Elementary School in the Bronx and re-met former classmate Marie (Santone), who had lived five blocks away when they were youngsters. They have now been married 26 years, and made a splash by attending their fiftieth elementary school reunion as a couple.

If it isn't reunion time or you can't get back home, some schools have events in far-flung cities to keep former students involved. Recall that this was the ticket for Mary (Gibbon) Clarke to call Dr. Mike Sperber, a college sweetheart from 1949. They had gone to school in Ohio at Oberlin, which was holding a function for alumni in Cambridge, Massachusetts. But rather than joining their former schoolmates, they talked for almost five hours, just the two of them. And they soon became a couple.

Whom to Consider?

If you're hoping to reconnect with someone who shares a part of your past, as we've seen there is no need to limit yourself to former sweethearts. (Usually that's a very short list.) Our couples make it clear that there are a variety of people to consider if you're searching on the Internet or searching your memory about connections you might revitalize with a phone call, a letter, or an e-mail.

Try friends from the old days. Twenty-eight years after they had last sung together, Bob McGarry emailed one line from a tune in *Hello, Dolly!* to his high school chamber choir friend, Deb (Giragosian). She immediately e-mailed the next line back. A few months later Deb moved from Massachusetts to Seattle, and they got married a year after one old friend sent another that first e-mail.

Sometimes it is even worth considering people you did not like. Fifteen years after graduation Robin (Faylor) Lewis e-mailed Jeff Baker, "the boy I hated in high school," when she was trying to reconnect with an old girlfriend from their school days in Garland, Texas. Lo and behold, Jeff turned out to be a terrific guy. They built a six-bedroom house for her two children and his three girls, and they married in 2003.

So go through the lists of classmates (often there are lists on Internet Web sites such as Classmates.com or Reunion.com) to trigger memories about your various schools—from elementary school on up. Consider schools other than your own. (Maybe you were friendly competitors, as Ed and I were, with kids from neighboring schools.) Muse on "what might have been" like Brenda (Elliott) did when she was demonstrating a Web site in February 2003 and checked out a high school she would have attended if she hadn't moved away from Santa Barbara, California, in 1987. She found John McNamara, whom she had known at La Colina Junior High School and zapped him an e-mail. He happily responded, and their correspondence bloomed into love.

Consider friends of your friends or, heaven help us, friends of your (back then) embarrassing brothers and sisters. What about camps you attended or summer jobs you worked? Camp Hillard is where Kate Coyne met Ron Martucci in their camp-counselor days. She married him 11 years later. Mull over your part-time jobs and try to recall the other kids working there. Were there trips you took to lakes or beaches or ranches or mountains, or grandma and grandpa's house? Whom did you meet there or in transit? One "Classmates in Love" story on Classmates.com tells of two teenagers who met on an Amtrak train in 1986. He came from California and she lived in Washington, so they lost touch after the "magical train ride." In 2002 he typed her name into the Web site, asking if she was the girl from the train. After five months of e-mailing and flying to see each other, she moved to be with him in California, and they made plans to marry.

Consider people you met through work early in your career. Actress Maddie Corman was 21 and doesn't remember 26-year-old director/actor Jace Alexander attending the premier of her movie *My New Gun* in 1992, but he thought she was very cute. They were quite familiar with each other's work by the evening in 1997 that she was in a restaurant where he was celebrating closing night for one of his plays. She felt strongly attracted. Two weeks later, when a friend invited her to play in a coed basketball game that Jace was joining, Maddie says, "I suddenly thought I could play basketball!" They started dating and were married in September 1998. "We admire each other professionally as well as personally," says Jace. "I knew so many people who knew him well," smiles Maddie. "We felt a sense of history in common."

Consider young people who might have visited your hometown. George Rogers of Scotch Plains, New Jersey, is looking for the girl from a "summer of '56 romance." Her name was Patricia, and she came from Missouri to Westfield, New Jersey, to visit her aunt, a friend of George's mom. She had her first "restaurant date" with him at a local diner, and he does know that her phone number at the time was Farmington 342.

Who else was in those extra classes you took over the summer to learn typing or languages or to prepare for the SAT? What about summer programs you attended in other parts of the country? Who comes to mind when you remember sports like tennis and skiing? Maybe you volunteered for organizations like the Red Cross or the March of Dimes, and Mr. or Ms. Right was there, too, only you were too young to notice. Think back: 4-H, band, joint Girl Scout and Boy Scout events, drama, debate, language clubs, Junior Achievement—there must have been someone you thought was interesting. Three decades ago a tennis-playing teenager wrote a letter complaining that there were only "ball boys" at the U.S. Open and ended up becoming the first "ball girl." Although it hasn't provided a romance yet, she loves the odds at that reunion! Make a list or just enjoy thinking through your past. Remember, you're looking for people with whom you have some common history. Congratulations if it leads to a happy romance, and bravo if you enlarge your circle of friends and fill your life with people who already have a reason to think you're special because you share a piece of their personal past.

If you decide to make contact, do reflect on where it might lead; there are a few precautions to take in order to protect your heart and perhaps help avoid hurt to other people. Reunited love can involve some big decisions. Be aware of the flashing yellow lights.

Chapter 13

Flashing Yellow Lights

ADMITTEDLY, NOT EVERY REUNION STORY IS A FAIRY TALE AND NOT every beau is Prince Charming just because he comes from the old neighborhood. Some efforts at rekindling love have been nightmares or simply sad stories that contain lessons well learned for anyone considering reuniting with an old flame.

The "go slow" flashing yellow lights include cautions about people who might take advantage of you, the affairs and divorces sometimes triggered by reuniting, and the particular issues children face when a parent rekindles a long-ago love. Reconnected sweethearts also often face difficult problems of long-distance commuting or wrenching relocation so they can be together while still meeting the needs of their children and keeping careers afloat. And sometimes there are shades of gray: The rekindled sweetheart isn't a bum, but he isn't a good match either. Often in such cases the effort to reunite leaves people not with love but with closure.

Because of the sensitive nature of their situations, a few people in this chapter preferred to withhold their identities. Others freely shared their names as well as their stories.

Go Slow

I had a few friends who tried to say "go slow" when Ed and I first reconnected, including my dear friend Ellen Levine, the respected editor-in-chief of *Good Housekeeping* magazine. She and her husband, Dr. Dick Levine, took Ed and me out to dinner shortly after we started dating. She says she intended to advise: "I don't care how great he is, slow down." A wise woman, that Ellen. But Ed was so dear and earnest and persuasive that she soon gave us her "seal of approval."

Reunitees like Ed and me are often in a hurry because we feel we have already lost so much time. Still, sage voices counsel that it is downright dumb to move too fast or give too much credence to what may turn out to be a fantasy. "The downside is it can move so fast you may be in it deep and married before you finally go 'Oh, my God. I'm in love with a memory, not a person!'" says therapist Ginny Fleming. "The problem is that the body remembers the feelings you had when you were 17 and in love. When you reunite, every phone call causes a high, like a narcotic. The danger is not going slow enough and really getting to know who this person has become as an adult."

Some who take a stab at reuniting are in for a shock. Maybe in the younger days she misread who he really was, maybe some of the qualities that were thrilling in a teenage boy are not so charming in an adult male, or maybe he has actually changed for the worse. Sometimes it just doesn't matter what happened—he's bad news now. That's what Sharon, a vivacious, witty New York City career woman in the entertainment industry, discovered when she spent a weekend with her college sweetheart.

"HE ARRIVED WITH A SUITCASE FULL OF ANTI-DEPRESSANTS"

A single professional woman, well respected by clients and competitors, Sharon, 42, was lonely in her personal life and hoping to find someone wonderful. At the urging of friends she mounted a search by phone and on the Internet, and was delighted when she finally reached Larry, her old college boyfriend. They made plans to see each other, and Sharon couldn't wait to reunite with the happy blond college boy she remembered from her youth. They had even discussed marriage before they broke up, so she was hopeful that when they met again, her lonely days would be over.

She was not prepared for the man who showed up at her door. "Larry arrived at my house," she recalls, "with a suitcase full of antidepressants."

He had been divorced twice, and his disappointment in life was written all over his strained face. When they went for a "nice" lunch, he cried. He also cried at the natural history museum and at a movie that was supposed to be a comedy. Sharon was stunned. She had recalled her past love as a self-confident guy who had a great sense of humor, but suddenly she remembered a number of serious reasons that he hadn't been the man for her then—and he wasn't now.

She got through the evening somehow, but when bedtime arrived, she felt scared of this man whom she could only describe as "creepy." She had already invited him to stay at her house, so he did. But she chuckles with some relief now when she remembers that he slept on the couch while she slept in her bedroom with her dog next to her bed and a tin can tied to her door to warn her in case he woke up in the night with any "ideas." Needless to say, they haven't seen each other since, and Sharon is still amazed at the change in her old boyfriend's personality.

It's nothing to be embarrassed about when a foray into reuniting doesn't work. Many people want to walk down memory lane with an old sweetheart, hoping that things will turn out well this time because of "nostalgia and some wishful thinking," says Dr. Iris SanGiuliano. "But you don't know what happened in the interim," she cautions. "Life has a way of changing all of us. Depending on what people have experienced, they may have become embittered. You may get an angry person. You may get all sorts of negative traits."

You hope for the best—that over the years you have both matured and grown wiser, more self-assured, more understanding. But people can change for the worse, developing such problems as alcohol or substance abuse, financial difficulties, legal crises, or mental health issues that make them radioactive as potential mates. These kinds of problems can be severe or intractable.

The wisest course it to keep your eyes wide open. That is precisely what a smart but lonely New York woman did *not* do when she received an exciting phone call from a long-ago love.

"HE WANTED MY MONEY"

It was a vulnerable period in Louise's life. She had been divorced from her husband for several years when she received a phone call from Greg, whom she had dated in college. "I was just shocked to receive his call after so many years. I remembered him as a hip, cool guy, and I was lonely right then, working really hard to lose the weight I'd gained during my divorce. He found me through a mutual friend, and he sounded so sweet and solicitous, I started falling for him."

When Greg invited Louise on a trip, she could hardly believe it was happening. "The truth is that he came on to me on the phone that night. He was so sexually provocative and I was so lonely that I agreed to meet him for a weekend in Vancouver and then drive down the West Coast.

When Louise arrived in Vancouver, she checked out six different rooms in the Wedgewood Hotel to find the "love-nestiest." But while she waited with bated breath for Greg to arrive, she looked out the window and spotted a strange-looking man repeatedly pulling in and out of a parking spot. It was Greg, and when he arrived at her door, he continued wearing his sunglasses the whole time they talked, including through dinner. Her antennae went up: Why didn't he want to look her in the eye? "I knew something was off," she says, "but I refused to acknowledge my discomfort with his behavior. I so wanted everything to go well." Ignoring her intuition, she took the trip with him to the famous Pike Place Market in Seattle, Washington. Then, with the sun shining on her face as they drove down the Oregon Coast, she says, "We were reminiscing and I was in heaven, as happy as I could be."

Later that afternoon Greg asked Louise if she wanted her own room. Again she refused to listen to her instincts and decided to share a room with him. Much to her disappointment, he stayed on his side of the bed, telling her, "I'm not sure whether I want this to happen." In the morning they continued their drive, but the next red flag appeared when Greg casually mentioned that he did not have the money to insure his car, the one in which they were traveling.

"I asked him how much he needed," she recalls. "It was the prudent thing to do rather than ride in an uninsured car. When he told me he needed $800, I took the money from my savings account and gave it to him. He promised to pay me back when we got home from the trip.

"The next day," she continues, "when we arrived at Big Sur, a beautiful town on the California coast, he disappeared for the entire day." She later learned that he was visiting another girlfriend. "It took that blow to make me see the truth," she says, and later she was chagrined and angry when his check bounced. "I must have had a big scarlet letter on me that said 'Available, vulnerable, can be taken in.' I received threats from Greg when I tried to get the money he owed me. He begrudgingly paid it back eight months later. It was such a painful experience. I guess I was taken in by the memory of his good looks and his athleticism."

Louise adds, "My advice to other women is 'Don't invest so much emotionally until you see the person again and spend some time with him.'"

Happily, her experience did not turn her against men or the possibility of reuniting with someone else. "I should have known better," she says, "when he put me in an uninsured vehicle and then took money from me. Sometimes the coolest guys on the campus aren't necessarily the ones that wear well for the long run."

Some advice that might have been helpful to Louise comes from therapist Suzanne Lopez, author of *Get Smart with Your Heart*. She says, "You have to ask pointed and direct questions. You have to go to where the person lives. If you have assets, you need to be smart about it and get a private detective to investigate and see who this person really is. You only know that he or she comes from your past. You don't know who the person is now."

Sometimes we have to acknowledge that we have been nourishing a fantasy. We often romanticize people—sweethearts and others—in our memories. We may so badly want the dream to be true that we'll take risks we would never consider with someone new.

Affairs and Divorces

High school or college reunions, despite the attendant "will I measure up?" anxieties, are highly anticipated events. It is fun to see how so-and-so turned out, who is divorced, who got rich and famous, and who didn't. And, of course, it is a chance to check out old boyfriends and girlfriends. Many times someone just wants to compare notes or maybe flash a little "since-you" success in the face of a former sweetheart.

And yet there are pitfalls that can turn an exciting, playful weekend into a big problem. Loretta Gruber is the founder of ElegantReunions.com and, as a professional in the field, has arranged hundreds of high school reunions. "A lot of people hook up that night," she says, "some single, some married. I've seen 'the walk of shame' on more than a few people's faces the morning after the big reunion dance."

The feelings triggered when people see their old crushes and former sweethearts can be far more intense than they expect. Especially after a few drinks, they may act on these emotions and have brief or even extended affairs. If either person is married, there can be painful fallout. However lost lovers cross paths again—reunions, the Internet, accidental encounters—if they fall back in love and aren't single, they sometimes find themselves faced with a profoundly upsetting choice to make.

Some decide to stay in their separate marriages, trying to compartmentalize or diminish their feelings for each other, and go on with life as it was. Others make a choice that admittedly brings pain to other people.

"NEITHER OF US WANTED TO HURT OUR FAMILIES"*

Gerald and Alicia, who were from different parts of the country, dated seriously during their days at a well-known university. He graduated first and went off to do military service. After corresponding for a time, they found the distance too much of a problem and ultimately lost touch entirely. Each married and had two children. Almost 32 years later Alicia, who was dissatisfied in her marriage, found Gerald through an Internet Web site and called out of the blue to see how he was. "My children were in college, and I was reminding myself that someone had loved me before I was just a taken-for-granted wife," she says. "I was hoping to feel attractive again." Gerald, also unhappily married with grown children, was delighted to hear from Alicia. They communicated sporadically at first, but within a few months they decided to see each other and began a passionate affair. "It felt like a cheating loophole," Alicia says, "as if it was okay because I knew Gerald before I knew my husband." Having fallen back in love, they decided to divorce their respective spouses. Gerald says, "I think my former wife and Alicia's former husband both thought at first

* Story is a composite of several couples who preferred to remain anonymous.

231

that it was just a temporary mid-life crisis." Alicia moved cross-country to marry Gerald. They regret the pain their relationship has caused their children. As for their ex-spouses, Alicia says, "They are good people, just not the right people for us. We hope they both find the same kind of love we have found." Alicia and Gerald are sorry about the distress resulting from their romance but feel they had no choice. "Neither of us wanted to hurt our families. It has caused a lot of emotional turmoil," Gerald says, "but Alicia and I knew in our hearts that we had to be together."

Dr. Nancy Kalish says that as a therapist she often hears from husbands and wives who are trying to figure out exactly what hit them when a partner left to be with a former sweetheart. "Often they are angry and bewildered. Sometimes they have a sense that the attraction of reuniting is so powerful, they couldn't have done anything to keep it at bay." That is the story of Howard who lost his wife to her high school love.

"WE MARCHED TO DIFFERENT DRUMMERS"

Howard and his wife were married in their early twenties in Charlotte, Virginia, and soon after started a family. He says, "When we got married, we genuinely thought we loved each other." But after 22 years of marriage, his wife ran into her high school sweetheart, fell back in love with him, and told Howard she wanted a divorce. He still doesn't know whether she intentionally searched for her old beau or encountered him accidentally. Howard says it took many years to get past the feeling that he had been betrayed. At first he was terribly upset and felt that his wife had thought of him as a meal ticket, providing cars, a pool, and a tennis court. He now says, "We just marched to different drummers." His ex-wife is still very happy with her reunited love. In the 18 years since his divorce, Howard has had one important relationship that is now over. He has taken a page from his ex-wife's book and is looking for a girl from his past.

One husband actually released his wife from their vows because more than 20 years into their marriage they learned that a sad twist of fate had kept her from her first love. Her high school boyfriend had joined the navy and written a letter proposing marriage, but it got lost in the mail. After reconnecting through the Internet, the woman and her long-ago sweetheart fell back in love. Her husband gave her his blessing and a divorce.

Kathleen and Dennis

"THE LOST LETTER HAD BEEN A TERRIBLE INJUSTICE"

Kathleen (Baney) was 14 and Dennis Reed was 16 when they fell in love at Baldwin Park High School in the San Gabriel Valley of Los Angeles County. He graduated in 1977 and enlisted in the navy. With Dennis often out to sea, the separation took its toll. Her friends warned, "He's probably got a girlfriend in every port." Kathleen answered, "No, that's not Dennis. He loves me. He's just not a big letter writer." She finally wrote that she needed some kind of commitment from him. He wrote back asking her to marry him, but the letter either never arrived at her parents' home or was accidentally tossed with the junk mail.

Kathleen thought her request had been ignored. Dennis thought maybe he had scared her away by suggesting such a serious step. He became despondent when she didn't respond and held back writing again because he didn't want to actually hear the bad news that she was turning him down. It was a classic case of crossed signals.

After a while Kathleen began dating David Wedgworth, turned down his proposal of marriage five times, and finally decided that since he was a good and loving man—and since Dennis was gone for good—she should accept. They married and had two children. A little later Dennis also married and had two kids. As the years went by, Kathleen and her husband discussed looking up their former sweethearts. David wanted to find his first love because he had always thought that an out-of-wedlock child she had borne might have been his. Although she loved him, Kathleen gave him the option of finding and going back to that sweetheart "if that's where he felt he belonged."

And in 2002, with her husband's blessing, Kathleen looked up Dennis's name on Classmates.com. She was saddened to learn from his biography on the site that his wife had died in his arms of breast cancer. She wrote of her sympathy. When he responded that her message had done his heart good, she was touched. By this time he was a staff sergeant in the Air National Guard in California, and she was living in Nevada. They exchanged more e-mails, and when they finally got a chance to see each other, she says, "our love was just as strong as it was before we tucked it away in our hearts and went on with our lives."

Kathleen is grateful to David, who had been her husband for 24 years. "He said the lost letter had been a terrible injustice, and he released me, giving me a divorce so I could marry Dennis." They were wed on September 13, 2003.

As unusual as their situation may sound, Kathleen and her former husband have great mutual respect for each other as parents and wanted each other to be happy.

Twenty-three years later, her new husband, Dennis, wrote in Kathleen's senior yearbook: "Now that I've found you, I don't plan on losing you again." To honor both men, Kathleen goes by the last name Wedgworth-Reed. David is still looking for his former girlfriend, and Kathleen says, "I will love my ex-husband forever for giving me my freedom to marry my first sweetheart."

One of the regrets Kathleen and Dennis express is that they won't be having children together, but they are pleased that the four children they have between them are at ease with their decision to reunite. That isn't always the case.

Children of Reunited Couples

When a parent remarries, whether it is to a former love or a new one, children often have deep anxieties. Whether young or grown, they may feel several upsetting emotions: Anger out of loyalty to their other parent; fear of being displaced; or worry that they will not be loved. With a parent's marriage to a reunited sweetheart there are additional questions: Because she's marrying someone from an earlier time, does Mom think the rest of her life—including me—was a mistake? Does she wish I had never been brought into the world, that she had stayed in the early relationship and had *other children* with him?

"If a parent starts to say, 'What would my life have been like if I had chosen him instead?' the implication is that the child wouldn't have been born and that you don't love him or her," explains Dr. Iris SanGiuliano. "It is important to reassure the children that you weren't sitting there thinking all the time of the lost love."

Many reunited couples take special care to tell their children that they do not regret the course their lives took precisely *because* the children are so important to them. As Tom Anton says of his 25 years apart from Sandi, which occurred because his mother hid letters they had written to each other, "We have a strong faith in God, and we believe there was a reason for this. I don't think of it as time lost because I have two beautiful children and I love Sandi's kids."

Usually couples whose children were upset about the reunion say that the passing of time helped. When the parents were patient and allowed their children to slowly get to know the new partner, much of the anxiety was resolved.

Sometimes there is a positive twist from the children's perspective. They may see this person from the past as a safe haven for their parent. One of Lois (Kenreich) Elser-Williamson's daughters even played a role in moving her mom's romance with Bob Williamson along. Jeanne knew that her mom and Bob had been high school sweethearts in the 1930s at Greenford High School. Lois, then in her mid-seventies, delicately asked her daughter for tips on how to pursue Bob without appearing too forward. Jeanne, who was directing a production at a local community theater, took matters into her own hands. She asked Bob to read for a part and cast him in the show so her mom would have lots of rehearsal time with her long-ago love. Meanwhile, Bob remembered that Lois had been his daughter Cheryl's high school English teacher; Cheryl assured him that Lois was "energetic and a lot like you." It turns out Bob is talented and went on to appear in several shows as well as to marry Lois. Another of Lois's daughters, Patricia, made an award-winning documentary about their reuniting entitled It Happened in Greenford.

As in the case of Lois and Bob, the adult children of potential reunitees sometimes go so far as to goose the romance along. The benefits can extend to the whole family if the parent becomes less dependent on the children for assistance with the needs of daily living and for companionship. And the youthful attitude that accompanies reunited love makes the parent happier and healthier.

Long Distance—Commute or Relocate?

One difficulty faced more often by reunited sweethearts than by new lovers is the issue of how to handle a long-distance romance. Lucky you if your reuniting honey lives nearby. But that's often not the case. You are simply more likely to end up with a long-distance relationship if you reconnect with an old love than if you date in your own vicinity. Nowadays, of course, if you are searching for a new love on the Internet, you may have the same problem, but you can screen out the prospects who live far away before you get attached. In reunited love the attachment is already there. Hello frequent flyer miles.

Some couples handle a commute well. Ed and I are bicoastal, traveling to see each other on weekends because I have kids in high school in the New York City area and he has responsibilities at his law office in California.

Cheryl J. Kagan lives in Tulsa much of each month with her

husband, Dr. Hilly Dubin, and their daughter, Brooke, but Cheryl regularly travels to Los Angeles and other cities for her work in public relations, a career she built before reuniting with Hilly.

TV producer/researcher Saryl Radwin and her rekindled sweetheart, optometrist Roz Rosenthal, commute to see each other on weekends because her work and her elderly mother are in Los Angeles and his job and his children are in San Diego.

Tom and Sandi (Russell) Anton commuted between Louisiana and Michigan for nine years after they got back together in order to finish raising their kids.

Kathie (Beck) and Joe Jensen saw each other once every eight weeks for the first two years of their marriage, until her kids were grown enough that she felt she could move back to Superior, Nebraska, where she and Joe had grown up and reunited at their thirtieth high school reunion.

Geraldine O'Brien and Jimmy Sibilia choose to commute each weekend between her home in Orlando and his near Miami rather than leave the great jobs they love and because he is still helping to raise his daughters. Geraldine sums up the feelings of many: "It's hard to be apart, especially considering the years we missed. We hate to say good-bye on Monday mornings. To make the best of the situation I try to do all my personal business during the week and put in as much time at work as possible so the weekends are really free for us to be together."

Other couples make a different but often tough decision. One partner or the other relocates and changes jobs or even careers so that they can be together.

Deb (Giragosian) left work that she loved as a financial auditor in Massachusetts, moving to Seattle and marrying former high school

singing-group friend Bob McGarry; she searched for a whole year before she accepted a very different post—administrator of their church.
Deb expresses the feelings of many rekindled couples: "After all those
lost years, we just couldn't stand being apart. I'd recently gotten a
promotion and loved my career, but his job was very secure. I made
the move and was able to spend a lot of time with his daughter. Now
I love my new job."

Anne Zehren left a fabulous job as publisher of *Teen People*,
moved to San Francisco to marry her old college friend Harvey
Anderson, and started a new business as a marketing strategy
consultant.

Kathy (Ciero) and her children moved from Illinois to a remote
part of Arkansas only six weeks after a proposal from her long-ago
family friend and sweetheart Jim Johnson. She married him in front
of the fireplace in their new house, surrounded by still-unpacked
boxes from the move.

After reconnecting on the Internet with John McNamara,
who'd had a crush on her in junior high, Brenda (Elliott) married
him and left Seattle with her children to join him in Reno, Nevada,
where he works as a firefighter,.

After reuniting with Chris Burgart at a thirtieth high school reunion, Kathy (Grant) married him and moved away from her adult
children in southern California to be with her husband up north.
She travels back every few weeks to get her fill of "grandmothering."

Heather (Lynn) married Scott Clark and moved with her three
children from Ann Arbor, Michigan, to New York, where he is a
sportscaster for WABC-TV.

Jim Petrausch left Florida to be with Renee (Shipp) in California, becoming her husband 36 years after he misunderstood her

hesitant reaction to his first proposal and then made the mistake of quickly marrying someone else. Now Jim and Renee have moved to Arizona for a new start together.

Bob Edinger, who only recently discovered that he has a 12-year-old son, Chris, by his high school sweetheart, Cathy (Rosania), sold his horse farm in Maryland and moved back to New Jersey. He married Cathy and now works as a mechanic. Explaining that he didn't want to upset his son's life with a move, he says, "I'd won two international championships with the horses and had done what I needed to do. Now I sign my paycheck and hand it to Cathy. I like being a family man."

Whether they choose to relocate, commute, or commute until they can relocate, most couples acknowledge it is a tough issue that involves a lot of give and take and requires a lot of understanding between them. But I can say from experience that it is worth the effort.

Closure

What about those reuniting experiences that are neither nightmares nor dreams come true? If it doesn't result in a long-lasting relationship, is it a waste? Some who tried reuniting didn't find love but instead found closure. That's what happened to James, who had always carried a secret torch for Nancy.

"SHE BROKE MY HEART FOR THE LAST TIME"

When James reunited with Nancy, his high school sweetheart, after 20 years apart, he thought his story deserved a fairy tale ending. It did have one, only it was not with Nancy.

They met at age 14 in junior high in Paramus, New Jersey. By 1973, at age 15, they had fallen in love. After dating for about seven months, Nancy decided James was too serious a guy, and she broke up with him. He was heartbroken.

James attended Boston University in Massachusetts, married, had a son, and moved to Hartford, Connecticut. In 1991 he went to his high school reunion. Nancy did not attend, but James learned from a friend that she was married, had a child, and was living in northern California. A few weeks later, with no romantic intentions, he called Nancy, and she was delighted to hear his voice.

James's marriage was troubled and, after 15 years, ended in divorce. When he moved into his own place in Hartford and started dating, he received a letter from Nancy saying that her marriage had come apart as well. They corresponded, talked on the phone, and decided to meet.

"When I saw her walking toward me for the first time in 20 years," James says, "my heart skipped. She looked more beautiful than I'd remembered, and we drove back to Boston together holding hands much of the way."

Their reunion quickly became a heated romance, but there was one problem: They were 3,000 miles apart. Still, they began a long-distance liaison that was infused with the drama of reuniting with a first love. "It felt magical," he says, "surreal and destined to be. It was as if my love for her had been hiding in a deep place in my heart all that time, and suddenly it was alive again, more incredible than ever."

But there were obstacles beyond the distance, including his four-year-old son and her four-year-old daughter. James and Nancy flew cross-country whenever possible and took several vacations as a couple in Europe. But within two years what had seemed like destiny to James disintegrated. "Just like when we

241

were 15," James says, "she ended the relationship. She broke my heart for the last time."

James moved on with his life, married a wonderful woman, and firmly believes that the reunion freed him from his fantasies about Nancy. "I think of her once in a while," he says, "and my thoughts are not bitter or angry. Some things that seem as if they're meant to be just aren't meant to be at all."

As James discovered, sometimes getting your heart broken the second time around is even tougher than on the first pass. "For some people it feels like 'I still can't make it work out; there must be something wrong with me,' especially if they are the one to be rejected again," says Dr. Sherry Bush. "If you have a fantasy about a person from high school and now at 50 you have the same crush and get dumped again, that can be devastating." But it may free you emotionally to embrace the future unfettered. Sarah, a dancer in Los Angeles, believes that freedom is what she achieved by attempting to rekindle a relationship with Craig.

"THERE ARE THINGS ABOUT HIM THAT WILL NEVER CHANGE"

Sarah met Craig at a party when they were both in their early forties. His record company (where he worked as an artist's rep) had relocated him from New York to Los Angeles, and when he and Sarah first saw each other, they felt as if they had known each other all their lives. They dated for about six months; Sarah could hear wedding bells, but the closer the couple got, the more Craig resisted committing. He had never been married; he was frightened of being tied down, and the rock-and-roll atmosphere of his workplace supported his penchant for instability.

He told Sarah that he had to back out of the relationship and that it was not her fault. "I really care about you," he assured her, "but I can't see my way clear to being with only one woman."

Sarah was deeply disappointed, but she moved on, eventually marrying a man in the fitness field. Craig had various girlfriends, but it was always the same. He would be powerfully drawn to someone, have a whirlwind dating period, and then back away.

When Sarah's marriage ended after eight years, she looked up Craig, and they became friendly again. Their romance returned with a passion. Craig tried his best this time, sending flowers and gifts, but his fear of making a mistake was still brewing beneath the surface. When Sarah felt her rekindled lover backing off again, she put an end to it herself, refusing to repeat the patterns that had left her so disappointed the first time. They have remained friends, and both are single. Sarah believes that their last period together gave her the closure she needed to move on not only physically but emotionally as well.

She says, "I understood this time that there were things about Craig that will never change. Now that I'm clear about that, I believe my commitment not to repeat a negative situation will only open up my chances to find true love again."

Sarah discovered within a few months that her second go-round with Craig wasn't going to work. Sometimes it takes a lot longer because we resist letting go of the fantasy. Our early romantic relationships are so significant to our identities that we hang on. Sometimes we do not allow ourselves to grieve when they end. "We need to mourn failed relationships," says New York City psychiatrist Dr. Marlene Marko. "That's the way to move forward unencumbered." Though she was self-sufficient and successful, a New York businesswoman found herself plagued by dreams and thoughts of her high school sweetheart until she got to know him better as an adult.

"GETTING TO KNOW HIM AGAIN FREED ME"

Fifteen-year-old Kris thought 16-year-old Joe looked very grown-up, even though he was only a sophomore in high school. "With his pronounced Adam's apple and large biceps," she remembers, "I thought he was beautiful."

Kris twirled the baton as a majorette for the band at their high school near New Haven, Connecticut, while Joe was a drummer. "We had our first conversation walking side by side after a parade," she recalls. He made a sarcastic remark, and I thought, "Oh, he's witty, too!"

They soon started dating, but after nine months Joe broke up with Kris. With so much ahead of them—high school graduation, college, perhaps graduate school—he worried that the relationship would be a distraction.

Kris was crushed. Her mother tried to soothe her lovesick daughter with that well-worn reassurance, "Don't worry. You'll have a hundred boyfriends before you find one you want to marry."

"You're wrong," Kris sobbed. "You don't understand. We're

meant to be together." To make matters worse, she ran into Joe everywhere in their small town.

In 1986, Joe went away to college—Kris was a senior in high school—and when he came back for Thanksgiving, he said he had made a terrible mistake and begged Kris to come back to him. They dated throughout college, although it was rough going. "He wanted me to be the same girl I was in high school," says Kris, "but I was asserting my independence. He was threatened by the silliest things and tried to control me. We argued a lot."

When Kris graduated from college, she landed a job, while Joe had been out for a whole year and was still unemployed. It soon became obvious that he was jealous of her independence and success. She sublet an apartment in Manhattan with some girlfriends, and the next thing she knew, Joe had rented a place down the street from her office. Feeling manipulated and smothered, Kris broke up with Joe in 1991. "It was hard," she says. "We'd been together for the better part of seven years, and we'd gone through so much together, like his parents' divorce and my grandfather's death. But my original vision that we were destined for each other had been slowly disappearing."

Joe took the separation hard, while Kris began dating and then married an older man, who was the polar opposite of Joe. "He was 12 years older," says Kris, "and I thought he was urbane and worldly. I know now that it was a rebound after the volatility of being with Joe. I was just exhausted by our intensity, and all the 'off again, on again' indecision. I wanted something stable."

Years later, after no contact, Kris dreamed of Joe repeatedly. While the dreams were not sexual, they were deeply emotional and left her feeling lost when she awoke.

Her response to the dreams, in part, gave her the courage to separate from her husband after a number of years of unhappiness. Through a friend she learned of Joe's e-mail address. "I'd mostly forgotten the bad things in our previous relationship, and I guess I glorified our soul connection because there was so little in my marriage. I wanted to know that connection again."

Joe answered Kris's e-mail, and they began a cursory correspondence, agreeing to meet for dinner so she could advise him on a career matter.

Kris remembers feeling safe with him when they were waiting for her taxi on that windy night. "Soon after, Joe moved south to be with his girlfriend, and we continued to send e-mails, becoming best friends and keeping each other current on the daily events in our lives. We still felt close, and we definitely had chemistry. But we never discussed getting back together, and there was his girlfriend to consider." Kris helped Joe through his graduate school applications, and when his grandmother died, he called her first.

But Kris was becoming painfully aware of the old problems. "He was calling me every night while he had a girlfriend. We'd talk for an hour—but never when I needed him, only when he needed me. I didn't feel comfortable 'pretending' to be together when he was involved with someone else. After a year I told him how I felt, but he couldn't face it. The old indecision—his inability to really commit to how he felt instead of what he thought he should be feeling—was rearing its head again."

She finally put an end to it—for good this time. "Getting to know Joe as an adult showed me that the things that had come between us when we were young hadn't improved. If anything, they had solidified. But I'm glad I did it. Otherwise, I might have always wondered. Getting to know him again freed me to meet and marry John," the true man of her dreams. "He's passionate and committed; he knows what he wants and doesn't let anyone stand in his way of getting it. But best of all he lets me be my best self and loves me for exactly who I am, not who I was or who he hopes I could be."

"The time I spent with Joe showed me I could feel love again just as passionately as I had as a teenager but with the wisdom and clarity of a 34-year-old. Because of Joe, I have a clearer sense of not only who I am but who I want to be with."

Kris feels that it was a healthy, valuable experience to spend time with her high school love and that she finally answered questions which might have always troubled her, at least subconsciously. She agrees with therapist Ginny Fleming who says, "You may have thought at the time that you were somehow at fault for the problems behind the breakup. When you reunite, you have a chance to unlock that and see whether personality differences or the other person's behaviors were at the core of the split. That's how a lot of healing happens."

So, fair warning: Reconnecting with a long-lost love, as our stories show, can have complications. But the commitment of couples who have embraced a second chance together is often beautiful and inspiring. Their weddings tend to have a special joy as the partners recapture something precious that was very nearly lost forever: happily ever after.

Chapter 14

Lost Treasure Found

"WEDDINGS ARE MARKERS IN PEOPLE'S LIVES," SAYS DR. IRIS SanGiuliano. "The commitment becomes more precious if you have come back together because you're completing something you weren't able to see through the first time around. You are finishing unfinished business. You are declaring yourselves."

There is a special poignancy in the wedding of a reunited couple. Rekindled lovers approach marriage with their shared life experience as youngsters *and* their significantly separate life experience as adults. It is a complex history but a cherished one as well.

We Are Gathered Here

For Ed and me, our wedding was a joyous, perfect day that felt 35 years in the making. He had his three gorgeous, loving daughters to stand with him as he made these "rest of our life" promises. I had my dynamite 17-year-old son, who escorted me down the aisle, and my exquisite 13-year-old daughter, who served as maid of honor and who, with incredible poise, sang "The Rose," leaving not a dry eye in the crowd.

When I say it was a perfect day, please understand: The limos were late, the bouquet started out yellow instead of white, red wine was spilled on several gowns, and we had to rescue our parents who were mistaken for onlookers and told to go away. So it's not that *nothing* went wrong. It's just that very few things could have shaken our happiness.

The weather was a drama, to say the least. Ed and I had dreamed of taking our vows under God's sky with the glory of nature blessing our union. We were north of New York City at a lovely estate with lush trees and the Hudson River in the background. The setting was a beautiful slate plaza with a stone balustrade overlooking the rolling lawn of Tappan Hill. Thunderstorms had been forecast, but up until about three in the afternoon, the sun shone coyly. Then, suddenly, huge rolling clouds appeared. Almost instantly they turned gray. The breeze intensified, and every time it blew through the leaves, we could hear a downpour threatening.

Moving the whole ceremony inside to the ballroom was an option. The storm would provide a dramatic backdrop through ceiling-high windows. But an outdoor wedding was our first choice if at all possible, so we asked our wedding coordinator for a worst-case scenario. What if the torrent came right before the procession started? We might not get all the flowers inside. We decided to risk it. But then, of course, we had to imagine a worse worst-scenario, as in: What if the storm struck *right in the middle of the ceremony*? Ed and I looked at each other for a moment and agreed: At least it would be memorable. We decided to go for it.

Ed hustled back to his dressing room to retrieve a lucky acorn his daughter Lauren had given him from her days at Stanford. Andrew blew on it like dice at a craps game, saying, "This acorn is going to get a real test today." Taking me aside, Andrew quietly tried to prepare me as a coach would prepare his athletes. "You can take it even if we have to go inside, Mom. You've handled tougher situations." There were no actual raindrops by game time, so the procession started. Guests later told us that they were crossing their fingers, holding their breath, and praying we would get through the vows before the deluge.

Escorted by their uncles, Lauren, Emily, and Joanna, in shimmery black summer gowns, led the procession. Caroline followed, regal with stems of dendrobium orchids nestled in the curve of her arm. I slipped my hand through Andrew's arm and started to step briskly.

"You look beautiful, Mom," he said. "Slow down and enjoy it." I took a deep breath, and he proudly walked me down the aisle to Wagner's magnificent "Bridal Chorus." As the last chord sounded, Andrew said, "I love you, Mom," gave Ed a bear hug, and stepped to the side.

Ed and I exchanged quick grins like mischievous teenagers daring Mother Nature. Then we began.

My best friend, Ellen Eisenstat, and Ed's brother Ron read from *The Diaries of Adam and Eve* by Mark Twain. It was too long in the original, so we had changed it around and hoped that Sam Clemens would approve our edits. Once we'd become daring enough to improve on Mark Twain, we also improved on Corinthians ("Love is patient . . ."), taking bits and pieces from the six versions we found. My dad did that reading without his cowboy hat because my mom said she wouldn't sit next to him if he insisted on wearing it with his tux. Ed's brother Dave read "Whole Love" from a book of Robert Graves's poetry given to us by our friends Ellen Levine and Cathie

Black. We could hear guests gasping behind us at the occasional thunderclap, but the skies let love triumph and there was a roar of approval as Judge Denise Cote pronounced us *at long last* husband and wife.

Then it was rock 'n' roll. When the band started "My Boyfriend's Back," pandemonium erupted. People jumped to their feet and cheered, sharing in our joy that, yes, he *was* back! We felt carefree, jubilant, and surrounded by love. I danced with my dad to "Hey, Good Lookin'," the song I used to hear him sing while he shaved in the mornings. My girlfriends Ann Moore, Angela Shapiro Mathes, Lisa Sharkey, and Clarice Joynes, showing the reverence usually reserved for the ceiling of the Sistine Chapel, examined my beaded Stuart Weitzman high heels. Blue crystals decorated each sole under the arch, spelling out the date and forming a heart. In a flash of ecumenical spirit, our dear friend Sue Leibman said she would feel that I was "more married" if Ed, in true Jewish tradition, came up and stomped on a wineglass. It shattered loudly, and everyone yelled, "Mazel tov!"

Music from the 60s and 70s kept people on their feet song after song. My friends Sara Moss, Nancy Atlas, Ellen Cooper Klyce, and Karen Mills showed the current crop of teens the Twist, the Pony, the Swim, and other dance steps we learned at slumber parties not so long ago. Ed's colleagues from Massachusetts, led by Chris Collins, had so much fun that they voted to "have the wedding again next weekend." My former chiefs of staff Mary Kilkenny and Kat Madaras, who remembered Caroline at age four in her "My Size Barbie" finery, teased that she had "upped her game" on the sophistication scale in her black satin gown. Our friend Jan Yanehiro led the San Francisco contingent in a slight exaggeration that *everyone* in their city sent congratulations that a son and daughter of the

Golden Gate had "bridged" the years. There were several rollicking toasts, including one in which Andrew was teased, "It's safe to say you now have more sisters than you ever thought possible!"

While we have yet to foist the wedding album on total strangers, with the slightest opening we share more details than the average person can tolerate. Ed and I never tire of talking about that glorious day. We were surrounded by our families and our dearest friends who had shown their love and loyalty many times over. There were even a couple of my high school friends who had whupped Ed's team in debate. (He might tell it differently, but that's the benefit of being in charge of the keyboard.) These friendships were a reminder of the circuitous route we, like other reunited couples, had taken to arrive at this day.

Do these couples regret the time they lost, the years they might have spent together if fate or choice hadn't parted them? Some do. Bob McGarry, who married Deb (Giragosian) 28 years after they sang together in high school quartets, says, "There's always a sparkle in her eyes and a smile on her face. It's a shame that I missed so many years of that." But many couples, though buoyantly joyful about reuniting, think the timing was just right.

Regrets? Too Few to Mention

David Bilon is philosophical about the 22 years between high school graduation in Columbus, Georgia, and his wedding day in 1991. "I'm happy where I am now with Fran. Sometimes I think I might not be here if we'd gotten married early." He feels that he learned a lot from being with other people during their years apart. "You acquire a certain wisdom," he says, "which makes you better in a subsequent relationship. In some ways I'm glad things worked out just the way they did."

That accepting attitude about "the years between" comes up frequently. Many reunitees believe that their time apart was put to good use or that they avoided hurting each other during that period. "We're not likely to have a lot of painful baggage with a past love," explains therapist Suzanne Lopez. "We're filled with the belief that anything is possible and that the whole world is in front of us."

"I could see where, if I was 65, I might be a little upset about the time lost," reflects 33-year-old Matt Wheeler who married his summer love 17 years after they met. "But a lot of it was hard knocks and we're better off in the end to have gone through that separately. I'm glad other people taught me the lessons that I can now live by with Alexis."

Carol Gregory is married to Mike Howell, whom she first dated in her teens and remet 28 years later at the American Legion hall during a hometown festival. "I think that if we'd had a family that young, it wouldn't have worked because he wasn't ready to settle down." He certainly *was* ready by the time they made the commitment to each other in their mid-fifties. "I never forgot her," Mike says. "I'm the happiest I've ever been in my life."

Some couples feel that their personal history simply took the right course, and they have no desire to spend time on regrets. Of course many of them had children during their time apart and declare they wouldn't change history because their children are so dear to them. There is an eloquence to the truths they have discovered: "Sometimes you have to grow up yourself a little before you know the value of what you have," says Joe Jensen, who married Kathie (Beck) 45 days after they remet at their thirtieth reunion. "You learn what's worth keeping and taking care of. Some people would call our reuniting fairy tale stuff, but I believe there are no accidents. We are lucky to have three great children between us. Everything has happened at exactly the right time."

Whether or not they have regrets about the years apart, rejoined couples are fervent about embracing the years ahead. Often that calls for a wedding.

To Have and to Hold

These ceremonies are as delightful and varied as the couples themselves. It's fascinating to see how clearly their personalities and stories are reflected in their choices. The invitation for Marjory Lehrer's wedding to Barry Spiro featured their school pictures from Erasmus High in Brooklyn on the cover and read, "Thirty-six years later . . . we found our second chance!" Gary Puetz and Carol Pedersen, who remet at a thirtieth high school reunion, used their prom photo with the caption "Still dancing after all these years" on their wedding invitation.

Trouble finding a wedding ring he liked led to a sentimental choice by J. R. Barberie. His soon-to-be-wife Ellen (Hector) remembered a ring she had given him for his eighteenth birthday, with a stone they had in jest dubbed "the black diamond." When they married in Vancouver, British Columbia, that teenage gift became his wedding ring. They had a nondenominational ceremony, but they acknowledged the two religions that had been a barrier in their adolescence when J.R. adopted Jewish tradition and, like Ed, stomped on a wineglass to the cheers of family and friends.

A lifestyle difference had come between Los Angeles publicist Cheryl J. Kagan and Tulsa optometrist Dr. Hilly Dubin. He liked the laidback Midwest, while she wanted the pump of a big city. Years later they found a balance. She would move to Oklahoma and travel to Los Angeles each month for business. Her friends insisted on celebrating the deal with a wedding extravaganza worthy of Hollywood. Cheryl said, "Whoever wants to be a bridesmaid, just wear a black dress." They ended up with a wedding party that included 10 bridesmaids (among them friend and client, actress Cybill Shepherd), four flower girls, a ton of ushers, and a Lhasa apso wearing a collar of pink and white roses. Instead of signing a guestbook, everyone autographed a huge photo of the couple taken in 1967 at The Palm Shore Club in Brooklyn, where they first met.

Her "punk" look attracted Matt Wheeler to Alexis (Grossman) the moment they met as young teens, but her grandmother hoped that Alexis might go "traditional" on her wedding day. Matt was happy that Alexis stuck with her maverick style: She hacked off her hair at the last minute and wore a red Chinese brushed silk dress that she spray-painted with black stars—a look he proudly describes as "Armani meets Dr. Seuss." On the front of their wedding invitation was a photo of the couple from the summer of 1985; the back panel had a shot of them in the same pose 18 years later.

On occasion the children of reunited couples help Cupid along. Renee (Shipp), who had grown up with Jim Petrausch in Wyoming, would have chosen a quickie wedding in Las Vegas just to get it done, but her daughter was adamant. "You've been waiting to marry this man for more than 30 years," she said. "You need to do it right." Following a formal church ceremony with six bridesmaids, the finally wed husband and wife gave each other a high-five.

In another instance a daughter came to the rescue. Two days before her wedding, Joy (Jemison), who was in her seventies, called it off like a nervous young bride. She and Sam Nichols, who had been separated by World War II and reunited after their spouses passed away, were set to wed in July 2000. But some minor personality conflicts scared Joy. Sam was grief-stricken; she was heartbroken. Sam describes how his daughter Michelle brought them back together. "Even though she had lost her mother not so long before and had loved her mother very much, Michelle knew that I was hurting. She was the one that helped repair the damage. She called Joy and said, 'My father is not very happy without you.'" The couple began exchanging letters again, and in July 2001 they were married in Michelle's Oregon rose garden.

Weddings are full of symbolism, but for reunited couples there is an especially rich history from which to draw. Often the setting is a potent symbol. Liza Huber, a star of TV's *Passions*, and Alex Hesterberg were elementary school classmates. After they reunited as adults, they got married in the same church where they received First Holy Communion together as second graders.

Their house with the white picket fence was a telling choice for Wanda (Hite) and Todd Lista's wedding ceremony. After years of living in big cities like New York and Los Angeles, Wanda had found her dream of love back home in South Carolina with her high school sweetheart.

Carol Channing and Harry Kullijian were married in the home of Roz and Mervyn Morris, who reintroduced the couple more than 70 years after their sweetheart days in junior high. The invitation to the wedding on May 10, 2003, showed a black-and-white photograph of Harry with his arm around Carol in 1933. Merv, of course, gave away the bride. A touching symbol of the past is the wedding ring that Harry gave Carol. She remembers seeing it on his mother's hand.

Hometowns beckon as wedding sites even when both bride and

groom have moved away. Heather (Lynn) and Scott Clark went home to Lima, Ohio, to marry. That's where they had met in junior high and where they reconnected 26 years later. They chose New Year's Eve so that old friends who had moved away would be home for the holidays. A former classmate who had become president of the Lima City Council was deputized temporary mayor so that he could perform the ceremony. Scott says, "It meant a lot to us to get married in our hometown because that's where it all began."

An archaeological dig in the Southwest was where love first bloomed for Leslie and Russell. Their reverence for antiquity led them to Pecos National Park, New Mexico, where they married in the ruins of a church that had been built in the 1500s on an Indian pueblo. "We chose the summer solstice," Russell says, "because we were experiencing a personal change of seasons, from not commit-ting to standing up in front of everyone, saying this is the best op-portunity life has ever given us."

Beverly (Gordon) and Riley Hodder are a living testament to that reunited couples' creed: "Nothing is going to stop us this time." When their justice of the peace forgot he was supposed to do the honors, Beverly and Riley went forward with a rip-roaring four-hour reception and even cut the wedding cake before he arrived and mar-ried them.

At the wedding of Jeanne (Trattner) and Michael Harris, his 40-something niece, Susan, toasted the couple. She recalled that when she was eight years old her parents had packed their luggage to attend this same wedding in Las Vegas, and then suddenly un-packed. There were no jitters for the bride this time, and Susan was now old enough to receive her own invitation.

These couples celebrated in their ceremonies what therapist Ginny Fleming calls "a feeling of longevity in the love that most newlyweds don't experience." The moment of becoming husband and wife is simultaneously a culmination and a new beginning.

From This Day Forward

At our wedding the dance floor was full late into the night. As the reception started winding down, I found myself in a huddle of close girlfriends: my assistant, Anna Solomou, who could now fully qualify as a wedding planner; Joannie Danielides, who had expertly chaperoned the photographers; Carol Traynor, who had helped Caroline give a shower for me; Kathleen Powers, whose three-month-old granddaughter Eve was the youngest "girl" at the shower; Dolores Casey, who gave me a "bride" baseball cap for the honeymoon; and Marilyn Silverman, whose antique handkerchief was my "something borrowed." Sisterhood prevailed—mission accomplished! Ed and I said our good-byes to friends who had come from afar, and soon only a few loving stragglers remained.

Upstairs in the dressing room I realized that I had a clothes steamer, jeans, sneakers, umbrellas, a boom box, an ironing board, and an unopened bottle of champagne to take home. I yelled downstairs, "Hey, is the girl in the white dress really supposed to carry all this?" My dear friends Liz Rye, Frances Mottola, and George Rivera of the New York Police Department came to the rescue, as they are professionally wont to do. They bundled everything, including the bride and groom, into the waiting limo, along with my daughter, parents, and a few lost souls who had missed their rides home.

Not wanting to let go of this wonderful day just yet, we started reminiscing about the rain that never actually came, about Ed's mom, Kathy, blushing sweetly when our parents were asked to stand for a round of applause during the ceremony, and about how moving it was watching my folks dance to "their song," "The Tennessee Waltz."

Ed and I looked at each other almost in disbelief. We had first held hands 35 years ago, and today we had committed to holding on tight forever. We had finished the unfinished business. We had declared ourselves. The words we said to each other during the wedding perfectly describe our happiness at reuniting:

"You have changed my life . . . brought me joy . . . healed my heart," I told him. "Where were you, my sweet love, all those other mornings of my life, when I could only hope that you would find me?"

Ed's words embraced me. "You are my lost treasure found, never to be lost again."

AFTERWORD

A S WE WENT TO PRINT, TWO COUPLES WITHIN THESE PAGES SAW their earthly unions come to an end. Joe Jensen died in his wife Kathie's arms. She says that in their church, marriage is not "until death do us part," but instead "for all eternity." She believes, "Joe is waiting for me." Carol Pedersen passed away with a gentle smile after looking one last time into the eyes of her beloved husband, Gary Puetz. He says, "We were so connected, Carol was the answer to 'why?' I will always keep my promises to her." Both couples felt that their marriages were "meant to be." I hope my telling their stories provides some comfort; certainly the beauty of their love survives.

ACKNOWLEDGMENTS

TWO PEOPLE ABOVE ALL MADE THIS BOOK POSSIBLE—MY LOVING husband and my cherished best friend, Ellen Eisenstat. Ellen, who is a brilliant writer, spent literally hundreds of hours reworking and editing these chapters. She said that the book had to reflect my sense of humor, which she feels has been, until now, a bit of a secret. When your best friend is also your "covert cowriter," there's a lot of fun to be had interspersed with the hard work. Thank you! Can we go shopping now? And my wonderful, smart, devoted husband put his legal skills to work for me on contracts and negotiations, so much so that we now privately refer to me as "Miss Pro Bono." He also did a huge amount of statistical research and editing to refine the work. Many late hours he stayed up with me to make sure that I didn't feel alone.

My publisher/editor at Hudson Street Press, Laureen Rowland, deserves much credit for conceiving the idea and managing the myriad aspects of getting it to press, for boosting the author with humor and confidence, and for her incisive editing. She is one of the "happening women" as I've told her—and now a lifelong friend.

Arthur Greenwald, who has had lifelong friend status for 25 years, put his remarkable talents to work improving the writing. He also advised me diplomatically but honestly when I hung on too long to paragraphs that had to go. His loving help made this book much better than it would have been otherwise.

Of course, my children, Caroline and Andrew, deserve and get my thanks every single day. Caroline, who poked a toe into the publishing world with her internship at *Seventeen* magazine, read various sections and provided the benefit of her fresh perspective. Andrew sometimes called after a golf match to ask, "Shall I come home now, Mom . . . or are chapters 1 through 10 on my bed?" Both of my wonderful children were generous about sharing their computers and desk space, and indicating their faith that this was a worthy effort. (They haven't seen the top of the dining room table in about a year now—it's been covered by manila folders containing research. Maybe I'll try to fix that.)

I now believe that, to borrow a catchy phrase, "It takes a village to write a book." My dedicated assistant Anna Solomou came in on weekends, made calls from home, and got to know the couples in this book almost as well as I did, as she fact-checked and requested photos. Joannie Danielides guided me through uncharted waters and has always represented me to my colleagues in the press with grace and grit. She and her wonderful business partner and husband Nick also made valuable contacts with several people who appear in these pages.

Fredrica Friedman believed in this book long before I did. I thank her for her hard work as my agent, her example of derring-do in traveling the world, and her passion for boosting the efforts of other women.

The close friends who helped me find couples and experts to interview lovingly got this project off the ground—Sue Leibman, Ellen Cooper Klyce, Brig Klyce, Carol Traynor, Jan Yanehiro, Barbara

Kasman, Gail Yancosek, Elizabeth Oster, Xena Galietti, Rachel Kolster, Bud Konheim, Kathleen Powers, Pat Baird, Jan Ryan, and Rita Anne Howard—romantics every one, they have my deep appreciation.

Thanks also to Joan Hamburg, the undisputed goddess of advice in New York for having me on her radio program, a visit that resulted in letters from many reunited couples.

Our friends Susan Lucci and Helmut Huber invited Ed and me to the lovely wedding of their daughter, Liza, where I unexpectedly discovered a reunited couple for the book because the handsome groom, Alex Hesterberg, went to elementary school with the beautiful bride.

The general counsel for Estée Lauder, my friend Sara Moss, introduced me to attorney Harvey Feuerstein, who contacted his son Mark Feuerstein to vouch for my integrity with Suzanne Pleshette, his costar on *Good Morning, Miami*.

Jan Yanehiro put me in touch with Mervyn Morris who put me in touch with Carol Channing and Harry Kullijian, who were married in his home.

You may be getting the picture by now—this book has the depth it does because friends reached out to friends on my behalf.

Cathie Black (president, Hearst Magazines), Ellen Levine, Deb Shriver, Pat Ganzi, Kate White, Pamela Fiori, Jerry Shevak, Atoosa Rubenstein, and Valerie Salembier, leaders all in the Hearst company, have my great respect and affection for cheering on this effort and for giving me such warm support in other endeavors as well. Victor Ganzi, president and CEO of the Hearst Corporation; Frank A. Bennack Jr., vice chairman of the board, the Hearst Corporation; and Bruce Paisner, president of Hearst Entertainment, Inc., have my deep gratitude for the wonderful opportunities they've given me to be part of that fine organization.

ACKNOWLEDGMENTS

Ann Moore, chairman and CEO of Time, Inc., is a fantastic advocate for women helping women and she is a dynamo I seek to emulate. Along with Nora McAniff and Pat Fili-Krushel, Ann enthusiastically encouraged me in this project and sent along ideas from the magazines at Time-Warner to help find rekindled couples.

Angela Shapiro, the president of Fox Television Studios, Inc., has been an amazing friend, supporting this endeavor, sharing her own fabulous humor to brighten up the toughest days, and being a superb example of integrity and grace. Among the other women who have been an inspiration both professionally and personally are: Jean Rather, Paula Zahn, Sondra Lee, Lisa Sharkey, Mary Mundinger, Beth Rudin DeWoody, Alair Townsend, Diane Sokolow, Amanda Mackey Johnson, Jennifer Raab, Debbie Wright, Esther Newberg, Sonia Armstead, Rochelle Brown, Dr. Lisa Callahan, Linda Stasi, Heidi Evans, Jane Hanson, Dr. Ida Schwab, Karen Mills, Camryn Manheim, Dennie Gordon, Dr. Audra Malerba, Jayne Weintraub, Eloise Maroney, Sherrie Rollins Westin, Lisa Gregorisch-Dempsey, Anna Quindlen, Liz Smith, Adele Rifkin, Nora Ephron, Judy Dobrzynski, Joan Rivers, Ann Biderman, Lynda Obst, Nicole Miller, Lisa Caputo, Dr. Barbara Edelstein, Maria Shriver, Nancy Daley Riordan, Sarah Jessica Parker, Kate Spade, Sherry Lansing, Marlo Thomas, Carol Higgins Clark, and Mary Higgins Clark.

Helene Brezinsky and Margaret Donohoe gave me their always-wise counsel. Their delight in this project when it was just an idea made me feel that it should be a go.

Jenifer, Valerie, and Meredith Estess, first introduced to me by our treasured mutual friend, Sue Leibman, inspired me, especially when I wrote the chapter on "crisis." Jenifer gallantly battled amyotrophic lateral sclerosis (ALS), and I sought to give this book the kind of humor that drew people to her as she and her sisters built a national campaign to find a cure for everyone with this ruthless disease by establishing Project A.L.S.

Marilyn and Dr. Fred Silverman and their daughters Marjorie, Cara, and Ellen; Kathleen and Krista Powers; Heather and Scott McBride; Lyssa, Andy, and Lindsay Benincaso; Dennis and Joanne Mulligan; Dolores and Ray Casey and their fabulous clan—Jeff and Audra, Darren and Stephanie, Ray Jr. and Marybeth; and Trudy and Michael Sullivan have over the years all provided my children with homes away from home, happy diversions, and consistent love. Others who have helped me provide my children with loving guidance are: Joe and Mary Olmo, Terence Mulvey, John Murphy, Don Costello, Kenny Walsh, Brian Carey, Beverly Galloway, Rosalie and Myles Tanaka, Maureen Lampidis, Suzanne Price, Abigail Penzell, Mahon Bishop, Leslie Waltzer, Peggy Carnival, Cathy Mary Mullan, the faculty and staff at the Convent of the Sacred Heart, at St. David's School, and at St. Joseph Regional High School, especially Coach Tony Karcich, Rita Anne Howard, Frank DeVito, and John Job.

My team from the First Lady days is always ready to come back to help when I call and I thank them for that loyalty: Mary Kilkenny, Kat Madaras, Clarice Joynes, Stephanie Sheehan, Cynthia Brickhouse, Christine Ennis, Carol and Gene Traynor, Karen and Charlie Kolster, Diana Robertson, Gogie Padilla, Susan McLain Friedman, Kathy Gershuny, Marilyn Siegel, Phil Wilhite, Joe Gelchion, Peggy Cohen, Lauren Caruso, and David Reese are top notch. Liz Rye, Frances Mottola, and George Rivera of the NYPD exemplify courage and honor.

Since our wedding is part of this story, a few particular thank-yous are in order. Stuart and Jane Weitzman presented me with the most exquisite high heels any bride has ever worn. Ed and I thank the Honorable Denise Cote for her time and words of wisdom in marrying us. My good friend the Honorable Nancy Atlas had set her schedule to perform the wedding honors and then, when a legal glitch intervened, still attended to make the celebration special. Nanci Grady and Liz Hendrickson, who remember Ed and me dating in high school, gave our wedding some fun historical perspective. Some of the other people who went to great effort to be there for us: Ron Oster and the Honorable Diana Wheatley, Dave Oster and Jeannette Fung, Elizabeth Oster and Michael Elliott, Steven and Marcella Oster, Louise and Lee Gunderson, Nancy and Jack Fetterman, Adele and John Prayias, Allen Levy, Nadia and Bob McConnell, Reese and Pat Schonfeld, John and Juliette Reverand, Donna and John Cristen, Lila Corn and Marc Rosenweig, Chris and Catherine Collins, Gayle and Chick Weiss, George and Catherine Thompson, Dave and Joy Layden, Peter and Ellen Durand, Rich and Gail Squar, Tom Ackland, Steven and Jan Anderson, Gail Cohen and Gary Hamblet, and Marty and Ellen Rosen.

Others who have shown much kindness to me and the children in various ways during this project and before: Jim and Joey Eichenberger, Jace Alexander and Maddie Corman, the wonderful producers of *Law & Order*, Joan and Bob Tisch and Billie Tisch, and their families, especially Laurie, her daughters Carolyn and Emily, and Andrew and Ann Tisch, Sammy Arthur, Milos and Martina Forman, Michael and Pam Hausman, Edward Norton, Cathy Giuliani and her husband Rudy, Paul Gleicher, Richard Leibner, Carole Cooper, Nancy Kay, and Dan Rather, Dr. David James, Howard and Carol Safir, Karen and Bill Clark, Rosemarie O'Keefe, Mayor Michael Bloomberg, Police Commissioner Ray Kelly, Deputy Mayor Patti Harris, Deputy Mayor Dan Doctoroff, Ester Fuchs, former Mayor Ed Koch, Mercedes and Sid Bass, Lally Weymouth, Ken and

Grace Hatton, Marty Richards, Jerry and Elaine Orbach, Suzanne Ryan, Victor Kovner, Joan K. Davidson, Diane Bondareff, Barbara and Bernie Leibman, Adis Vila and Adis Fernandes, Dr. Gail Furman, Judy Kramer, Karen and John Klopp, Jessie Pollack, Truda Jewett, Libby Zimmer, Mark Roithmayr, Dr. Burt Grebin, Roy Chinnici, Rob Corona, Susan Brown, Tom Ginocchio, the moms in the football stadium at St. Joe's, especially Kathy Dolan and Julie Pickett, Bob Gilbert, Christine Wilson, John and Judy Gross, Ed Foote, John Galietti, Susan and Michael Mukasey, Elliot Cuker and Noeline Hession, Angela Hession, Bobbi Waldman, Paul Critchlow, the Honorable Leslie Crocker Snyder, Jon Sale, Rob Karin, Linda Wachner, Bibi Kahn, Derrick Pike, Kevin McManus, Anna Venditti, Fred Cerullo, Maren Pedersen, John Corporon, Susan Tick, Dr. Spencer Sherman, Mye David, the Demarest family, Morty Davis, Eileen Finn, Josie Natori, Joan Alexander, Christine Prekopa, Marcia Lee, Pam Arnone, Shelli Sonstein, Joan Chin, Todd Ciaravino, Therese McManus, Arie and Coco Kopelman, Ali and Joe Torre, Stacia Haskins, Bob Leider, Jill Beach, Helen Jeanne Nicastri, Diane Jaramillo, Lauren Bright, David Rosengarten, Dr. Patricia Wexler, Carla Singer, Norma and Jeff, Wanda, Carlie, Randy, and Chris Wilhite, Norman Smith, George Constant, Dr. Ralph Lopez, Rita Baron Faust, Susan McDermott, Jonathan Disick and his family, Dan Byrne, Brian Patton, Leonard and Elaine Esposito, Mayra Melendez, Al Rodriguez, Roxann Hayes, Miriam Valentin, David Ryan, Angel Matos, Jimmy McCaffrey, Frank Serse, Sergio Conde, Aida Virola, Vincent Beckles, Nestor Landron, Tibor Kerekes, Brendan Duffy, Richie Marsilanus, Lenny Marino, Arty Goldberg, Ed Hennessy, Steve Hines, James Musso, Jimmy O'Brien, Kevin Keane, Robin Maples-Everett, Brian Scully, Jerry Montanez, Palo Dedvukaj, Victor Correa, Jennifer Lance, Rene Gonti, Charlie and Stacy Solomou, Chickie (Carmela) Piazza, Coach Rod Meyers and his wife Nancy and Coach Jim Kubinski of Duke University, the Quagliano family, Dr. Romeo and Ann Marie Solon, Dr. Allen Lubarr, Dr. Joel Mark, Dr. Ed and Suzanne Davies, and my wonderful aunts and uncles.

Andrea Cagan, Danielle Friedman, Joanne Kaufman, and Saryl Radwin helped with researching and editing the book. I appreciate their good-spirited hard work. Contact information for people who might belong in the book came from several generous people: William White, Debbie Johnson, David Klatell, Kathleen Vach, Marian Wiseman, Jeannine Frank, Jeanne Jemison, Susan Stautberg, Susan van Berg, Glenn Rifkin, and Kate Flannery all have my sincere gratitude for helping in this way.

I especially extend my heartfelt thanks to the people whose experiences you'll read about in My Boyfriend's Back. They devoted their time, answered many fact-checking queries, and welcomed me into their lives. A few of the details and names have been changed or withheld to protect the privacy of those who so generously shared their stories.

Thank you also to the scientists and therapists who gave me the benefit of their knowledge, most especially: Dr. Helen Fisher, Dr. Iris SanGiuliano, Dr. Sherry Bush, Dr. Marlene Marko, Ginny Fleming, MFT; and Colleen Konheim, CSW. Also generous in this regard were: Dr. Carolyn Perla, Estelle Schecter, Dr. Nancy Kalish, Vicky Firstenberg Hillman, MA; therapist and author Suzanne Lopez, Dr. Herb Barrett, Dr. John Stine, Dr. Linda Waud, and Dr. Lucy Brown. Dr. Neil A. Busis, Chief of the Division of Neurology at University of Pittsburgh Medical Center, Shadyside, Pittsburgh, Pennsylvania, reviewed some of the chapters to ensure consistency with scientific and medical knowledge.

Our Families

To Ed's mother, Kathy: I am indebted to you for raising such a kind, honorable, loving son and for welcoming me into your family with so much love. I thank Ed's siblings and their spouses for their enthusiasm and hospitality during the course of this project. Ed's daughters, as you've read, have good hearts and good humor among many other wonderful qualities. Their deep love for their dad, and his for them, is a beautiful thing to observe.

My mom and dad, Gwen and Bob Kofnovec, have set a lifelong example of tenderness and partnership in marriage and steadiness in always being ready to help all of their daughters and grandchildren (I am blessed with sisters, nephews, and a niece). I learned how to be a truly loving and encouraging mother by watching their dedication to family. My parents set the standard for love in my mind and they set it high. Mom and Dad, I cherish you and thank you from deep in my heart.

QUESTIONS FOR DISCUSSION

1. A common experience among rekindled lovers is instantaneous reattraction. What do you think explains this phenomenon? Why is the feeling often more intense than what people experience when meeting for the first time?

2. What appears to be the most potent catalyst for rekindled love? Why? Find three examples in the book and discuss.

3. Have you ever rekindled a relationship? If so, what happened? If not, have you ever considered rekindling a relationship? What about it is appealing? Do you know people who have reunited with someone? How do their relationships seem different than others?

4. What do Carol Channing and Harry Kullijian (p. 27) as a couple have in common with Cheryl Kagan and Dr. Hilly Dubin (p. 156)? One example is that both women as young ladies were attracted to the boys' musical ability. Find several other commonalities. What conclusions do you draw from the comparison about love in general?

5. Why do you think reunited couples can easily overlook signs of the passage of time in each other's appearance? What term besides "Young Eyes" would you create to explain this experience?

6. Many reunitees report that their sexual lives are more vivid than they would have expected. Why do you imagine this is so? Might this have something to do with trust?

7. Which current or historically popular songs have rekindled love as a theme? (Some examples: "Back in My Arms Again," sung by the Supremes, "Old Flame" sung by Alabama, and "Second Time Around," sung by Frank Sinatra.) Choose one, find the lyrics at www.lyrics.com, and decide which chapter of *My Boyfriend's Back* best explains the story.

8. Consider what accounts for the extraordinarily high "stay together" rate of reunitees. What are its implications?

9. Why do you think the topic of rekindled love triggers such interest even among people who are not personally involved? What does its existence say about hope?

10. Choose a film (comedy or drama) that features rekindled love as its theme. (See chapter 2, p. 33 for ideas.) Analyze the differences between the male and the female perspective. Was the conclusion of the film satisfying? Explain your reaction.

11. Discuss why the theme of reunited love seems to resonate with every generation.

12. A concept of "destiny" permeates the remarks of many rekindled couples. Do you believe there is a force at work that explains their belief that their reunions were "meant to be"?

13. Many reunited couples describe "synchronicity" in their stories. Tom and Sandi Anton, for example, discovered that during their years apart, "we found out we'd both named our first child Katherine, drove minivans, and worked in stained-glass as a hobby. We even liked the same merlot." What other couples in the book had this experience and what does it mean? Have you yourself ever experienced this kind of synchronicity—in a relationship, a friendship, even a job search?

14. Is there value in spending time with a former sweetheart even if it doesn't result in a rekindled relationship? Why is closure, discussed in chapter 13, so important?

15. What can be learned from the romances of reunitees that other people can apply to their own marriages or significant relationships?

ABOUT THE AUTHOR

Donna Hanover is the host of the nationally syndicated television program *Famous Homes & Hideaways*, now its fifth season (produced by Hearst Entertainment and Fine Living Network). She was the First Lady of the City of New York from 1994 to 2001.

Ms. Hanover received her BA from Stanford University in political science in 1972 and her master's degree from the Graduate School of Journalism at Columbia University in 1973. Soon after, she began anchoring the news and producing television and radio programs in cities throughout the country, including Danbury, Connecticut; Utica, New York; Columbus, Ohio; Pittsburgh, Pennsylvania; and Miami, Florida. While anchoring news on WPIX-TV in New York City from 1983 to 1990, she was also a correspondent for the television show *Wall Street Journal Report*, contributing stories on entrepreneurs, women on corporate boards, and many other topics. Her piece entitled "Advertising by Plastic Surgeons" won her a Pinnacle Award from American Women in Radio and Television in 1986.

Prior to her hosting duties for Hearst Entertainment, Ms. Hanover was a correspondent with WNYW-TV FOX 5's *Good Day New York*, and she anchored *Good Day Sunday*. She became known for adventure stories where she flew with the Blue Angels, trained with the FBI at Quantico, skated with the NHL Rangers, danced with the Rockettes, and ran plays at training camp with the New York Giants. She also hosted *In Food Today* on the Food Network, and *House Beautiful* on A&E.

An accomplished actress, Ms. Hanover portrayed Ruth Carter Stapleton in *The People vs. Larry Flynt*, directed by Milos Forman. Her other films include *Keeping the Faith, Superstar, Someone Like You, Series 7, Celebrity, Ransom, Running on Empty,* and *The Dream Team.* Her most recent film is *Noel,* starring Susan Sarandon and Robin Williams, directed by Chazz Palminteri. Ms. Hanover has appeared on television in *Sex and the City, The Practice, Family Law,* and *Ally McBeal,* and has a recurring role as Judge Deborah Bourke on *Law & Order.* She also starred off Broadway in the highly acclaimed *The Vagina Monologues.*

In addition, Ms. Hanover has written for *Good Housekeeping* magazine, including profiles of Bette Midler, Nell Carter, Shirley MacLaine, and California State senator Jackie Speier.

Ms. Hanover is known for her dedication to Project A.L.S., the March of Dimes, St. Mary's Hospital for Children, and Race for the Cure. She resides in New York with her children, Andrew and Caroline, and enjoys a bicoastal life with her husband, Edwin A. Oster, an attorney. She and Ed married on August 3, 2003.